# THE RISE OF THE

# CORPORATE COMMONWEALTH

LOUIS GALAMBOS AND JOSEPH PRATT

# The Rise
# of the
# Corporate
# Commonwealth

## U.S. BUSINESS
## AND PUBLIC POLICY
## IN THE TWENTIETH CENTURY

Basic Books, Inc., Publishers

NEW YORK

LIBRARY OF CONGRESS CATALOGING-IN-PUBLICATION DATA

Galambos, Louis.
   The rise of the corporate commonwealth.

   Bibliographic references: p. 267.
   Includes index.
      1. United States—Industries—History—20th century.
   2. Industry and state—United States.   3. United
   States—Economic policy. I. Pratt, Joseph A.
   II. Title.
   HC103.G29   1988        338.973        87-47784
   ISBN 0-465-07029-9

To our quest for the perfect Baltimore crabcake—a search
that sustained us when good words were hard to find

# Contents

# List of Figures

# List of Tables

# *Preface*

It has recently become fashionable to bemoan the inflexibility and inefficiency of American business and political institutions. The attacks are mounted by business school pundits who are themselves under assault for having contributed to the nation's current problems, by liberal commentators who have traditionally been skeptical of business contributions to American society, and by a potpourri of writers who are feeding on the current widespread anxiety about the nation's economic outlook. Their diagnoses are varied. But all seem agreed that the patient is seriously, perhaps terminally, ill.

History tells us that the plans for the funeral are a bit premature. The business system in the United States has weathered just this sort of crisis before; the current difficulties are in fact the second such major challenge that the American system has experienced in this century. Throughout its history that system has been unusually flexible. Our business and governmental institutions have changed in decisive ways over the past century, accommodating to numerous ⬧ and complex developments in the environment at home and abroad. If there is a central theme to that history, it is the flexibility of the American business system.

But should history be used this way—to analyze contemporary problems? We think so. Some critics of the American business system have used a snapshot taken during the 1980s; we offer instead a dynamic picture of a nation and a business system with long traditions of successful adaptation to change. Some commentators have urged us to look to Japan and other countries for guidance in redesigning our society. But that sort of cross-cultural borrowing holds great risks, for institutions well adapted to one culture are not likely to function as effectively in a different setting. We believe Americans should look more closely at their own past for guidance in strengthening the business economy. Only by understanding the manner in which our private and public institutions have evolved can we place our current problems in a context that takes account of the strengths as well as the weaknesses of our modern organizations. The history of our own institutions— the American style of business and public policy—is the logical starting point for a discussion of the changes needed to revitalize the business system today.

Of central importance in that tradition is the corporation. The present-day firm did not spring full-blown from the Second World War experience, nor did our administrative state take its current form in the last few years. Both institutions developed slowly. They developed together, and they emerged from an historical process marked by conflict, shaped by various ideologies, and punctuated with misdirections as well as startingly successful innovations in the public and private sectors. That historical path toward today's corporate commonwealth deserves to be walked at least once by all those who are concerned—as we are—by the nation's current dilemma.

The record of the past especially deserves consideration by those students who will in a few decades become leaders of our most important business and governmental organizations. We have written this book with them in mind. Our hope is that this history will better enable them to make constructive use of the fundamental concepts they learn in courses on economics, political science, organizational behavior, business and public policy, corporate strategy, and business management. We hope, as well, to arm them for dealing with a world that often seems too complex and too hostile to be mastered by a mortal administrator in business or government. Others have tried, many have succeeded, and that history deserves to be known.

In reconstructing the past we drew heavily upon the research of others, including our colleagues, our students, and the several authors whose books we have edited. We cannot thank them all individually here, but we have tried to indicate in our bibliographical essay as many of these helpful friends as we could remember. If we left you out, we apologize and offer to correct the omission in our next edition.

Others read our manuscript and tried valiantly to correct our mistakes. These hardworking contributors included Mike Bisesi, Chris Castaneda, Raymond Corey, Paul Deisler, Meg Graham, Naomi Lamoreaux, Bob Lewis, Kenneth Lipartito, Paul McNulty, Jan Miller, Ed Perkins, Bette Stead, Paul Tiffany, Richard Vietor, and Dow Votaw. We were also blessed by having at Basic Books a skillful and concerned editor in Steve Fraser, who read our chapters as we drafted them and gave us many helpful suggestions. He was also patient, as was Martin Kessler, Basic's publisher and president. If this array of talent left any errors in this book, we ourselves take full responsibility for them.

Both of us were helped in many ways by our respective institutions and by the staff they provided. The Johns Hopkins University was supportive of the work on this project, and we would in particular like to thank Sharon Widomski and Betty Whildin for their efforts on our behalf. Similar assistance was received from Texas A & M University and the University of Houston. The latter school provided considerable secretarial help—including most prominently Darla Selman—and released time for Joseph Pratt, who became NEH-Cullen Professor of History and Business at the University of Houston while this manuscript was being written.

As custom enjoins, we would like to extend our final appreciative remarks to our families and friends. They were always the first to come to our aid and the least demanding of thanks, but without their tolerance, interest, and affection, this book could not have been written.

Louis Galambos
THE JOHNS HOPKINS UNIVERSITY

Joseph Pratt
THE UNIVERSITY OF HOUSTON

# THE RISE OF THE

# CORPORATE COMMONWEALTH

# Part One

# J. P. MORGAN'S WORLD

J. P. MORGAN and Lee Iacocca: it is difficult to imagine two businessmen more different in background and in style than the financier and the automobile manufacturer. Yet each is, we think, an appropriate symbol for the American business system in his own time—Morgan for the American way of doing business in 1900 and Iacocca for that of the 1980s. The gulf between the two men accurately measures the extent to which business and the public setting in the United States have changed in this century. Hence we begin this history with an account of J. P. Morgan and his perspective on business and government; we conclude with an analysis of the world according to Iacocca.

Morgan embodied the values of the responsible business elite in America at the turn of the century. A private, inner-directed man, he was a dominant influence in the crucial investment banking industry. Largely unchecked by the government, labor unions, or foreign competitors, Morgan and his peers exercised substantial influence over some of the most productive sectors of the fast-growing American economy. They were influential in particular in that part of the business system operated by very large corporate combines and the banks that served and sometimes controlled them.

Iacocca and his business setting could scarcely be more different. A self-promoter who relishes the spotlight, he plays to the hilt his celebrity role as chief executive officer of the giant automobile firm he rescued from the brink of bankruptcy. As the successful white knight of the Chrysler revival, Iacocca has become a symbol of the efforts American firms have made in the 1980s to recover their competitive edge. If Iacocca's story is repeated by other ailing companies, then the federal government will be more deeply engaged in that recovery than a man like Morgan could have imagined. In that sense Iacocca is also the fitting symbol of the new role the government has come to play in the business system.

In Morgan's day a small elite in the business community had far more power than any businessperson, Iacocca included, can exercise today. The business leaders of the 1980s do not command; they negotiate—with Congress, with organized labor, with federal and state agencies, with well-funded interest groups, all of whom constrain their choices. Moreover, the organizations the business leaders run have changed in startling ways. It is this new institutional framework—private and public—and its evolution that is the central concern of this book.

The rise of the large corporation in J. P. Morgan's era marked a decisive shift in the nation's business system. In manufacturing, transportation, communications, and distribution, giant corporate combines were organized to bring order to their industries' markets and to exploit major technological innovations. As these institutions developed, businessmen found new ways to achieve efficient production, to encourage innovation, and to maintain control of their economic and political environments. New corporate structures were created, and managers learned how to handle larger and more complex operations. These changes, internal to the business system, also measure the gulf between Morgan and Iacocca.

The government's role shifted decisively in three major areas in this century: single-industry regulation, cross-industry regulation that set rules under which all businesses operate, and government-directed activities that indirectly shape the nation's business climate. These categories are useful, for they indicate that government as such did not grow; what developed were specific governmental functions performed by specific institutions.

These categories are also handy in providing a rough chronological guide to the expansion of federal involvement with business. Over the decades since the beginning of the century the focus of governmental innovations gradually shifted from single- to cross-industry regulation and then to government-directed functions. During the 1920s it began to appear that further adjustments between business and government might be unnecessary, but the crisis of the 1930s launched another phase of governmental expansion. The result was a new accommodation between business, government, and labor that proved quite durable in the prosperous American era from the Second World War to the late 1960s. Since then a new crisis has developed, and once again the corporation and the federal government are changing in response to a threatening situation. To understand these present problems and the changes taking place, one must look first to the history of our modern business and political institutions. The best place to start is in 1900 in the era of J. P. Morgan.

# CHAPTER 1

# The View from the House of Morgan

Y OU COULD have walked into his office unannounced. In the fall of 1900, the country's leading financier sat at his desk in plain view, the door open, while he studied the reports and memoranda accumulated in the operation of J. P. Morgan & Company. All you needed to do to meet John Pierpont Morgan was to step into his office and introduce yourself.

But you probably would not have chanced it—even to meet Morgan. The few steps into his office would have carried you over the very broad gulf that separated the gentlemen who were members of the New York Yacht Club from the common people of America. Morgan had served for two years as commodore of the Yacht Club. Indeed, he spent most of his summer evenings on his own yacht, *Corsair III.* There he entertained his friends, wealthy men like himself who were accustomed to private yachts and private railroad cars. Earlier that year, when Morgan had gone south for a vacation, he had taken more than a dozen companions along in three private railroad cars attached to the Florida Special. Men who lived as

Morgan did were as certain of their station in life as any American can be, and J. P. would have explained that to you—very quickly and very forcefully.

That was another reason for not venturing into his office. Morgan's power was personal as well as financial. He was a big man with intense eyes that burned with energy. His nose—broad, ugly, and bright red—might have diverted your attention briefly while he gave you the lecture you deserved. Morgan was sixty-three years old and accustomed to command. Brusque, brilliant, and decisive, he would have sent you back to the corner of Broad and Wall Streets with a sharper understanding of those personal traits that made for success in American business.

Morgan himself once explained that success was all a matter of character. In his business of investment banking, character was of course extremely important, as it always is when large sums of money are lent. But in saying that, Morgan as usual was saying too little about himself. He was failing to describe his vital, constructive role in the great transition that was taking place in American capitalism at the turn of the century. Morgan was a builder, an architect of organizations. His products were some of the most formidable of our past and present-day corporations, giant transportation and industrial combines that from his day to ours have been major forces in the American economy.

Morgan's creations followed a pattern shaped not only by the economic setting but also by the particular personality of this formidable man. He would have scoffed at this idea, of course. But from our perspective we can see clearly that Morgan's personality helped position him to play a central role in the strategic transformation that took place in the economy during those years. His obsession with bringing things under control was the critical element. In every aspect of his life, J. P. Morgan revealed a compulsive desire to bring haphazard reality under tight control. When dining out, as he did frequently, he insisted on the same table in his favorite restaurant. When he spent time with his family on a Sunday, there would always be a round of hymns—the same hymns every time. In travel, in family life, in his regular church activities, this intense man relentlessly imposed control on everything around him.

That, too, was his fixed purpose in the most important of his business activities. There was ample disorder in the rapidly expanding business system of turn-of-the-century America to keep several J. P. Morgans busy. In those years the country's bountiful natural resources were great magnets that pulled investment capital and labor into new enterprises. The nation did not lack the kind of people willing to guide this critical process of development. The entrepreneurs of that day took high risks. They put their own capital and credit on the line to seed new companies. They had to fend off competitors, discipline a frequently unruly labor force, and manipulate the political system when it stood between them and the resources they needed. When they succeeded, their firms frequently drove out of business less efficient producers and companies making older, less desirable products. This process of "creative destruction" was one of the outstanding characteristics of American business in the nineteenth century.

The oil industry was typical of this style of resource-centered business. Oil production in the United States had already grown by over 100 percent in the twenty years prior to 1900, yet the business stood on the threshold of another, even more decisive burst of rapid expansion as the great fields of the southwestern United States came into production. The Gulf Coast wells were amazingly rich, and aggressive businessmen like Joseph S. Cullinan of the Texas Company made them the foundation stones of new and very successful enterprises, in the process accumulating great personal fortunes. Theirs was the American dream writ large. But viewed from the particular vantage point of J. P. Morgan and Company, Broad and Wall Streets, these developments had a negative, even threatening aspect. They destroyed the control that John D. Rockefeller's Standard Oil Company had achieved in the oil industry during the years before 1900.

From Morgan's point of view Rockefeller had followed a perfectly natural course of business evolution. He had sought and achieved a dominant position at one stage in the process of transforming oil from crude in the ground to a marketable product available to the consumer. Refining was the first crucial link in the process that Rockefeller brought under control. He persuaded the refiners to join forces in a so-called horizontal combination (see figure 1.1), rather than to compete. As that goal was being accomplished, and it took many years, he also strengthened the Standard Oil Company's position by combining vertically—that is, by integrating transportation and distribution and then oil drilling and production with his refining operations. Rounded out in this way, Standard Oil was in position to impose a substantial measure of control over prices, production, and thus profits in the industry. Because of its large size the combine could also hold down unit costs, concentrating its heaviest production runs in its most efficient refineries. Because it was vertically integrated, it could eliminate transactions costs between refining and transportation, for instance,

FIGURE 1.1

### Horizontal and Vertical Combination
### in the Oil Industry

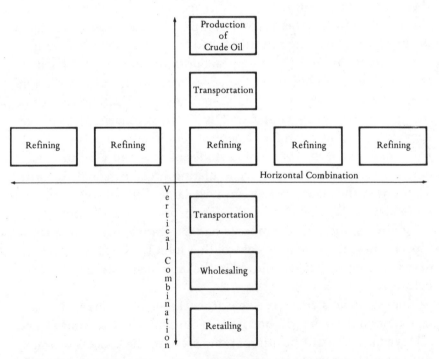

Horizontal combination brought together the various firms performing one function such as refining. Vertical combination brought together the enterprises performing different functions in the sequence from acquiring raw materials to selling finished goods or services to consumers.

and sell its high-quality products here and abroad at prices that encouraged mass distribution—the counterpart of Standard's capacity for mass production.

By 1900 Standard Oil had achieved most of the goals Rockefeller had set for the organization. It controlled about 90 percent of the domestic industry. It was able to curb price competition, keeping prices and profits in the industry relatively stable. It was a highly efficient producer of finished products and was able to distribute and market its goods over the entire United States and in a number of foreign countries. But the sudden growth of the oil industry in the Southwest and West upset this situation, as new entrepreneurs and new firms challenged Standard's dominance.

Morgan confronted the same sort of quandary in the iron and steel industry. There the disruptive factor was not new ore discoveries, however. It was worse: it was Andrew Carnegie and his efficient producing units, which were putting competitive pressure on the steel firms Morgan had helped to organize. In an effort to bring competition under control, Morgan had backed the merger of five companies into Federal Steel. He had placed the reliable Judge Elbert H. Gary in charge of this combine of steel products manufacturers. But this move had no sooner been completed than Carnegie threatened to expand vertically into steel products, a move that would launch a debilitating wave of price competition and might well send Federal Steel and Morgan's other firms into bankruptcy. It was something to ponder as Morgan silently played solitaire—his favorite card game—in the quiet evenings.

For years now Morgan had been working relentlessly to bring these kinds of competitive situations under control. There were profits to be made by all where the pressure of price competition could be relieved. Morgan had first encountered this problem in the railroad industry. Railroads had extremely high fixed costs—costs they had to pay for their bonded debt, for example, whether the road had any business or not. This encouraged each separate company to try to get all the business it could, at almost any price. Price wars were common on the competitive through routes. In 1874–75 these struggles had forced the roads to cut the average rate on goods shipped between New York and Chicago by almost 30 percent.

Morgan could no more tolerate this kind of self-destruction than he could doing business with men like Jay Gould and Daniel Drew, two Wall Street speculators with dubious reputations. Morgan started as early as 1886 to hold meetings for the officers of competing lines to encourage them to eliminate cutthroat competition by stabilizing prices and market shares. Later he sought a more lasting solution, merging various lines into great railroad systems that were virtually self-sustaining insofar as they controlled the feeder lines that provided the through roads with traffic. Morgan was able to bring these companies into line in large part because the severe depression of the 1890s had brought them to the edge—and often over the edge—of bankruptcy. That settled, Morgan was satisfied to leave the reorganized companies alone, so long as they were headed by reliable officers who would keep competition under control.

By 1900 Morgan saw many other opportunities to implement his business strategy of combination and control. In iron and steel he had plans laid for the greatest combination of all—the United States Steel Corporation, the first billion-dollar company. He would buy out Carnegie, merge the several producers of finished products, round out the new firm with ample ore and coal fields, and bring order to this vital industry. He had his eye on the maritime industry as well, and the telephone enterprise also seemed ripe for reorganization. The Bell System had for years controlled the telephone industry by way of its patent rights, but after the patents had expired in 1894 and 1895, independents had sprung up, in rural areas as well as in the cities, to challenge Bell. Intense competition and the industry's large capital requirements made the telephone a likely candidate for restructuring à la Morgan.

The great financier was thus placing his mark on the American economy primarily by fostering combinations in capital-intensive industries in an effort—not always successful—to bring the market under control. Morgan was not averse to entrepreneurship, to the promotion of innovations. He was a major factor in the young electrical industry in the United States and abroad. He had been intrigued by Thomas A. Edison's inventions and in fact had installed an electric generating and lighting system in his own home at 219 Madison Avenue in 1881, long before the invention had been perfected. Morgan soon discovered the price of premature innovation. The wiring frequently shorted out, his neighbors complained about the noise from his generator, and then the system started a fire that ruined his library. Morgan nevertheless persisted, both in using electricity in his home and in financing the Edison power companies that were providing electricity to America's largest cities in the 1880s and 1890s.

Electricity was, however, the exception. Steel was the rule for the Morgan undertakings. There he reorganized a mature, capital-intensive industry, in this case using a holding company, a firm that owned or held the stock of other corporations in the combine, to bring most of the industry's major producers into one firm. U.S. Steel controlled enough of the nation's ore supplies to make entry very difficult for potential competitors. The Steel Corporation made over 50 percent of the basic iron and steel in the United States and an even higher percentage of many finished products, such as wire nails. It could to a substantial degree control prices and influence market shares; its policies on these matters emphasized stability. It was, from Morgan's perspective, a very successful enterprise that brought and maintained order in one of the country's leading industries, a situation that yielded ample profits for all.

Morgan's contribution to the business system was thus to bring under control relationships between heretofore competing firms. He had less to do with the effort going on during these same years to improve controls within the corporation. Every combine went through a long process of administrative consolidation as authority and lines of communication were gradually centralized and standard forms of accounting were applied to the company's operations. It frequently took several years to clarify relationships between the chief executive and the several departments in the business. Businessmen previously accustomed to running their own companies often found it difficult to accept orders from the combine's central office.

While each such company developed at a particular pace and in a particular way, the most common pattern that emerged involved functional departments reporting to a central office under the day-to-day direction of the company's president. Each of the departments—typically manufacturing, transportation, and marketing—

was normally headed by a single manager who could thus specialize in the administration of just one of the business's several activities. Committees of these several managers usually studied and made recommendations on major decisions facing the business, such as financing expansion or deciding where to market the company's products.

The committee system notwithstanding, decision-making in this type of corporation was highly centralized and the authority of the chief executive officer (CEO) generally unchallenged. He of course had to report to a board of directors—this was where Morgan would normally have his representative—but so long as the firm was successful, the CEO could anticipate few specific directives from that front. Morgan's main concern was to have the right person in the vital position of CEO. Once assured on this point, the financier was concerned about general measures of performance, not specific decisions. The major constraint on the executive's authority came not from above, but from below; the large size of the business and the immense amounts of detailed information flowing on a regular basis to the top were too much for a single executive—even one with an excellent staff—to monitor and absorb. The CEO had to depend upon middle managers and committees to see to that. The CEO was thus both beholden to and the master of an intricate network of managerial relationships, most of which involved a high degree of functional specialization. It was this type of organization that gave birth to professional business management in the United States.

Viewed from the House of Morgan, the center of the U.S. business system consisted of corporate giants of this ilk and their closely related banks. Out beyond them in the next of several concentric circles were the smaller businesses and banks that filled the niches between the dominant firms. Even further out were the small farmers and individual businesspeople in real estate, professional activities, retail stores, and the service industries, all sectors of the economy that were still highly competitive and seemingly beyond the sort of control Morgan and others had imposed at the center. Beyond even that ring were the consumers and laborers, atomistic and largely passive in the Morgan schema. Like the small producers they seldom were highly organized, and Morgan did not really want to see them bring their activities under control.

Insofar as this business system needed coordination, it was provided by markets and the gold standard. While Morgan's combines
were designed to thwart short-term market forces, active and
smooth-functioning markets still had a critical role to play in the
economy over the long term. The New York stock market just
beyond the door to J. P. Morgan & Company was a perfect example
of what an effective market could accomplish. In effect, the stock
exchange gathered capital from all over the country and even
abroad—since the 1890s, from small investors as well as large—and
channeled these funds to businesses in need of them. Similar markets existed for most of the country's basic commodities. All were
kept synchronized, as were the international money markets, by the
gold standard for currency. The gold standard ensured that market
transactions today would have a similar value tomorrow. Money
lent this year would be paid back next year in a stable currency.
Only a few years before, the gold standard had been under fire from
those Americans who sought to encourage inflation, but in 1900,
with President William McKinley reelected, the gold standard
seemed safe and with it Morgan's style of capitalism.

Protecting the gold standard was one of the few things that Morgan was certain the government could properly do to affect the
economy. Protecting private property was another. That would include providing police protection and a fire department to help if his
library burned again. Matters of health were properly within the
purview of the state, as were questions of national defense. Otherwise, Morgan's economic world was largely private, not public.

The nation's foremost financier had thought a good bit about this
question in recent years, because many people in the country were
calling for a more active, more powerful state. Since the depression
of the 1870s, western and southern farmers had been looking to
impose controls of their own sort on the nation's economy. Unlike
the controls J. P. Morgan created, these farmer-fostered programs
would have brought political authority to bear on economic affairs.
Monopolies would have been eliminated in transportation, communications, and manufacturing; the railroads would have been
regulated; the currency would have been inflated in a systematic
manner to help creditors; and farmers would have been given direct
support in various ways. Some of the agrarian agendas had been

supported by other interests, including some businesses, and a small part of their program had been enacted. In 1887, Congress had created the Interstate Commerce Commission to regulate the railroads. Three years later it had passed the Sherman Antitrust Act, ostensibly to establish opposition to monopoly and restraint of trade as public policy throughout the country.

This was all disconcerting to Morgan. Even though the forces of agrarian protest had seemingly crested in 1896 (when the farmers' Populist Party had joined with the Democrats in an unsuccessful effort to elect William Jennings Bryan), even though William McKinley's election in that year apparently rang the death knell for those politicians seeking to jettison the gold standard, the rumblings of reform would not go away. Throughout the country there were middle-class reformers who called themselves "progressives" and were deeply concerned about the concentration of economic power.* They were complaining too about the way labor was treated in this country and about the severe problems of cities like New York. Morgan was active in a number of private philanthropies aimed at dealing with the problems in New York City. That was not enough. The reformers in New York and other cities wanted to supplant private welfare with a public system. On these and other fronts, including the control of working conditions for women and children, the progressive reformers were looking to impose public control over matters that had up to this time been left in private hands—too often, they thought, in powerful hands like those of J. P. Morgan.

Confident that men of his class and station could control economic affairs far better than any regulatory commission, Morgan had always thrown his considerable support behind those candidates like McKinley, who seemed satisfied that America would continue to prosper most if it changed its government least. McKinley (1897–1901) was a Republican. But Morgan was happy to sup-

---

*The progressive reform movement, which began at the local and state levels in the 1890s, attempted to address through government a variety of problems stemming from rapid industrialization and urbanization. Generally, progressive or liberal reformers sought to increase the powers of government. They tried as well to break the power of the often-corrupt ward-level political organizations in the cities. Frequently they looked to nonpartisan experts—on regulatory commissions, for example—as the best means of strengthening the hand of government.

port Democrats, too, so long as they were solid-gold, reliable Democrats like Grover Cleveland (1885–1889, 1893–1897). For William Jennings Bryan and others who spoke for the forces of reform, Morgan had only contempt shaded with some uneasiness about what the future held for American government. Morgan saw himself as the best friend that government had ever had, whether it was the state or city government in New York or the federal government in Washington, D.C. During the depression of the 1890s, he had demonstrated his loyalty by coming to the rescue of the government in a monetary crisis. Congress, locked in a struggle with the White House, would not pass legislation needed to restock the U.S. Treasury with gold. As foreign and domestic investors became nervous, a serious gold drain developed, bringing the government to the edge of default. Morgan intervened. In cooperation with New York banker August Belmont and the Rothschilds (a powerful European banking firm and family), Morgan helped to restock the U.S. Treasury with gold and dampened the flow of the precious metal out of the country.

This episode epitomized the Morgan style of political economy. The elite of the financial system lent a helping hand to the president of the United States, dealing on a personal basis. The nation benefitted, as did all those financial interests in the United States and Europe that had a stake in keeping the country on the gold standard and out of default. Order was preserved. Meanwhile, Morgan and his colleagues made some money on the transaction, a proper reward for the risks they incurred and the authority their names brought to this tense situation. The control imposed was personal, elitist, ad hoc, and profitable to the private interests involved. The balance between private and public power was struck much to the advantage of the private sector.

This was the style of business and government Morgan wanted to preserve, and in 1900 he had reason to believe that the America he saw from the House of Morgan might remain intact. His favorite party, the Republican Party, was in the driver's seat in national politics. Liberal reformers were still protesting about the "trusts," but the GOP had consolidated the gains it had made in the decisive election of 1896, and the agrarian movement seemed to have been stopped in its tracks. The Supreme Court had virtually nullified

both the Interstate Commerce Act and the Sherman Antitrust Act,
leaving Morgan's combines in transportation and manufacturing
apparently beyond the control of public authorities.

Moreover, these great corporations appeared to be bringing to
their respective industries the measure of control that was needed
to assure peace and profits. The national economy was booming.
The stock market was easily absorbing the new securities sold to
finance mergers, whether promoted by Morgan or by other investment bankers. One can understand why Morgan enjoyed so much
the opportunity that fall to orchestrate the wedding of his daughter
Louisa to Herbert Satterlee, a partner in his firm. As usual J. P.
controlled every detail of the occasion: the tapestries, the flowers,
the large ballroom erected for this single occasion at 219 Madison
Avenue. Twenty-four hundred distinguished guests had an opportunity to enjoy the hospitality of the man who more than any other
symbolized the power and wealth that American business had
achieved by 1900.

CHAPTER 2

# The Entrepreneurial Firm
# and the Morgan System,
# 1840–1900

AS A CHILD John Pierpont Morgan had become familiar with a far different sort of business from the great corporate combines he constructed at the turn of the century. In Hartford, Connecticut, where he spent his early childhood, the Morgan family was deeply involved in what were typical businesses of the 1840s. J.P.'s grandfather, Joseph Morgan III, had invested in the Aetna Fire Insurance Company and then in the Connecticut River Banking Company. Hartford was a transportation center in the fast-growing New England economy, and the elder Morgan found opportunities to invest his capital and organizational talents in a hotel, a canal company, and then a railroad. He was in this regard like many other American businesspeople who built locally centered networks of complementary enterprises. Ties with a bank were important for capital and for facilitating commercial transactions. Transportation ventures further enhanced the local economy, bringing more visitors to stay at Morgan's Pavilion Hotel and more customers for the real estate in which Joseph Mor-

gan also invested. This complementary portfolio of local investments was woven together by a web of personal ties in the community and in the regional business system.

J.P.'s father, Junius Morgan, was a businessman with the firm of
Howe and Mather. The company ran a general merchandising business with a store in Hartford and a trade in wholesale dry goods that
stretched out from Connecticut into the growing cotton economy of
the South. The cotton grown in the South was spun and woven in
the mills of New England and then shipped back to the South as dry
goods by businessmen like Junius Morgan. Of course Morgan also
handled other products when he made his lengthy trips through the
South, dealing face-to-face with the customers of Howe and
Mather. His ties were broader than those of his father, but both men
traded with people they knew and trusted; Joseph Morgan had
personally visited the local agents who wrote policies for Aetna.
Junius extended credit to his customers; he stood to lose money if
they went under during a depression such as the one that had
shaken the business system between 1837 and the early 1840s.
Character was important if one were to survive—or, as was the case
with the Morgans, be very successful—in this business setting.
Personal ties were more important than organizations, and most
businesses were run by a single proprietor or by partners like Howe
and Mather, whose firm became Howe, Morgan and Co. in 1850.

## THE NINETEENTH-CENTURY FIRM

Throughout the United States in the 1840s and 1850s this style of
business, the entrepreneurial firm, played a crucial role in the nation's rapid economic expansion. In most of the businesses of that
era, one or two men made the major decisions about the firm's
long-range goals and its means of achieving those objectives. These
were the entrepreneurial decisions, those that most affected the
business's allocation of resources, and the great strength of this type
of enterprise was its ability to innovate, to perform the entrepreneurial function. There were no committees to slow the process
of innovation, no layers of bureaucracy that had to sign off on

changes. Within the firm the process of entrepreneurship was firmly in the grip of the owner, who might at most have to consult with a partner and perhaps some fellow businessmen or a lending institution if the undertaking had been financed through a stock sale or a loan.

Obtaining capital and credit for the firm was one of the businessman's most important activities. The United States in the 1840s and 1850s was a capital-poor country, and few of the institutions that twentieth-century firms routinely turn to for financial support were available. The urban exchanges did not handle stocks; those securities were considered too risky to be traded in that way. Besides, few enterprises in manufacturing or distribution were incorporated. Most were partnerships. Banks seldom lent money on a long-term basis to such businesses, although they might extend commercial credit, usually for thirty, sixty, or ninety days. It was, however, no easy task to obtain loans even on these terms. The businessman had to be known personally by the bank's officers and had to have a solid reputation.

In this setting the normal course for someone starting in business was to draw upon personal and family savings and often those of a partner for start-up capital. If one or more of the partners had been in business before, working for someone else, they might have a strong enough standing to obtain credit from suppliers of the raw materials or finished goods they needed. But working capital was normally in short supply, and the entrepreneurial firm had a very slim margin for error.

Typical of the businesses of that era was the lumber enterprise young Frederick Weyerhaeuser launched in Rock Island, Illinois in the 1850s. A recent immigrant from Germany, Weyerhaeuser had worked for a time at a sawmill, which failed during the panic of 1857. By that time he had acquired enough capital to buy the bankrupt firm's lumberyard and then lease its sawmill, but cash was so scarce that he bartered his goods, trading lumber for farm animals or produce, just to keep his tiny business afloat. After a few years of successful operations he had accumulated enough assets to buy the sawmill at the sheriff's foreclosure sale. Going into partnership with his uncle, he put up $4,616.51, of which over $3,000 was in cash and the rest was in assets ranging from a buggy to seven hogs and a brass collar. In effect Weyerhaeuser and his uncle bet most of the property they owned that another recession would not threaten their venture before they got their feet solidly on the ground. In their case they won the gamble and soon had a thriving, solvent business. But the margin for this kind of business was narrow, and the risks—most of them beyond the businessman's control—were all too numerous.

In addition to obtaining capital and credit, the owner-entrepreneur was responsible for the firm's technology—the tools, machines, and systems the firm developed to produce particular goods or services. In distribution and finance that might not be very important, but in manufacturing, transportation, and communications, technological matters were central elements in business success. The American economy in the nineteenth century was experiencing a revolutionary transformation from handwork to machine production and from human and animal power to water and steam power. In electricity and chemicals, new scientific concepts were creating unusual business opportunities. To take advantage of these situations, however, the entrepreneur had to harness new technologies. Given the limited resources of the entrepreneurial firm, that usually required the businessman to have some technical ability in order to make decisions about technological matters.

Even in the textile industry, which experienced a higher degree of specialization than most antebellum businesses, the owner-entrepreneur had to be closely involved in basic technological decisions. The machinery used to spin and weave cotton and wool was changing rapidly, as were the sources of power. Many producers in small or medium-sized businesses were directly involved in making these changes in the production process. Joseph Schofield of Philadelphia, a cotton manufacturer, was typical of this breed. An immigrant from England's Lancashire textile district, he got his start in the 1840s by operating a small mill for another manufacturer, using his own family as part of his work force. Soon he had accumulated enough capital to go into business for himself in a partnership. His sons, who took over the business after their father died, continued the tradition of hands-on management. They worked in every part of their mill and directly supervised the installation of the new machinery they bought after their first year of operation. By 1860 they had thirty-two employees and a business that was continuing to grow. But in this case and many others like it, business-men still had to be jacks-of-all-trades, including the mechanics of the production process. In the very large textile factories of Lowell, Massachusetts, there was more specialization of function, with the superintendent directing the technology, but such companies were the exception, not the rule, in American business in the 1840s and 1850s.

## LABOR RELATIONS IN THE ENTREPRENEURIAL FIRM

In textiles and other industries in which production was being shifted to the factory, the businessman had to muster a new kind of disciplined labor force and keep employees on the job more steadily than had been the case in the past. This was a traumatic change in the nature of work. The sun and the seasons gave way to the clock and the machine. Adjusting to this new order was difficult for employees, as many labor historians have noted. It was also a difficult shift for the businessman, who had to manage in a country in which labor was in short supply and much of the population was literally on the move, changing residences and occupations frequently. "Churning" is an apt expression for the mobile American population of the time.

In even a small factory, the employer was likely to have a superintendent or foreman who was directly in charge of the work force. But all important decisions about the hours of work (they were long) or about wages (they were high by European standards) had to be made by the boss. The entrepreneur seldom had to deal with organizations of workers; not until 1842 did it become clear that unions were not illegal conspiracies. Whether the workers were organized or not, however, the employer's relations with the work force tended to be adversarial. To a considerable degree the workers and the employer had different interests. The businessman was under pressure to hold down labor costs, and indeed the entire move to the factory was in large part a means of substituting capital for labor in a manner that would reduce the cost of production. When prices fell, as they did regularly, the businessman was quick to cut wages. If workers resisted the cuts, the employer would replace them or shut down entirely if that would save money. The flexibility of the entrepreneurial firm extended to labor relations, and the two-edged sword that cut costs also periodically left the workers without jobs or with sharply reduced incomes.

In both the factory and the small shops characteristic of American business in the 1840s and 1850s, workers periodically attempted to protect their interests through joint action. Handicapped by the absence of a strong class tradition in this country and by the embryonic nature of their local organizations, laborers were nonetheless able to win some immediate victories when business conditions were favorable and employers were reluctant to lose sales. When demand slackened, however, and the balance of power shifted toward the owner-boss, the workers were unable to prevent wage cuts and changes in work conditions. It was not until the late 1850s that skilled hands in a few industries were able to develop trade unions, so-called "pure and simple" unions,* capable of surviving through an entire business cycle. In the meantime the tradition of adversarial labor relations—a hostile relationship that fell short of class warfare but normally involved conflict and could easily drift toward violence—became the norm for the entrepreneurial firm. Owner-entrepreneurs directed their attention primarily toward disciplining the work force and cutting labor costs. In the factory, in particular, business made no effort to take advantage of the worker's own entrepreneurial talents. Specialization of function and machine production actually worked in the opposite direction, as did the general tone of labor relations in the era of the entrepreneurial firm. The businessman provided the innovative impulse. Workers who had entrepreneurial instincts had to strike out on their own, as some did during the generally prosperous years prior to the Civil War.

## BUSINESS AND SOCIETY IN PRE–CIVIL WAR AMERICA

For business in America these were, on balance, good times economically and politically as well. The American style of federal

---

*They were "pure and simple" because they focused on questions such as wages and hours and avoided reform politics and utopian plans for the reorganization of society.

government left most of the important decisions about controls on or support for business in the hands of local and state authorities. The elaborate system of checks and balances set forth in the Constitution ensured that this situation would be difficult to change. The major political parties—the Democrats, the Whigs, and later the Republicans—all had their centers of gravity at the local level. There businessmen could make their influence felt directly, and many did. Enjoying a position of high standing and frequently of influence in their local communities, they were able to sustain a political climate friendly to capitalist endeavors. Aside from their direct involvement in this highly personalized brand of politics, they had many advantages, the greatest of which was a cultural setting attuned to "making it" in a material sense. The antibusiness sentiments that were to emerge in the late nineteenth and early twentieth centuries were minor themes in the 1840s and 1850s, except perhaps in the South. What did vibrate through America was praise for the creator of new ventures, whether on the farm, in transportation, or in manufacturing and commerce. This materialistic culture was translated into specific political accomplishments when the states and localities supported internal improvements, encouraged resource use, eased the route to incorporation, and carefully protected property rights. The entrepreneurs of that day could expect few threats and much support from government.

In this setting the owner-innovator was an active participant in a congenial political system, the master of his labor force and technology, the main agent in obtaining capital and credit, and the primary factor in buying the firm's supplies and marketing its products or services. In many cases markets were local or regional, but rapid improvements in transportation and communications were beginning to break down barriers to interregional trade in antebellum America. Junius Morgan's trips to the South were a typical feature of commerce in this era. The distribution network was an intricate web of wholesalers and retailers, each of whom dealt in a series of markets, and most of whom had little control over the prices they paid or received. Businessmen set their prices at the level dictated by the market; they were in essence "price takers" in a market system that resembled the neat models of theoretical economics.

As the economy grew and their markets expanded, businesspeople behaved more or less as Adam Smith suggested they would and began to specialize in one particular product or service. This tendency was marked in the two decades prior to the Civil War, and the trend toward functional specialization by firms and within them as well would continue through the rest of the century, eventually reshaping most aspects of the American business system.

During the antebellum years the pace of growth in the business system was uneven—even more so than it is today—and on the downswing of the cycle, businesses were usually forced to cut prices. As margins narrowed, they cut costs as well, but costs were less flexible than prices. Businessmen faced with this problem often adopted the tactics Adam Smith had outlined and tried to get their competitors to agree to hold the line on prices. Where markets were narrow and competitors few, this tactic could get a firm through the bad times. But small companies had few resources to fall back on when demand and prices were falling. Price agreements were impossible to enforce in the courts and hence unstable.* A more successful approach was to establish a niche for one's products or services through differentiation. Few products were standardized, and differentiation was a viable means of ensuring that a firm's business would, to some extent, be insulated from all but the worst declines in demand and prices. Special trademarks and strong personal ties with customers were common means of achieving this goal. Extending credit to customers was another approach to the same problem.

Where all else failed, bankruptcy might be the result, especially during an extended downturn such as those following the panics of 1837 and 1857. The failure rate for the entrepreneurial firm was high, even in good times. But bankruptcy was accepted in antebellum America as a common problem, one that was individual, not social, in nature. Many a businessman failed in several attempts to get a successful enterprise going. There was, moreover, no end of entrepreneurs willing to step forward when one faltered. By present-day standards, the business system of that day was chaotic:

*American common law was averse to restraint of trade and monopolization. In Germany, by contrast, such arrangements were legal and enforceable contracts, and businesses frequently developed price and production agreements (so-called "cartels").

information was more limited than it is today, and the risks of investment much higher; price competition was often fierce, and shady practices were common. But the system had tremendous vitality. The ability to innovate, to strike out in entirely new directions and to do so quickly, was the greatest asset of the entrepreneurial firm of the 1840s and 1850s.

## THE HEYDAY OF THE ENTREPRENEURIAL FIRM

That vitality was tested in the 1860s, when the Civil War twisted the American economy out of its normal path of development. The war struck hard at the nation's leading manufacturing industry, cotton textiles. The business of dealing in and transporting cotton— like most southern commercial ventures—was disrupted by the war and the northern blockade of the region's leading ports. In New England the cotton textile firms, which were some of the nation's largest businesses, were forced to close their doors when they were unable to obtain cotton. Unlike most businesses of that day the largest of the cotton manufacturers used the corporate form of organization and drew upon the capital of a relatively large group of mercantile investors. These mills, which integrated spinning and weaving and were for their time highly efficient, had since the 1820s dominated the national market for textiles; the regional economy of New England suffered severely when they stopped production. Other northern businesses as well were hurt by wartime inflation, by the short supply of labor, and by the inability to get to markets in the South.

But one of the great assets of the entrepreneurial business was its flexibility, and in the North and West businessmen were able to adjust to and take advantage of wartime conditions. Some producers found demand increasing sharply. Military contracts for firearms and munitions, boots and shoes, uniforms, and provisions were lucrative. In the agricultural regions of the Midwest, horse-drawn farm machinery was creating a revolutionary increase in productivity, and the combination of a shortage of labor and high prices for farm products stimulated the demand for the products of the

McCormick Reaper factory and the Deering Harvester Company, among others. Western cities, especially Chicago and Cincinnati, did a booming business in agricultural products, which were moved from the farm to the customer through a complex network of commission merchants, manufacturers, wholesalers, and retail stores. Most of these enterprises were small by today's standards. Most (excepting the retailers) were functionally specialized. All were influenced directly by the prosperity in the North.

With business support and without southern opposition, Congress was able to pass a number of measures designed to encourage economic expansion even more: subsidies for the transcontinental railroads; land for the settlers who would ship their products on the railroads and buy more farm machinery, nails, and axes; tariff protection for the manufacturers of these and other products; and a national banking system for those who would help finance all these transactions.

In the South, businesses were less fortunate. The war at first stimulated some indigenous industries but ultimately crushed many of the region's businesses. By the end of the war, the loss of capital, physical destruction, and a flood of worthless paper money had wiped out most of a generation of entrepreneurs.

Reconstruction imposed additional burdens on southern business, but it did not prevent a rush of capitalists coming from the North and West eager to make good use of the South's natural resources, its relatively cheap labor, and its demand for modern products and services. They helped push the development of the region's railroad system. Lumber and lumber products also attracted entrepreneurial attention, as did the region's large supplies of coal and iron ore. Northern and southern businessmen also began to work together to promote cotton textile mills in the southern Piedmont. By the 1880s business in the South was beginning to recast the economy of a region long overly dependent upon staple agriculture for its livelihood.

Although it was fast recovering from the war, business in the South fell even further behind the North and West, where great surges of economic expansion were taking place. It was a fine time to be in business almost anywhere in the United States. From the late 1860s through 1893, the American economy grew at an unusually high rate (see table 2.1). Heavy investments in railroad construction were a prominent feature of this phase of growth, but what was most unusual was the breadth of the development and the multitude of economic opportunities it created. American businessmen were quick to take advantage of these opportunities: in oil, which could be turned into kerosene for growing urban and rural markets; in coal and minerals; in lumber and wood products; in manufactured goods for what had become the world's largest domestic market; and in the transportation and communications needed to link together an unusually large and diverse nation.

These years were the heyday of the entrepreneurial firm. Most of the nation's business was done by this type of enterprise. In moving the nation's abundant agricultural commodities from the farm to the consumer, for example, the crops were gathered for shipment by local merchants and the owners of elevators and other local storage facilities. They were handled in shipment by commodity brokers and commission merchants and normally were sold on an open exchange. Cotton, for instance, was bought and sold on the New York exchange as well as on a number of regional markets in southern cities. Wheat, corn, hogs, and beef all moved to market along

TABLE 2.1

Rates of Growth per Year of the U.S. Economy, 1859–1902

Annual Increases

| Successive and Overlapping decades | National Product (%) | Product per Capita (%) | Population (%) |
| --- | --- | --- | --- |
| 1859–69 | 1.99 | −0.39 | 2.39 |
| 1869–79 | 4.95 | 2.56 | 2.33 |
| 1878–82—1888–92 | 3.73 | 1.44 | 2.26 |
| 1883–87—1893–97 | 3.10 | 1.05 | 2.02 |
| 1888–92—1898–1902 | 4.04 | 2.20 | 1.80 |

SOURCE: Simon Kuznets, "Notes on the Pattern of U.S. Economic Growth," in Edgar O. Edwards, ed., *The Nation's Economic Objectives* (Chicago: University of Chicago Press, 1964), 16. Unless otherwise indicated, all the information in the following tables is from U.S. government sources, including the annual *Statistical Abstracts* and *Historical Statistics of the United States, Colonial Times to 1970*.

similar paths, handled by small firms run by their owners or a set of partners.

Even in manufacturing, where one might have expected economies of scale to have been important, the entrepreneurial firm produced most of the nation's products. In chemicals there was a thriving industry centered around Philadelphia. Typical of the companies of that day was the plant Henry Bower built to convert the wastes of the Philadelphia Gas Works into sulfate of ammonia. Bower had been trained in chemistry at the Philadelphia College of Pharmacy and had learned the business working as an importer of chemicals. He personally conducted all of his firm's research and development, directed its production, and handled sales, most of which were to other producers in the Philadelphia area. Bower was successful in all three functions. He developed a new process for manufacturing glycerin and pushed his firm into other products, including acids and prussiates. As the industry expanded and demand grew in the 1870s, the Bower interests thrived and diversified their product line, while keeping a focus on industrial chemicals for a largely regional market.

Similar situations existed in the production of metal and wood products, most foods, and ready-made clothing, and in new businesses such as photographic supplies and electrical equipment. Production and distribution were largely in the hands of small enterprises controlled by an owner-entrepreneur or a set of partners.

## THE RISE OF THE COMBINE

Successful as the entrepreneurial firm was in promoting business development, in a number of industries this style of organization began to give ground to a new type of enterprise. What, then, were the limitations of the entrepreneurial firm? Why would it be squeezed into a new and less powerful role in the economy after the turn of the century? It was (and still is today) a highly innovative mode of business organization, able to adapt to new conditions and thus to exploit the manifold opportunities arising in the fast-changing U.S. economy. But the entrepreneurial firm lacked the capital and administrative resources needed to achieve economies of scale in mass production and distribution. It was long on the ability to innovate and short on operating efficiency. Most of the businessmen of that day did not even know what their unit costs were; they were, as we have seen, "price takers" who used only the most rudimentary forms of income and asset accounting. Most lacked the power to influence the markets in which they bought or sold— another weakness from the businessman's point of view (but not from that of the customer).

One can appraise any business in terms of its ability to perform three major functions: innovating, achieving efficiency in day-to-day operations, and maintaining control of its external environments. Successfully carried out, these functions produce profits and the growth of the firm. Clearly the small firms of the nineteenth century were best suited to perform one of these functions: innovation. In that regard they were well attuned to the business landscape of a rapidly expanding nation with abundant resources. Many of these businesses were outstanding successes, reaping the advantages of entrepreneurship in the form of high profits. But it was difficult for them to protect those profits over the long run, to ensure that the owner or partners would ultimately be replaced by equally effective leaders or to reduce risks by exercising control of their markets. Nor could they normally achieve a high degree of efficiency in production or distribution.

To some extent, of course, the three functions involve tradeoffs in any business. A high degree of operating efficiency is unlikely in a firm constantly engaging in innovative behavior. Nor is a high degree of control—by a monopoly, for instance—generally associated with an unusually high level of entrepreneurship. What one should look for in any business system is the balance struck between these three functions by its typical firms. In nineteenth-century America, the normal firm was long on innovation but short on efficiency and control of its external economic relationships. Only in control of its political setting, as we saw before, could the entrepreneurial business be said to have excelled in this third function (see figure 2.1).

FIGURE 2.1
## The Three Major Business Functions
## and the Entrepreneurial Firm

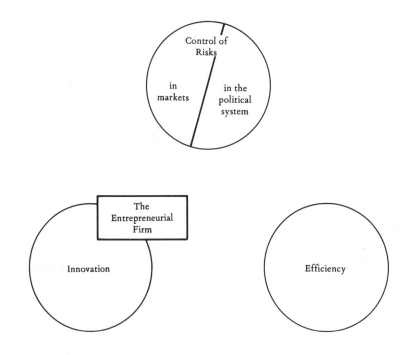

The balance is heavily on the side of the innovative function. Control of the firm's markets is weak. In the nineteenth century, entrepreneurial firms had relatively favorable political relationships. Efficiency of operations is low with this style of firm.

In a number of industries, this situation led businesses to develop a new type of organization, the centralized corporate combine. In the fledgling telegraph industry of the 1840s, for instance, the interests holding the Morse patent had at first licensed a series of small enterprises to construct lines between some of the country's leading business centers—New York, Philadelphia, Boston, Buffalo, and St. Louis. When competition arose, it too initially took the form of a loosely united federation of entrepreneurial firms using local capital to build sections of an opposing telegraph network. But in the 1850s, these partnerships yielded to a corporate form of organization, and a series of mergers made the Western Union Company the dominant firm in the industry. By 1866, Western Union had absorbed all its major competitors and was the largest firm doing business in the country (capitalized at over $40 million).

The combine effectively eliminated price competition in long-distance transmission. In addition to achieving economies of scale—in purchasing, for example—it enjoyed economies of system by integrating formerly competing firms into a single network. All of the stations were now interconnected and the resulting economies made the telegraph a natural monopoly. Western Union's wires linked the sender to all of the major urban centers in the United States. But to profit from these advantages, the firm's leaders (the former chief competitors were on the executive committee) had to bring their business under control in a style alien to the American business tradition. They created a set of regional organizations, each one under the authority of a general superintendent who supervised various district superintendents and reported on a regular basis to the executive committee. Information, collected in a systematic way, flowed up the business to the top; orders flowed down through the region, to the district, then to the manager of a station. This line of command was similar to a military structure of authority. The line officers ran operations and made the company's most important decisions. They were assisted by the staff, including the lawyers who worked with the executive committee. For technical assistance, the committee could turn to the firm's electrician. The line-staff organization would become a common feature of American corporate enterprise.

In this style of centralized combine the various functions performed by the owner of an entrepreneurial firm were divided among specialists. The heads of Western Union did not deal with their customers on a face-to-face basis. Nor were they directly involved with the labor force or the technology; the managers and superintendents handled the work force, and the electrician's staff was in charge of the company's technology. The executive committee made the combine's entrepreneurial decisions. They tended the $40 million in capitalization, approved or disapproved the operations of the regions and districts, and made the significant decisions about personnel and the allocation of resources—for example, when to support and when to terminate a joint Russian-American telegraph line to link the United States to Asia and Europe.

The combine was characterized by specialization of function, centralization of authority, and a new balance between the three major functions of the firm (see figure 2.2). Down the line, officers of the combine no longer made the kinds of quick decisions that the partners in an entrepreneurial firm had routinely made. Reports had to go to the executive committee, the staff had to be consulted, orders had to flow down the line. Some part of the combine's ability to innovate was sacrificed to achieve greater control of the firm's external market environment. Nevertheless, the members of the committee were well positioned and well informed to make major decisions for the system as a whole. When they did, a firm like Western Union could bring tremendous resources to bear to achieve its objectives. It could borrow money on favorable terms—no longer was working capital a problem—and could finance most of its expansion through retained earnings. It could muster substantial technological and legal resources. For Western Union, a company in a new industry using a relatively new technology, this advantage was particularly important. Western and other similar combines thus became more efficient performers of routine tasks.

Western Union's committee could not of course stay directly in touch with local developments—in the labor force or in politics—throughout its far-flung business empire. The new breed of business administrators (the managers and the superintendents) did not have the same ties to their local political system that the small entrepreneur normally had. The combine was thus left vulnerable to labor problems and to political opposition. But on balance the immediate profits to be gained by eliminating competition and by reaping the advantages of economies of system and scale far outweighed the liabilities of the combine. Western Union's profits and the value of its securities reflected the advantages of this style of corporation.

The railroad business experienced a similar pattern of development at mid-century. Expansion had at first been undertaken by a series of separate lines. Because of their needs for capital in amounts that were inordinate for that time, most of these roads were organized from the beginning as corporations. Competition was fierce, however, and these small lines were not able to sus-

FIGURE 2.2

## The Three Major Business Functions
## and the Corporate Combine

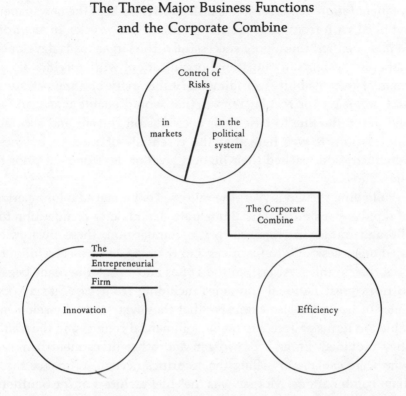

In a combine such as Western Union, the balance moved away from innovation toward greater control and efficiency.

tain themselves on the basis of their own traffic. Soon efforts were made to combine these separate firms into larger through systems linking major commercial centers. The western trade was all-important, and to tap that market a number of railroad leaders formed trunk lines: the New York Central, the Pennsylvania, and the Erie. In the 1850s this process of combination resulted in several lines of about 500 miles in length, but it was not until 1860 that one could travel from New York to Chicago on a railroad under one management.

The railroads were under even greater pressure than the telegraph company to develop efficient modes of internal administration and techniques for controlling competition. Their fixed costs were extremely high, and it was essential to keep traffic moving efficiently.

Moreover, they had to coordinate traffic to avoid collisions; their frequent failure to perform this task effectively kept the newspapers supplied with front-page stories of spectacular wrecks. In an effort to manage their lines more successfully, the larger roads developed elaborate systems of functional organization, with specific allocations of responsibility, a rudimentary hierarchy of administrators, and provision for regular reports that would enable managers up and down the line to base their decisions on current and accurate information. It was here that the essentials of modern business administration reached their highest level of development prior to the 1860s.

Following the Civil War, the railroads experienced a long period of rapid expansion, technical integration, and fierce competition for through traffic. In response to the competition, these businesses tried unsuccessfully to fix prices and then, again unsuccessfully, to pool their traffic.* At last, in the 1880s and 1890s the roads began to form great national combines including from 5,000 to 10,000 miles of track, lines so extensive that they were virtually self-contained in terms of access to major commercial centers and the traffic they provided. Enter J. P. Morgan and other investment bankers, who were capable of selling the securities needed to finance these giant combinations. Morgan was the chief architect of the Southern Railroad Company and the New England system, and during the severe depression of the 1890s he became involved in the reorganization of numerous other roads. By the end of the depression, the American railroad network was dominated by these great combines, all of which were characterized by elaborate bureaucratic systems run by professional managers. While these combines had lost some of the entrepreneurial edge of the typical nineteenth-century firm, they had certainly strengthened their market controls and their administrative systems in an effort to ensure their long-run profitability, à la Morgan.

By that time, similar changes had taken place in a number of manufacturing industries and in some related areas of the country's

---

*The pools and price-fixing agreements are usually referred to as *loose combinations* or *cartels.* In most industries business leaders experimented extensively and unsuccessfully with loose combinations before adopting the more drastic course of amalgamating their firms in a combine by way of common ownership.

distribution system. In the oil industry, from the Civil War until the 1880s, the entrepreneurial firm had been the common form of enterprise, but John D. Rockefeller and his colleagues in Cleveland, Ohio changed that situation, introducing a new measure of corporate control beneath the banner of Standard Oil. That combination had, as we have seen, virtually eliminated competition, sometimes using a ruthless style of business that left the public uneasy and the nation's elected officials on edge. Powerful as it was, the firm could not entirely ignore the public, nor could it disregard the task of operating efficiently the large enterprise that had been created. In Standard Oil the internal response was a functionally departmentalized, centralized style of corporation, with the major decisions made by a series of committees operating out of the company's headquarters. Standard operated its own pipelines and began to manage its own wholesale distribution, to make its own barrels, and finally to acquire and operate its own oil wells. By the end of the 1890s, Standard Oil had developed into a highly efficient, vertically integrated combine, one that realized economies of scale and provided American consumers with low-cost, high-quality products.

While Standard Oil had yet to resolve its differences with the public, the giant oil firm was an extremely efficient producer-distributor of standardized products, and it began to innovate in new ways as well. Because of its large resources, Standard could afford to employ a talented scientist to find ways to use midwestern crude oil with a high sulfur content. After successfully solving the problems of refining Lima (Ohio) crude, Standard became a major producer as well as refiner of midwestern oil. Later, other combines would see the value of such research and would not, as Standard did, disband their labs after developing a single major innovation.

Standard charted a path of business development that numerous other producers would follow, some of them with great success. In tobacco James B. Duke reversed the order Standard had adopted and integrated vertically first; later, after he had built the largest firm in the industry, he merged with his four major competitors to form the American Tobacco Co. In meatpacking the innovative Chicago-based firms that introduced refrigeration to the industry followed a similar growth path, with somewhat similar results. In sugar, the Havemayers followed the Standard Oil pattern more closely, achieving a dominant position in production and purchasing by creating an efficient and powerful combine, the American Sugar Company. By the early 1890s this new type of enterprise had achieved a controlling position in a number of important branches of communications, transportation, manufacturing, and distribution.

## THE OUTLOOK FOR BIG BUSINESS IN 1900

Morgan and others were absolutely certain that the combines were the wave of the future. They had stabilized competition in several major industries, protected the property of their owners, and introduced effective administrative and financial systems within the firm. The successful combines were more efficient in mass production and distribution than the entrepreneurial firms they had replaced. They were also using their large resources to develop technological innovations beyond the reach of their smaller rivals. To Morgan and others it seemed only a matter of time and the right economic circumstances before the rest of American business would be consolidated under the control of centralized combines.

Still, there was reason to debate this outcome, to question whether big business would indeed come to dominate what was already the largest capitalist economy in the world. For one thing, not all the combines had succeeded. The depression of the 1890s was punctuated with the bankruptcies and reorganizations of a number of giant firms. Not all, it seems, were able to achieve economies of scale or system; not all were able to prevent the entry of competing entrepreneurial firms capable of besting their larger rivals. In the telephone industry after Bell's patent rights had expired, a large number of smaller competitors had successfully entered the field to challenge Bell's position.

It was unlikely that the combines would ever be able to innovate as effectively as their smaller rivals. In businesses where the technology was changing rapidly, for instance, the early centralized combines often seemed slowfooted, unable to make up through control and efficiency what they had lost in flexibility. Power they had, and as Standard had demonstrated with Lima crude, they could innovate in ways alien to the small enterprise. But on balance efficiency and control, not innovation, were the strong suits of the large corporation.

It was also unclear in 1900 whether the combines would be able to achieve successful control of their external political settings. The rise of the great corporation had provoked an intense social and political reaction in the 1880s and 1890s. Farmers and their organizations had attacked the power of the combines; small and medium-sized businesses had condemned the behavior of firms such as Standard Oil and the giant railroad systems; reformers were crying out for new efforts to regulate or break up the "trusts."* If the opponents of big business had their way, government and not the corporation would control the structure and performance of the American business system. Labor too had protested the concentration of wealth and power that was taking place at the turn of the century. Trade unions of skilled workers were gaining strength in many industries. If organized labor had its way, corporate management would be forced to share its control of the means of production and distribution with the unions.

From their offices in New York, the new corporate leaders ordered their employees to deal with these threatening movements. But there were, as it turned out, no good substitutes for the business leader involved with labor and politics on a community level and aware on a day-to-day basis of how different social groups were responding to business developments. Managers fumed and issued dire prophecies, but the public concern about the giant corporation and other aspects of business behavior persisted. Thus it was not at all clear in 1900 that Morgan's style of large enterprise would be allowed to develop, even where there was every economic and business reason to anticipate that it would triumph.

*The combines were widely referred to as trusts or monopolies, regardless of the precise manner in which common ownership was achieved and regardless of the extent to which they dominated their industries' markets. Technically a trust refers to the use of a legal trusteeship—Standard employed this device for some years before turning to a holding company—to establish the all-important element of centralized ownership. A monopoly exists only when there is one producer of a good or service for which there is no available substitute. The public and media ignored these technical distinctions in discussing the so-called "trust movement."

# Part Two

# THE SYSTEM IN FLUX,

# 1901–1939

Despite the public's anxiety about the trusts, subsequent generations of business executives have looked back to J. P. Morgan's world with nostalgia. In that golden age of business autonomy, CEOs all seemed to be great builders, government apparently knew its proper place, and "big labor" did not yet exist.* Decision-makers in the emerging corporate combines had the power to run their firms as they saw fit, and the results seemed to be as beneficial to the nation as they were to the businesses involved. This vision of the past focuses on one part of the history of Morgan's era, particularly its startling record of technological and organizational change and of economic growth.

There was another, less attractive side of J. P. Morgan's world. There were abuses of power, practices wasteful of human and natural resources, and growing tensions between the corporations of that

---

*The American Federation of Labor, a federation of craft or trade unions, was the largest labor organization in the United States. In 1900 the AFL was growing rapidly, but it still included only a small percentage of the American workforce.

day and those who were less well organized to control their desti-
nies. Efforts to ease these tensions and solve what seemed to be the
society's major social and economic problems inevitably followed in
a political system that was open and democratic. In the first four
decades of the twentieth century, while a new generation of business managers was trying to expand and improve the system of
production and distribution, others in the society were grappling
with the difficult problems of innovating in the public sector. How
should industrial workers and other citizens organize to pursue their
self-interest? What were to be the functions of the government in
an economy dominated by struggles among giant combines? Could
the government be used to establish a measure of control over the
corporate system in the interests of groups other than business and
of the society as a whole? Should the political system help those
other groups of Americans achieve the sort of economic security
that big business appeared to be winning for itself?

Such questions were the focus of intense public debate from 1900
to 1939. Out of those debates and the accompanying political struggles came a new American commonwealth, a corporate commonwealth, that was more open to diverse inputs and more concerned
with equity than the Morgan system. The new commonwealth was
as well less certain of its long-run goals. Big business still played a
very prominent role in making the central economic decisions in the
new system, but by the Second World War, big government and big
labor had become important partners in this enterprise.

This intricate process of accommodation was not, of course,
unique to the United States. In nation after nation, similar changes
occurred as the rise of large enterprise, industrialization, and sustained economic growth altered traditional power relationships,
redistributed income and wealth, and changed the texture of life.
Most other nations began this process, however, with a well-devel-
oped set of national political institutions and a long tradition of
public involvement in the economy. Not so in the United States.
Here public administration was a new art, and the dominant traditions favored private gain, not public service. Americans were skeptical about the expansion of public power, and in political debates
they placed the burden of proof on those who favored a stronger
government. The demands of electoral politics also encouraged fre-

quent stops and starts in policy-making and simplified political debate to the level of campaign slogans and symbolism. The nation's frequent elections and mass voting often led to debilitating confusion of purpose in framing public policy. So too did the bewildering array of interest groups which competed for the right to shape public policy and thus influence business behavior.

The confusion was multiplied by the manner in which the great centralized business combines that provoked so much discussion at the turn of the century continued to evolve during these decades. The CEOs of these businesses developed new means of dealing with political change and with their labor force. One of the most vexing problems business leaders faced involved their efforts to keep their corporations innovative and flexible; private administrative systems, like public bureaucracies, had a tendency to strangle the innovative impulse. Efficiency in routine operations, control of the market, and immediate profits frequently pushed entrepreneurship into the background. But to remain viable over the long run, businesses had to change—sometimes quickly. Technologies changed, as did markets. As executives struggled to achieve a workable balance between efficiency, control, and innovation, they altered the business system and compounded the difficulties of developing a new mode of political economy.

Difficult as the transition was, by the time of the First World War Americans had worked out a new political accommodation with business. Corporate management now had to share some of its power with the government and concerned interest groups. From the beginning of U.S. involvement in the European war through the end of the 1920s, this accommodation—we will call it the "corporate commonwealth"—appeared to have solved many of the problems and relieved many of the tensions generated by the business system of J. P. Morgan's world. New modes of cooperation became popular. The United States experimented with associative, noncoercive techniques for guiding business behavior in constructive directions. While most businesses retained in this setting most of the preogatives of private property, power in the corporate commonwealth was diffused more than it had been in Morgan's prime. Labor relations appeared to be drifting toward a new and less adversarial posture, especially in the nation's larger firms. Prosperity generated in part by business's new-found ability to exploit modern science and engineering promised to supplant conflict with consensus. But then the 1929 panic on Wall Street and the ensuing depression turned the commonwealth on its head. This first major crisis of the modern order drove society to strengthen again the authority and reach of the national government and once more to shift control of some elements of business behavior from the corporation to the commonwealth.

# CHAPTER 3

# *The Expanding Public Presence, 1901–1930*

$$H$$ISTORIANS OF REFORM
frequently describe sweeping developments in business-government relations in the years from 1901 to 1930, but actually the process of change was piecemeal, uneven, and at times haphazard. "Government" did not suddenly change; what did change was the government's policy toward a particular industry, either through the passage of new laws or through the application of antitrust* to a firm or group of businesses. The CEOs of large companies experienced this process as a series of attacks, now from one side, now from another. They frequently responded in kind, countering a thrust here and perhaps taking the offensive on another front. They were concerned and often irritated. They developed a strong sense that they had somehow lost the favorable public standing they had enjoyed through most of the previous century. They were right.

---

*"Antitrust" refers to the public policy (state or federal) based on judicial decisions, laws, or constitutional provisions prohibiting monopoly and behavior that contributed to monopolization or restraint of trade. These decisions, laws, and provisions have a long legal history in the United States and in England.

Factory workers, farmers, and small businessmen were also dismayed by the changes taking place in the United States. They often felt threatened by the large corporations at the heart of J.P. Morgan's world, and they looked to government for help. Other Americans less directly involved with the powerful new business organizations joined their voices to the chorus appealing for a new brand of political economy. The national government responded to their pleas with policies that were innovative in impulse, if not always in results. In an effort to bring stability and greater public acceptance to the railroads and utilities, political leaders developed a new American form of independent regulatory commission. They sought to punish unfair trade practices and to soothe public fears over the trend toward monopoly by passing and enforcing antitrust laws. To assert greater public control over the nation's banks, they created the Federal Reserve System. Taken together, these three innovations in the public sector marked a significant turning point in business-government relations and in the development of the modern U.S. administrative state.

## THE INDEPENDENT REGULATORY COMMISSION

Private control of transportation and communication systems, financial institutions, public utilities, and some forms of energy production and distribution prompted widespread, organized concern in the early twentieth century. Each of these business activities came to have its own particular degree of "publicness," in this country and abroad. Each involved substantial resources. Each had become vital to the smooth functioning of the economy. Although the specific rationales for government involvement varied, the general impulse underlying the emergence of regulation was everywhere the same: to limit the power of private interests to manipulate either the entire economy or significant parts of it to their advantage. Autonomy in these businesses seemed to place too much power in the hands of a few individuals.

The political choices were clear-cut but difficult to make. One was to tolerate private control, subject only to competitive pressures from other, similar private interests. This laissez-faire approach rested on the traditional American faith in the marketplace as an effective regulator. The power of companies supplying gas lighting, for example, would be constrained in the short term by the threat that other gas utilities might undersell them and in the long term by the possibility that new competitors, such as electric companies, would emerge to take away their customers. But of course the long term is seldom of interest to consumers and voters experiencing what they think are immediate abuses of power. Wholly private control of vital industries seemed increasingly untenable to a growing number of Americans in the late nineteenth and early twentieth centuries.

Another option was public ownership. If these businesses were indeed "public," the government could simply acquire and run them as it did the postal service or the U.S. Navy. This alternative had numerous adherents, even in J. P. Morgan's world. In the 1890s the Populists and others had come out strongly for government ownership of the railroads. Many small communities had municipal utilities. Yet public ownership faced an uphill struggle in the United States. The traditions of private property and limited government were deeply rooted. Nor for that matter were state and local governments or even the federal government well equipped to administer large-scale enterprises. The national government had few administrative agencies and little expertise. The "state" as we know it today was just beginning to take shape in J. P. Morgan's day. Given the public hesitancy about the growth of government, it is not surprising that the United States turned to public ownership less often than most other industrial societies (figure 3.1).

Since these businesses were not to be controlled solely by either private owners or the government, America developed a curious innovation, a hybrid institution commonly referred to as the independent regulatory commission. The American variant on a type of agency earlier introduced in Great Britain was a political and intellectual compromise. It provided a means of doing something about the problems that were receiving public attention without forcing existing executive agencies to take on the thorny issues involved in regulation. It was a conservative compromise because it left the property and the most important decisions about it in private hands.

FIGURE 3.1

Extent of State Ownership of Business, 1978

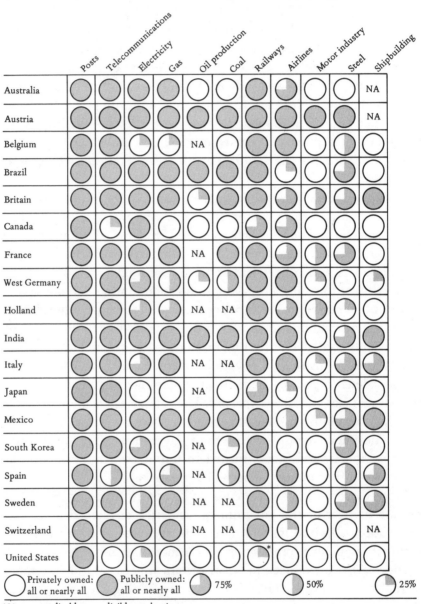

SOURCE: *Harvard Business Review*, March-April 1979, p. 161.

The independent agency seemed to promise Americans a way to have more government without having more politics.

In the early years there was little systematic effort to analyze which sectors of the economy and which types of business were best suited for regulation. Instead, the process proceeded piecemeal in response to the demands of those—including some business-men—who were most effective in exerting pressure on the legisla-ture and the executive branch. The list of businesses ultimately regulated was not the end result of an overview of the functions most suited to public control. Indeed, there was little tendency to perceive the various regulatory agencies as parts of a whole.

## REGULATION OF THE RAILROADS

First to be regulated was the railroad industry. In spite of J. P. Morgan's considerable efforts, the nation's primary transportation network experienced disturbing upheavals in the late nineteenth century. The railroads included many of the largest and most highly organized businesses of that age. Because they were the backbone of the nation's transportation system, they were the object of in-tense public scrutiny. Railroad rates affected almost every substan-tial economic activity. Railroad financing dominated the nation's capital markets. The more flamboyant railroad executives provided the nation's newspapers with some of their best public symbols of "big business."

Shippers dependent on the railroads generally viewed rates as too high and too unpredictable. Both complaints were justified. The roads had grown rapidly, with little concern for how any single firm might fit into the national transportation system. Market forces frequently led to the construction of costly competing lines and in turn to chaotic cycles of cutthroat competition. Rates were unstable and often discriminatory. Where competition did not exist, shippers were charged high rates for relatively short hauls. Small shippers (including farmers) who could not bargain effectively with the roads had to pay the top rates, while larger interests received husky dis-counts.

Faced with mounting pressure to do something about this situation, Congress began to sift through various proposals for reform. Many professional railroad managers, led by Albert Fink, the father of cost accounting, favored the use of government sanctions to enforce the decisions of private associations—so-called pools—designed to bring order to the industry. But this brand of cartelization was politically unrealistic. Too many voters and too many of their elected representatives feared the power of the railroads. Nationalization was similarly unacceptable. The federal government could not have afforded to buy the railroads even if it had wanted to do so; the total bonded debt of the roads far exceeded that of the national government. The independent regulatory commission emerged as a politically viable alternative.

Congressional debate focused on the two general approaches to regulation used by the existing state commissions. In most eastern states these bodies were advisory. They had the authority to investigate and even to publicize conditions but not the power to set rates. Amid a strong wave of agrarian protest, many of the midwestern and southern states had created stronger commissions, with legal powers to set rates and enforce their orders. These organizations had often been aggressive in their attacks on real and perceived abuses. Charles Francis Adams, a prominent spokesman for the "weak" advisory commissions, captured the tone of the "strong" rate-setting commissions:

> They were where they were, not to study a difficult problem and to guide their steps by the light of investigation. . . . On the contrary, they were there to prosecute. The test of their performance of duty was to be sought in the degree of hostility they manifested to the railroad corporations. In a word they represented force.

Coercion as opposed to cooperation was the watchword of the strong commissions. Whether strong or weak, however, these state agencies could not regulate businesses that operated across state lines. The Supreme Court removed any doubt on this matter in 1886 when it ruled in *Wabash* v. *Illinois* that only the federal government had the authority to regulate interstate commerce.

Congress therefore acted, somewhat reluctantly passing the Interstate Commerce Act of 1887 and imposing public control over business decisions that had been solely in private hands (see box). This deft piece of political juggling met the call for regulation by creating what appeared to be a "strong" independent regulatory commission, with power over railroad rates, but the law was actually ambiguous about the agency's authority. The broad mandate of the Interstate Commerce Commission was to make rates "just and reasonable." The law dealt specifically with a number of controversial practices, flatly prohibiting the practice of charging higher rates for short than for long hauls. But the measure allowed an exception if the rates had not been arrived at "under substantially similar circumstances and conditions" or if the commission decided it was dealing with a special case. Thus the statute invited the ICC to waffle on important issues.

The ICC's weaknesses quickly became evident. The setting of "just and reasonable rates" required good information about the costs of railroad services; considerable expertise was needed to ana-

---

THE INTERSTATE COMMERCE ACT OF 1887

The Act created the Interstate Commerce Commission (ICC), consisting of five members appointed by the president for six-year terms. Leading features of the Act included the following:

"All charges made for services by carriers subject to the act must be reasonable and just. Every unjust and unreasonable charge is prohibited and declared unlawful."

"The direct or indirect charging, demanding, collecting, or receiving for any service rendered, a greater compensation from any one or more persons than from any other for a like contemporaneous service, is declared to be unjust discrimination and is prohibited."

"It is made unlawful to charge or receive any greater compensation in the aggregate for the transportation of passengers or the like kind of property under substantially similar circumstances and conditions for a shorter than for a longer distance over the same line in the same direction, the shorter being included within the longer distance."

"Contracts, agreements, or combinations for the pooling of freights of different and competing railroads . . . are declared to be unlawful."

"All carriers subject to the law are required to print their tariffs for the transportation of persons and property, and to keep them for public inspection at every depot or station on their roads."

lyze this data; the agency needed unambiguous authority to force compliance; to exercise effective control the commission (no less than railroad management) needed to have a strategic overview of the future of American railroads and the general transportation system. But the ICC originally had neither the data, the expertise, the authority, nor the strategic vision that it needed. Nor could it look to other similar organizations as models. Its halting development foretold many of the problems that would arise with single-industry regulation in other sectors of the business system.

The authority of the ICC to require the testimony of witnesses and the submittal of records on matters under investigation was quickly challenged in the courts. Even when the ICC obtained the records it needed, the wide diversity of accounting practices in the various corporations made the information difficult to use. Not until 1906 was this problem solved; the Hepburn Act of that year empowered the ICC to prescribe a uniform system of accounts. Only then could the agency develop the first requirement of any effective management system: a steady flow of reliable and consistent information.

The commission still lacked the expertise needed to interpret this information, however. Under the original law, there were five commissioners, a number later expanded to seven and then to eleven. But how was the government supposed to find the "experts" that could make an independent agency work? The law forbade the appointment of commissioners with "immediate railroad affiliations." But who then would staff the commission? In the early years there were hardly any trained specialists who would fit the bill; the first business school in the country, the Wharton School at the University of Pennsylvania, had opened its doors only in 1886. Economics was just beginning to take shape as a systematic discipline. There were plenty of lawyers and engineers to appoint, but few of those who had knowledge of the railroads were untainted by immediate affiliations. One such attorney, Thomas Cooley of the University of Michigan and the Michigan Supreme Court, distinguished himself in early service to the ICC. But people of this sort were hard to find.

Meanwhile, the ICC bogged down in the task of sifting through mounds of complaints on a case-by-case basis. This approach reflected in part the limited discretion allowed under the original act. Before 1906, the ICC had the power only to investigate rates upon complaint and void those found to be unreasonable. While the commission was judging each case and the courts were reviewing it, the original rate stood. Indeed, on appeal the courts reheard the information previously presented before the ICC. The Hepburn Act finally gave the ICC authority to strike down a specific rate and then decree the highest rate that would be allowed. The 1906 law also made the ICC's rulings binding pending court review; later, in 1910, the Mann-Elkins Act (see box) gave the agency power to suspend rates until the commission reviewed the case. This latter measure further enhanced the commission's authority by requiring the railroads, not the ICC, to prove the "reasonableness" of a new rate. Court review of the commission's decisions remained a problem, but by 1910 many of the procedural difficulties that had prevented the ICC from being effective had at last been eliminated.

Attention then shifted to what should have been the central regulatory question from the first: deciding how the ICC could determine reasonable rates. Value of service, a market test, had been the standard used by the railroads before the creation of the ICC. In general, shippers were being charged as much as they could be forced to pay without taking their business elsewhere. The ICC developed a different concept of reasonableness and tried to set rates that would be fair to shippers while providing sufficient revenue to the railroads to yield profits for their owners and to safeguard their ability to maintain and expand service. The formula used by the ICC (and by most state utility commissions) called for a fair rate of return on a fair value of investment, and this was the concept written into law in the Transportation Act of 1920.

"Rate-of-return" regulation filled a pressing political need, but it was in practice a very difficult formula to apply to specific rates on specific commodities. Using statistics of questionable validity, the ICC established figures for fair levels of investment through what was in effect a political bargaining process. After setting the rate base and rate of return, the ICC distributed a company's total revenue needs across its entire rate structure while trying to be as equitable as possible, bearing in mind pressures from competing carriers.

---

THE EVOLUTION OF THE ICC SYSTEM OF REGULATION, 1906–1980

1. *Hepburn Act (1906)*. Strengthened the ICC by giving it the power to declare existing rates unjust, to set maximum rates, and to prescribe railroad accounting practices.
2. *Mann-Elkins Act (1910)*. Gave ICC power to suspend announced rates pending an investigation; created a Commerce Court.
3. *Valuation Act of 1913*. Required ICC to ascertain value of all railroad properties.
4. *Transportation Act of 1920*. Made "fair rate of return on fair value of property" the goal of rate-making; gave ICC power to oversee pooling of railroads, to set minimum rates, and to regulate railroad securities.
5. *Motor Carrier Act of 1935*. Initiated limited regulation of trucking.
6. *Transportation Act of 1940*. Required ICC to establish a national transportation policy.
7. *Transportation Act of 1958*. Allowed ICC to guarantee loans to railroads to finance capital investments in roads, equipment, and maintenance; gave ICC oversight of discontinuation of passenger services.
8. Creation of Department of Transportation (1967): Transferred long-range planning functions from ICC to DOT.
9. *Railroad Revitalization and Regulatory Reform Act of 1976*. Gave ICC more flexibility in rate-making and gave railroads freedom to lower prices.
10. *Staggers Rail Act of 1980*. Provided for deregulation phased in over three years; began to loosen controls on rates, mergers, and abandonment of unprofitable routes.
11. *Motor Carrier Act of 1980*. Opened entry to new competitors and began the process of deregulation of rates.

---

Working on a case-by-case basis, the agency slowly ground away at this almost impossible task.

Ultimately the ICC brought rates under control, but the agency had no way to encourage the regulated firms to be either efficient or innovative. Indeed, regulation had the opposite effect. It discouraged flexibility and innovation in a business that was already mature, that was leveling off after a long era of expansion. What the ICC stabilized was a business system that was unbelievably complex, badly overbuilt, and heavily in debt. The Interstate Commerce Act had outlawed pooling—which railroad managers might have used as a vehicle for planning—without providing the commission with any alternative means of shaping the evolution of the transportation system as a whole. The Transportation Act of 1920 finally addressed this problem, granting the ICC power to oversee the consolidation of the nation's railroads. But the commission was atuned to control, not structural innovation. The inertia-bound agency failed to use the powers granted in the 1920 act to foster reorganization aimed at eliminating weak lines and weak financing. Instead, the agency plodded ahead, setting rates in case after case as the nation's railroad system stagnated. Neither innovative nor efficient, most of the leading corporations in this industry foundered, as did the ICC.

## REGULATION OF PUBLIC UTILITIES

The evolution of numerous state utility commissions in the years from 1901 to 1930 mirrored significant parts of the ICC's history. Like the railroads, the public utilities were capital-intensive companies that were the focus of careful public scrutiny and considerable political controversy. Many observers counted electric, gas, and steam manufacture and distribution as natural monopolies, since the heavy investments needed to attain economies of scale made the building of duplicate, competitive facilities wasteful and inefficient.* The early urban utilities had grown in response to the investment decisions of numerous individual entrepreneurs, but these local businesses had then frequently been consolidated into larger regional systems. Public officials in the cities and states were quite content to have these large enterprises provide their services, but they were suspicious of the power these corporations possessed. The political issues raised could not be ignored. Most urban dwellers were dependent on these privately owned companies for essential services such as heating and lighting. They had no alternative suppliers to whom they could turn. As a result, state after state joined the Progressive Era parade toward control of public utilities

---

*Similar conclusions were reached about water companies, most of which became municipally owned and operated enterprises, and about street railways, most of which were regulated and many of which were taken over by urban governments.

by independent state regulatory commissions. The commissions that emerged shared many basic similarities and problems.

Local communities had long exerted some control over utilities through franchise requirements, but as the scale of these undertakings grew, so did the demand for stricter controls to protect the public by assuring a supply of necessary services at reasonable cost. Some communities opted early on for public ownership. Most large cities, however, chose to use some form of rate regulation. The relative merits of state versus local control came in for considerable debate, with major utilities generally supporting state authority as the lesser of two evils—perhaps because it made relations with the regulatory system easier to control and certainly because it was more efficient than having different rules for each municipality. As it turned out, the creation of these state commissions also served the important function of legitimizing privately owned utility systems throughout much of the nation.

Some states established new agencies to regulate the utility companies, but others merely turned to their railroad commissions and directed them to shift some of their resources to this new task. Whichever approach they used, the commissioners encountered most of the difficulties that had already arisen in railroad regulation and arrived at similar solutions. They had to determine how best to create a fair and durable system of rate regulation. The general guideline of a fair rate of return on a fair value of investment sounded fair. But again, the trick was in actually embodying the concept in practical decisions. For the utility regulators, determining the fair value of investment presented several theoretical and procedural dilemmas. The utilities favored the use of the replacement value of investments in determining the rate base. This was an inflationary age, and the utilities were under pressure to expand and to adopt new and increasingly expensive technologies. Replacement value would enlarge the rate base and give the firms larger returns for funding these improvements. As the state commissions matured, however, they generally leaned toward using original value of investments as the simplest way to determine a rate base. Alas, the original data had often been lost, was buried beneath accounting adjustments made during past mergers, or was obscured by watered stock—stock for which the company did not receive

assets equal to the value of the shares—that had been issued during
the mergers. Commissions faced another difficult challenge in determining the proper way to calculate depreciation on past investments. These were thorny problems and the task of determining an
acceptable rate base on which to figure a fair rate of return preoccupied most of the public utility commissions (PUCs) through
1930.*

While the PUCs were focusing on rate-making, however, businessmen like Samuel Insull were transforming the utility businesses
by consolidating separate companies into large systems. Insull and
other organization-builders were making the all-important decisions about financing, management, and technology in these businesses. Regulation had in effect bogged down over the technicalities
of controlling rates, leaving the major business decisions to be made
in the private sector. All too often these private decisions left the
utility corporations overburdened with debt and vulnerable to a
major downturn in the economy.

By the end of the 1920s other fundamental problems were beginning to appear among the nation's railroads and utilities. Rate regulation as practiced by the independent regulatory commissions
affected the finances of individual companies, but the commissions
had little authority or inclination to shape the broad financial or
operational aspects of a series of businesses that together accounted
for a significant part of the capital invested in American industry.
Public rate-making did not encourage the companies to apply new
technologies vigorously nor to improve their efficiency in the hundreds of small ways that creative managers use to cut costs and
increase output. As constituted, public authority was poorly
equipped to deal with long-range adjustments in markets or technologies.

Was it obvious by 1930 that single-industry regulation was in
trouble? No. In certain regards this public innovation had been
highly successful. The government had gingerly asserted control
over the rates charged by selected corporations while leaving ownership and management of most aspects of their operations in pri-

*While many of the public utility commissions were responsible for more than one
industry—gas and electricity were often combined, for instance—they tended to treat each
industry separately in the regulatory process.

vate hands. This was a distinctively American approach to balancing public and private interests. By the end of the 1920s, independent regulatory commissions that set rates based on a fair rate of return on a fair level of investment had become an accepted part of the American system of political economy. By that time, too, the initial efforts to control the power and abuses of business had in many cases begun to blend with the regulated companies' desire to achieve similar ends—to stabilize prices and market shares, for example. This unanticipated consequence of regulation would itself ultimately become a serious problem. But from the perspective of the late 1920s, there was ample reason to believe that the regulatory commissions were a successful governmental innovation that was gradually being improved as Americans gained experience with this form of political control. The shortcomings of the commissions would, it seemed, ultimately be corrected.

## CROSS-INDUSTRY REGULATION

While single-industry regulation soothed popular fears of the power of the railroads and utilities, many Americans remained concerned about the trend toward concentration across the economy as a whole. Those who had grown to adulthood in a world of small local businesses had no ready frame of reference for dealing with the new world of J. P. Morgan. There was reason to believe that over the long term big business was bringing less-expensive goods to ever-greater numbers, but many citizens, aroused by spectacular abuses of private power, were skeptical of these claims. A growing perception that wealth and power were being concentrated in the hands of ruthless people unconstrained by law or by considerations of the public welfare fed the political agitation for new policies. Large segments of the public looked for redress—or at least for reassurance—from government at all levels. Gradually the political system responded by asserting new authority to shape aspects of the entire business system.

Seldom before had the federal government sought to regulate business as a whole. The initial efforts to define cross-industry controls generated a great deal of political heat while shedding little light on the options available to the government. The political bargaining over the new measures was intense, and the debates were often confused. When laws were passed, administrative and legal conflicts over enforcement frequently thwarted those who sought coherence in public policy. Government officials tended to pursue specific ends with specific policies, seldom examining the ways the various programs would affect each other or the long-term implications for a business system experiencing major changes in technologies and markets. Confusion of purpose was often the result.

This was true in the case of antitrust policy, seen by many as the centerpiece of a general government program for business. Certainly opposition to monopoly became a central political issue for an entire generation of Americans. From the passage of the Sherman Act in 1890 to the onset of the First World War, debate over the trusts* and arguments about the efficacy of antitrust were significant issues in electoral politics. Admittedly, the policy itself had more political significance than economic impact: its primary effect was felt in two major industries, oil and tobacco. But as a political matter, the antitrust movement played a significant role in shaping the society's initial response to big business.

Antitrust measures promised to provide a distinctly American solution to the public policy choices presented by the rise of the giant corporation. A law controlling market structure would encourage competition, thereby removing the need for further regulations. Antitrust laws would thus curb the power of big business "naturally" by restoring free markets without building up a big government. Almost a century after the rise of the corporate combine, it is easy to scoff at this "romantic" vision, but to scoff is to read our own more or less comfortable acceptance of big business into the past. The power of the Rockefellers, the Carnegies, and the Morgans inspired widespread fear and antagonism at the beginning of the century. Antitrust offered one means of striking at their concentrated power, promising an end to the abuses of the corporate combines.

*The label "trust" continued to be applied during these years to all large corporations, generally with a negative connotation.

Symbolically the policy worked. It gave Americans a sense of control over the great corporations. It made excellent political theater, and politicians—from the members of Congress in 1890 to Presidents Theodore Roosevelt (1901–1909), Woodrow Wilson (1913–1921) and Herbert Hoover (1929–1933)—instinctively grasped the political potency of antitrust rhetoric. "The trusts" could be tamed. "The people" could be restored to sovereignty. The problems of economic concentration could be solved. Perhaps no economic policy of government in modern American history has offered greater symbolic benefits—or more difficult practical problems of enforcement.

Theodore Roosevelt's role in this political drama was especially important. His contribution was significant because he was the first activist president in the modern era and dramatic because of his personality and his ability to sustain the image of a vigorous, powerful chief executive. Historians later noted that the effervescent "trustbuster" actually used the law fewer times than his corpulent, conservative successor, William Howard Taft (1909–1913). Never mind. The American people were convinced that Roosevelt had thrown down the gauntlet to the trusts, asserting the authority of the federal government. J. P. Morgan and his fellow moguls had been challenged for the first time. Roosevelt's background helped position him to play this unusual role. A patrician by birth, an extrovert by nature, a Republican by choice, he had done a stint in the West, establishing his virility as a cowboy before returning to the urban East. Roosevelt had further enhanced his public image by service during the Spanish-American War. His heroism under fire established, T. R. had returned to the United States to election as governor of the state of New York. In this post, as always, the young governor carefully nurtured his ties with party regulars while cultivating with equal care his role as an agent of reform, a concerned spokesperson for the commonweal. Elected vice-president of the United States in 1900, he was abruptly thrown into the nation's top office the following year when President McKinley was assassinated. As he had done in New York, T.R. worked both sides of the street. He saw no conflict in attacking one of J.P. Morgan's or E.H. Harriman's railroad combines and then accepting large campaign contributions from both financiers. He was deeply convinced that he could distinguish the bad combines from the good ones. He also persuaded the American voters that he could perform that difficult feat and protect their interests from the trusts. In 1904 they reelected him to the presidency by a large majority. Roosevelt gave the progressive reform movement its first national leader and its first vigorous proponent of the antitrust policy.

In making specific policy choices, President Roosevelt and the legislators and judges of that era could refer to the common-law prohibitions* of "combinations in restraint of trade" and of "attempts to monopolize." But the legal applications of these prohibitions had developed in a premodern economy that bore little resemblance to J.P. Morgan's world. Before the passage in 1890 of the federal Sherman Antitrust Act (see box), many states had passed statutes or constitutional provisions prohibiting monopoly, but few had enjoyed much success in enforcing these laws against corporations whose activities reached across state lines—as did those of most large firms. As had been the case with railroad regulation, difficulties in applying state laws had pushed the debates over antitrust measures toward Washington, D.C. There a strong consensus on the need for action developed, and legislators of all regions and of all political persuasions in the conservative Congress of 1890 had supported some form of antitrust law. The Sherman Act passed in the Senate with only one dissenting vote as professional politicians acknowledged the necessity of closing ranks and passing a measure that would deal with "the trust problem."

The Sherman Act, labelled "an act to protect trade and commerce against unlawful restraints and monopolies," attempted to codify the common law while applying it to a modern context. The language of the law was far from precise, since it did not specify business practices that would henceforth be seen as evidence of restraint of trade or attempts to monopolize. The task of interpreting these phrases fell to the courts. The act created no enforcement or information-gathering agency, leaving these functions to district attorneys under the direction of the U.S. Attorney General. Violations were to be brought to the attention of government officials by

---

*The "common law" is based upon precedent, the previous judicial decisions; statutory law, by contrast, is based upon acts—that is statutes—passed by a legislature.

---

The Sherman Antitrust Act (1890)

Section 1: "Every contract, combination in the form of trust or otherwise, or conspiracy, in restraint of trade or commerce
among the several States, or with foreign nations, is hereby
declared to be illegal. . . ."

Section 2: "Every person who shall monopolize, or attempt to monopolize, or combine or conspire with any other person or
persons, to monopolize any part of the trade or commerce
among the several States, or with foreign nations, shall be
deemed guilty of a misdemeanor. . . ."

Section 3: "Every contract, combination in the form of trust or otherwise, or conspiracy in restraint of trade or commerce . . . is
hereby declared illegal."

Section 7: "Any person who shall be injured in his business or property by any other person or corporation by reason of anything forbidden or declared to be unlawful by this law, may
sue . . . without respect for the amount in controversy, and
shall recover threefold the damages by him sustained."

---

those whom the monopolies had harmed. A strong incentive to sue
competitors was provided by section 7 of the act, which stipulated
triple damages for those injured by violations of the law. Antitrust
law was thus created to be a self-enforcing measure to foster competition.

As the courts defined the specific content of the antitrust law,
they in effect constructed a legal filter that stopped the progress of
some combines while allowing others to proceed unhindered. In
1911 the Supreme Court stopped Standard Oil and American Tobacco, breaking up both as illegal monopolies in restraint of trade.
Price-fixing and pooling arrangements routinely failed to make it
through the courts. But in 1920 one of the largest corporations of
its day, U.S. Steel, passed the court test. Most of the combines of
that era were never charged with antitrust violations. The antitrust
laws, however loaded with political symbolism, thus did not fundamentally alter the nation's new brand of corporate capitalism.

The stipulations against "attempts to monopolize" and "conspiracies in restraint of trade" nevertheless gave many a corporate
officer pause, in part because these guidelines were so vague. Even

after the Clayton Act in 1914 specified certain categories of competitive practices as illegal, the laws still provided no effective guidance on the central economic question raised by the combines: how could the government determine the level of concentration in an industry and then decide when one company's market share threatened to forestall effective competition? The Supreme Court's "rule of reason" (1911) gave the government discretion to distinguish between companies that had amassed their economic power legally and those that had used illegal means. But neither judges nor the Department of Justice could specify in advance what patterns of behavior would constitute legal forms of business activity.

The confusion stemmed in part from the lack of a generally accepted goal for the antitrust policy. It was clear that many Americans feared big business, but it was equally clear that they wanted the economic growth and the products and services associated with large enterprise. Hence public officials compromised, allowing most of the combines to proceed unchallenged while selectively prosecuting a handful of highly visible corporations.*

Even this limited effort was hampered by the lack of reliable information. Theodore Roosevelt and Congress sought to bolster the government's capacity to monitor business activities with the creation in 1903 of the Bureau of Corporations. Staffed with investigators and empowered to collect economic data, the bureau had the dual roles of finding and publicizing information and of recommending legislation to the president. These roles were not necessarily incompatible, but tensions quickly arose over the way the president used the new organization. The bureau sought to avoid problems by looking for information where it was most likely to support the President's program—that is, in businesses he had already adjudged to be "bad," notably in meat-packing, oil, and tobacco. The bureau's investigations of these corporations were anything but detached. In its initial study of the oil industry, for example, its investigators sought out longtime critics of the Standard Oil Company and in effect asked them, "How bad is Standard Oil?" In 1914, the investigative powers of the Bureau of Corpora-

---

*The government was less selective in its handling of loose combinations such as price-fixing agreements. These were routinely prosecuted, and where sufficient evidence of restraint of trade existed, the courts normally struck down these agreements.

tions were transferred to the newly created Federal Trade Commission, an independent regulatory agency that also had the power to prosecute business misconduct.

In the same year, Congress passed the Clayton Antitrust Act, which specifically prohibited various categories of trade practices. But still corporate leaders and other critics of the antitrust policy wanted more clarification. Debate centered on a proposal that the FTC be given the power to offer advance rulings to businesspeople concerned about the legality of their corporation's policies. Such authority would have gone a long way toward removing regulatory uncertainty. But advance approval would also have pushed the FTC into the gray area of quasi-judicial authority, thus raising serious questions about the separation of powers.* This provision was dropped from the bill, and neither the FTC nor the Department of Justice would give businesses the assurances they wanted in advance.

Neither the presidents, the regulatory agencies, nor the courts put forward an effective measure of concentration that could be understood by potential offenders and used as the linchpin of antitrust policy. Nor did any part of the government begin to wrestle effectively with the questions of economies of scale and system and how, exactly, they should be treated in public policy. Technologically and organizationally the business system was changing in fundamental ways, but public officials had yet to work out how society could best capture the long-range economic benefits offered by modern large-scale enterprise while maintaining a satisfactory level of competition.

Antitrust thus remained more a political than an economic policy. It should not be dismissed, however, as mere political posturing. On the contrary, it served several critical political functions. It was a much-needed safety valve for public concern during an era of rapid business change. Curiously, antitrust measures actually helped legitimize the role of the large corporation. Monopoly or near-monopoly became acceptable in most cases only when it was accompanied by extensive regulation, but oligopoly (that is, a market dominated by a few leading firms) generally passed the antitrust test

*Under the Constitution the power to interpret the law in this way was reserved for the judiciary. The power to apply the law was vested in the separate executive branch.

and provided most combines with the degree of market control that they needed to stabilize their industries over the long run. Along with railroad regulation, antitrust laws also helped legitimize a new and stronger role for the government in the nation's business life. In a country that had long had a weak central government, this was a significant step in the evolution of a modern public sector.

Nevertheless it is difficult to avoid the conclusion that these ends could have been achieved with less confusion and tension. Most corporate executives viewed antitrust as one of a series of new threats to their autonomy and to their ability to plan coherently for their company's future. The fact that the laws were not enforced systematically increased the uncertainty. From a corporate perspective, "good" and "bad" trusts existed in the eye of the beholder— usually an "opportunistic politician." The threat of antitrust prosecution was nonetheless real, and a wise executive who headed a large corporate combine had to prepare for the worst.

A separate (though indirectly related) government policy toward competition was the tariff. In the years from the Civil War to the 1930s, tariffs had gradually become more protective and more inclusive. Protection against foreign competition was an important component in the rise of big business in a few major industries, notably sugar and tin-plate manufacturing. The head of the "sugar trust," H.O. Havemeyer of American Sugar, generalized too broadly from his personal experience when he suggested that "the tariff is the mother of trusts." Although correct for the sugar industry, this conclusion did not apply to most other corporate consolidations. Nonetheless, Havemeyer's statement reflected the opinion of many contemporaries. Both the tariff and antitrust laws dealt with competitive conditions, although the distinction between domestic and foreign competitors prevented policy-makers from molding these two programs into a unified business policy.

The government did not officially recognize the relationship between competition at home and the efforts of foreign firms to supply the U.S. market. Antitrust policy was framed in largely domestic terms, as though U.S. business did not operate in a worldwide economy.* In the 1920s, the government actively encouraged

*The only exception was the Webb-Pomerene Act of 1918, which allowed U.S. firms to cooperate in developing foreign markets.

American firms to challenge the businesses of other countries—
especially Great Britain—but while the United States looked overseas for markets and resources, its tariff policy remained strongly
protectionist. In contrast to Great Britain's free trade, the U.S. government aggressively built political barriers to protect its business
system.

Like antitrust, tariff policy evolved from an intricate combination
of political forces. Tariffs were a major source of government revenues during the years before the 1930s. Indeed, as supplemented by
estate taxes and taxes on liquor and tobacco products, they provided
the bulk of the government's peacetime revenues. Beyond considerations of public finance, Congress was guided by intense lobbying
by affected industries when it set the tariff schedule. Favors once
granted proved difficult to repeal; a favorable tariff schedule came
to be regarded as almost a natural right by many businesses.

The tariff and antitrust, the nation's fundamental policies toward
competition, were thus implemented on a case-by-case basis. No
national planners designed tariff schedules to foster the long-term
expansion of crucial domestic businesses or to secure the place of
American companies in international competition. Similarly, antitrust policies were determined piecemeal by the Department of
Justice and the courts. By making antitrust policy company-specific
and defining tariff policy on an industry-by-industry basis, the
government assured that both policies would be ad hoc and relatively unpredictable. In response to the resulting uncertainty, every
separate company had to seek ways to protect itself from antitrust
action while lobbying—usually through its industry-wide associations—for as much tariff protection as Congress would give it. The
American way of political decision-making thus shaped an ambiguous outcome to the long, intense public debate over competitive
policies.

## GOVERNMENT-DIRECTED ACTIVITIES: THE FEDERAL RESERVE

The final important departure in the powers of government in the
years from 1901 to 1930 was the creation of a central banking

system. Before the passage of the Federal Reserve Act (1913), the government exercised only limited control over central banking functions. The country relied instead on the good will and good intentions of private bankers. The creation of the Federal Reserve Board ("the Fed") was a necessary first step toward government control of the nation's financial system. It embodied a growing recognition that central banking was of necessity a public function in an industrial, urban society.

In a practical sense, the coming of the Fed signalled the demise of the world of J.P. Morgan. He above all others was the symbol of the control that private investment bankers had exercised over the financial system. Morgan had earned his power through a lifetime of practical experience in international banking. Because he was almost universally respected for his clear grasp of the inner workings of the economy, Morgan was able to exert considerable influence on the nation's financial system at the turn of the century. The acid test of the capacities of Morgan and his peers came in 1907, when a severe panic threatened to plunge the nation into a prolonged depression. When several large New York City banks appeared on the verge of collapse, Morgan stepped forward to stem the tide. For assistance, the seventy-year-old banker commanded the cooperation of the city's best and brightest bankers, many of whom had been trained by Morgan and his associates. Under his direction, this cadre examined the records of major banks to determine which were fundamentally sound and which might be beyond saving. Using this information, Morgan sought to mobilize the financial support necessary to shore up the strongest institutions. The funds to accomplish this difficult task came from several sources. First, Morgan brought numerous prominent executives together in his library. He explained to them the seriousness of the situation and solicited their contributions to a fund to support the banks. He made a similar appeal to heads of major banks active in the New York clearinghouse. Additional funds came from the transfer of local and federal government holdings to distressed banks. Finally, the nation's de facto "central banker" arranged the controversial acquisition of Tennessee Iron & Coal Company by U.S. Steel, thereby removing one important threat to banking stability, the large outstanding loans from major New York banks to the troubled

Tennessee Iron & Coal Co. This last piece of the financial puzzle required the approval of President Theodore Roosevelt, who allowed the Steel Trust to make this acquisition in the interest of financial stability.*

When the dust had cleared, the nation's financial system was largely unscathed. But fundamental questions had been raised by the events of 1907. Skeptics in Congress wondered aloud if the country should remain so dependent on private initiatives in times of national crisis. Morgan was a man of integrity. But could a private banker—no matter how able and ethical—continue to fulfill the functions of a central bank as the economy grew larger and more complex? Who would shoulder this burden when J. P. Morgan died? Would citizens in the South and West continue to allow northeastern bankers to dominate the nation's financial system?

As Congress began to grapple with these questions, its sense of urgency was heightened by the consolidation of several major New York banks. The House of Representatives held extensive hearings to investigate the nation's banking and currency problems. Representative Arsene Pujo headed the investigation, and the Pujo hearings (1912–1913) produced systematic evidence proving what everyone familiar with banking took for granted: that power over the nation's financial system was concentrated in the hands of a small number of New York bankers. Information on interlocking directorates† made public for the first time provided excellent political ammunition for those seeking reform. At the pinnacle of the banking system, the investigating committee found an "inner group" consisting of the three most prominent bankers in New York: J. P. Morgan; George Baker; and James Stillman. Their lines of influence reached into the economy through the financial ties between the major banks these men ran and the industrial concerns they had financed. The committee concluded:

---

*The acquisition was questionable because it increased the concentration of resources under U.S. Steel's control, giving that firm even greater ability to block the entry of potential competitors.

†This refers to the fact that the boards of directors of many different firms included representatives from a small number of leading banks, investment groups, and prominent families. It was assumed that these directors used their positions to control the policies of the various corporations involved.

> There is an established and well-defined identity and community of interest between a few leaders of finance, created and held together through stock ownership, interlocking directorates . . . and other forms of domination over banks, trust companies, railroads, and public-service and industrial corporations, which has resulted in great and rapidly growing concentration of control of money and credit in the hands of these few men.

With that, the committee ended its hearings, having generated both the information and the indignation to push Congress toward bank reform.

The gods spared J.P. Morgan an encounter with the new era: he died in Rome in 1913. But while the unofficial central banker of the United States was being laid to rest, Congress was putting in place the rudiments of a new system. Banking reform had a high priority in the early years of the administration of Woodrow Wilson. He oversaw the design of a politically acceptable plan that embodied essential elements of central control while soothing the public's fear of the so-called money trust. The compromise that emerged in The Federal Reserve Act of 1913 sought "to furnish an elastic currency, to afford means of rediscounting commercial paper [and] to establish a more effective supervision of banking in the United States. . . ."

Congress devised a decentralized system, with twelve district banks, headed by a weak Federal Reserve Board in Washington. These were "bankers' banks" in that they both served and regulated existing banks. Unlike the two U.S. national banks of the early nineteenth century, they could not make loans to or accept deposits from the general public. Each Federal Reserve bank was a corporation whose stock was owned by the member banks in proportion to their capital. Each was run by nine directors, three of whom were representatives from banks in the district, three from commercial interests, and three appointed by the Fed. At the top of the pyramid stood the Federal Reserve Board, which initially consisted of five presidential appointees, the secretary of the treasury, and the comptroller of the currency. Congress hoped to insulate these appointees from short-term political pressures by giving them ten-year appointments and making them full-time employees. Their terms later were increased to fourteen years.

The structure of the Federal Reserve embodied the warring impulses that had wracked Congress during the debates on banking reform. The search for an efficient central system could not be separated from the equally intense search for additional controls over the activities of the money-center banks. The fear of centralized financial power in the hands of either the big city bankers or of government officials susceptible to their influence shaped the choice of a decentralized system with limited control from Washington or New York. Many other aspects of the law as passed—from the selection of members on the district banks' boards to the long terms for the members of the Federal Reserve Board—reflected this desire to protect the new system from the inordinate influence of either bankers or politicians.

Congress purchased these safeguards at a high price. Decentralization without a strong mechanism for defining overall policy proved to be a significant handicap as the Fed sought to define its central banking role in the decades before the Great Depression of the 1930s. The powers to set reserve requirements of member banks, to establish the rediscount rate (that is, the rate at which member banks borrowed from the Fed), and to buy and sell government securities provided the Fed with the tools it needed to manage the nation's currency and to begin to manage normal business cycles. But the lack of a clear focus hampered the Fed in applying these policy tools. Indeed, decentralization encouraged the very result which the framers of the act had so feared: the centralization of power in New York City banks. Given the weakness of the Federal Reserve Board in Washington, it was hardly surprising that the district bank in New York quickly emerged as the guiding force in the Fed's operations. Under the leadership of Benjamin Strong, the New York Reserve Bank took the lead in coordinating the open market operations of the entire system. Indeed, to many contemporary observers Strong became the symbol of the Federal Reserve system. New York—which was, after all, the nation's financial capital—retained effective control over the flow of currency in the American economy.

While these changes were taking place, the Federal Reserve lost a race with history. Its officials struggled to understand its powers over the economy and to fashion more effective means of using its monetary tools. But the design of the Fed made effective central control difficult. It had been placed on top of a set of powerful private financial institutions, which had grown accustomed to exercising de facto central banking functions for more than half a century. It had to make its choices in response to intense political pressures from various regions of the nation more concerned with regional needs than with the overall functioning of the nation's economy. Above all else, it came into being at a time when the business system was changing rapidly, yet it had no appropriate theoretical framework for analyzing these changes. As a result, the Fed was as poorly prepared as most Americans were for the economic cataclysm that befell the nation in the 1930s.

In all three areas of business-government relations—the industry-specific policies handled by independent regulatory commissions, antitrust and tariff policies that crossed industry boundaries, and government-directed activities by the Fed—a similar pattern of development was evident. There was a general shift from a wholly private to a mixed system of public and private controls. Policies aimed at promoting corporate enterprise were now blended with policies protecting the interests of other groups, including shippers and consumers. More attention was given to the national welfare and less to the welfare of particular businesses. A distinct shift in power had taken place as the world of J.P. Morgan gave way to this more complex brand of political economy, America's corporate commonwealth.

To business executives trying to chart a course that would provide their companies with the right balance between efficiency, innovation, and control, these changes in the public sector were disturbing. Control of the firm's markets was complicated by the reality or threat of antitrust action. The political environment of the firm had become far more complex and far more difficult to control. In those businesses subject to rate-of-return regulation, some of the most fundamental managerial decisions about prices and production had been shifted from the private to the public realm. The firms involved could still influence those decisions, but so could other organized groups that took an interest in the industry's performance. In some industries, most notably the railroads, neither management nor the regulators had come up to the challenge of learning how to make the corporate commonwealth work effectively over the long term. In other businesses the agencies and CEOs were more successful. Agency staffs accumulated the information and analytical tools they needed to perform the regulatory function properly. Managements learned how to maintain efficient and innovative organizations in this new setting.

As it turned out, the changes were not nearly as dramatic as the devout reformers had hoped or the threatened businessleaders had feared they would be. The process of change was slow and halting. Entirely new political institutions were being created and fitted into a government that had been designed more than a century before with an eye to preventing the growth of the centralized power of the nation. The establishment of institutional control in the public sector was further constrained by the lack of consensus on the changes that were needed and by the unwillingness to pursue policies which might have undermined continued economic growth.

Moreover, it became apparent in the 1920s that business had not suddenly lost all of the good will that Americans had traditionally expressed toward private enterprise. With some significant exceptions, most Americans were still intensely interested in material progress. They were still convinced that the best way to achieve that progress was through private, not public, enterprise. This favorable cultural setting provided the country's corporate leaders with opportunities to win back some of the independence they had lost. They would never really get things back to the happy situation they had enjoyed in J. P. Morgan's world. The administrative state in America would continue to grow, and more groups would organize effectively to protect their interests. Power had been diffused, and that trend would also continue. But in the twenties U.S. businessmen and women would make important adjustments in their own behavior that would soothe some of the political tensions that had arisen in the years before the First World War. As a result they would hasten the broader acceptance of big business as an integral part of the new commonwealth.

CHAPTER 4

# Business
# Consolidates Its Control,
# *1901–1930*

To THE LEADERS of most
American businesses in the years before the First World War, political problems were distressing but they were not the most pressing
difficulties that had to be overcome. The thorniest issues were in the
marketplaces where goods and services were purchased and sold,
where capital and labor were obtained, and where the forces of
competition and technological change were focused. The managers
of a large enterprise had to learn how to balance the firm's need for
innovations against the need for control—that is, for a relatively
stable environment. To ensure the corporation's long-term success,
they also had to achieve a high degree of efficiency in mass production and distribution. These goals were in part contradictory, and
compromises had to be devised and implemented.

Corporate leaders frequently began their search for an appropriate strategy by attempting to achieve total control over their relevant markets, either through a monopoly or through loose combinations designed to contain the forces of competition. That was what

71

John D. Rockefeller and others had done in the late nineteenth century. Normally that phase of business strategy gave way, as it did with Rockefeller's enterprise, to an acceptance of less than total control and an accommodation with oligopoly, the domination of an industry by a few large firms. In the oligopolistic setting managers normally learned to restrain the manner in which they competed—eschewing, for instance, intense price competition that could be debilitating to the entire industry. They avoided for the most part the sort of speculative behavior so characteristic of the entrepreneurial firm of the previous century and cultivated a long-range perspective on the firm's performance. The planning horizon of the giant corporation stretched out far into the future.* Managerial outlooks on profits and competition gradually came to be attuned to this new business setting, but the transformation took place slowly and was a source of considerable uncertainty for management.

Within the firm, too, there were significant problems to be solved. In the nation's largest enterprises managers were responsible for very large amounts of capital, complex assets that had to be used efficiently if the business were to prosper over the long term. No longer could executives exercise direct control of the firm's assets and work force, as J.P. Morgan's father and grandfather had. They had to work through several layers of managers, supervisors, and foremen, and in many cases thousands of workers. They needed information that would enable them to judge performances and to evaluate whether personnel down the line had followed orders. In particular they needed to know which of their business policies were working and which were not working very well.

Efficiently running the vast business empires arising out of the consolidation movement was in itself a major accomplishment. But in addition corporate managers had to keep their organizations innovative if they were to stay abreast of the times. Efficiency called for large-scale standardized operations, and change necessarily interrupted those routines. But new technologies had to be developed and patented before they could slip into the hands of competitors. New challenges from other firms at home or overseas had to be met.

*One of the casualties of the recent wave of mergers and hostile takeovers appears to have been this long-range perspective. This development and its implications are discussed in chapter 10, "Reconstruction Begins."

New goods and services had to be bought and sold in distant markets that the corporate officer could no longer visit directly on a regular basis. In a setting changing as rapidly as the American economy was in the first three decades of this century, even the largest and most powerful corporations could not long remain static. Innovation, like efficiency, had to be managed. Much of the internal history of business in the years 1901 to 1930 is a study of how and to what effect business managers were able to achieve those sometimes conflicting objectives and to acquire a measure of control over their firms' market and political settings.

## *ADMINISTRATIVE CONSOLIDATION WITHIN THE FIRM*

Since most of the large firms of that era were created through mergers of competitors, the initial managerial task was to establish an effective organizational structure. The managers started by centralizing authority over their geographically dispersed and disparate types of organizations. Some of these organizations were still run by their former owners in the immediate aftermath of merger, and thus the process of centralization might involve a conflict of wills as well as an effort to create and impose a new business system. Normally these skirmishes were short-lived, but even after peace was restored, the problems of achieving a high degree of efficiency were formidable.

Most businesses adopted a pattern of organization comprised of functional departments, each of which had its own line of command and staff services. In the Du Pont Company for instance, separate departments were charged with responsibility for manufacturing the company's basic products—explosives, cellulose products, paints and chemicals—as well as for engineering, for purchasing, and for selling the firm's goods (see figure 4.1). Atop this structure was the firm's central headquarters, with its legal and financial staffs, controlled by an executive committee and a chief executive officer. A similar form of organization was adopted in most American businesses engaged in large-scale manufacturing and distribution in the early twentieth century.

The advantages of this type of corporation were that it encour-

FIGURE 4.1

The Centralized Structure at Du Pont

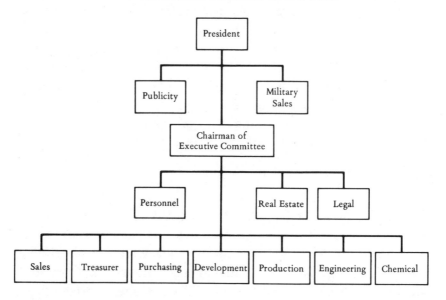

SOURCE: Alfred D. Chandler, *Strategy and Structure: Chapters in the History of the Industrial Enterprise* (Cambridge, Mass.: MIT Press, 1962), 74.

aged a high degree of functional specialization. One could build a lifetime career moving up the line in a single department, becoming an expert in manufacturing or in selling smokeless powder, for instance. The highest position in each function was that of vice president, and all the vice presidents served in the central office. Directly under them were the department directors, who ran operations on a day-to-day basis. Performance in these positions and those down the line could be carefully measured, because each manager had a designated area of responsibility, an area whose output and costs were recorded and evaluated regularly by the heads of the departments. The executive committee and the CEO in turn evaluated the departments, appointed the department directors and decided what specific responsibilities they would have, and made the firm's crucial entrepreneurial decisions about where to invest its resources. The CEO and the finance committee were responsible for seeing that the business had the resources it needed.

Usually this meant deciding when to borrow money, when to sell stock, how much growth to fund by way of retained earnings—a recourse that the successful combines increasingly came to use—and what dividends to pay.

As one might imagine, the managers up and down the line in this type of corporate enterprise had an almost insatiable desire for better information about their areas of responsibility: what were the important elements of cost? who was improving or falling behind? The result in most corporations was a new emphasis upon cost accounting, a practice largely foreign to the nineteenth-century entrepreneurial firm. Between 1900 and the First World War, most large businesses learned for the first time what their unit costs were. No longer was depreciation left to be paid out of undistributed earnings. Business decisions, including those about prices and production runs, could now be made on the basis of a full and accurate knowledge of costs. The efficiency and return on investment of different departments of the firm could be computed and compared.

In its most extreme and abstract form, the movement toward careful measurement of performance and of statistical reporting came to be known as "scientific management," which had a great following in America in the early decades of the twentieth century. As devised originally by Frederick W. Taylor, scientific management was essentially a systematic technique (and "systematic management" would have been a more accurate name for the practice) for breaking a job into its various components, for measuring performance, and for managing the behavior of the performers, in this case the firm's employees. The ethos of scientific management was probably more important than the specific techniques of control advocated by Taylor or the other prophets of the movement. Most large enterprises were actually wary of Taylorism and were more inclined to devise their own methods of management than to adopt the Taylor package. But the ethos of control, of using more active and systematic forms of management throughout the entire firm, from the head office to the shop floor—that spirit spread rapidly through American business in the first decade of the century.

On the floor of the factory, work forces had for several decades been increasing in size without experiencing fundamental shifts in organization. Foremen had long controlled their own gangs of employees, frequently subcontracting for the work performed. That system left to the foreman the basic decisions about which employees to hire, how much each would be paid, and how much each would do in a workday that normally varied from eight to twelve hours a shift. In most corporations the foreman-centered mode of operations was not supplanted until after modern techniques of control had been extended from the boardroom down through middle management; then, at last, bureaucratic techniques of organization replaced the personal authority of the foreman on the shop floor.

In some cases the old style of workplace gave way not to systematic management but to a new form of machine process, the assembly line. Henry Ford was the great pioneer of this process and his crucial innovations were introduced during the years 1910 to 1914. At the Ford Motor Company the employees were arranged along a moving assembly line, with each performing one discrete function as the frame and other large components of the automobile moved along to their destination, the yard where the car waited for distribution to the company's network of sales offices. The assembly line controlled the pace of work in the Ford plant. One of the primary managerial tasks was to organize the parts and processes so that the line could move smoothly and by 1914 the men could assemble over 1,200 Model T chassis in an eight-hour day. The assembly line greatly increased the degree of control that management could exercise over the labor force. Through specialization and mechanization, Ford achieved increases in productivity that enabled the firm to price automobiles low enough to tap a mass consumer market.

As the Ford Motor Company and other manufacturing firms grew, their owners and managers usually found reasons to extend their control beyond the business's primary functions, in this case the manufacture and sale of automobiles. With extensive capital tied up in plant and a large work force mobilized, managers were under great pressure to keep the factories running at a high capacity.* To keep unit costs down, they had to avoid interruptions in

---

*In the less capital-intensive entrepreneurial firm, the businessman was under less pressure to keep running because more of his costs were variable (they stopped when he shut down) and less were fixed (they continued whether he was running or not).

the supply of materials and parts, and the surest way to do that was by way of vertical integration, bringing suppliers within the firm. The same was true for the distribution network: to ensure a smooth flow of products to markets around the United States and (to a lesser extent) overseas, businesses began to bring the transportation, wholesaling, and even retailing of their products under common ownership. In this manner they could not only move very large volumes with minimal disturbances to the flow of goods but maintain quality control. They could also make profits from what had formerly been market transactions with other firms. Finally, they could block the entry of competitors who might attempt to invade their markets or sources of supply.

Typical of the firms that integrated vertically was one of Ford's competitors, the General Motors Corporation, which the dynamic William C. Durant founded in 1908. Durant brought together in his loosely joined combine the producers of several different automobiles—including Buick, Oldsmobile, and Cadillac—and the manufacturers of numerous components such as lights and other electrical elements, transmissions, gears, and engines. Unlike other such vertically integrated companies, however, General Motors let the several distinct companies in the combine enjoy a high degree of autonomy. They were consolidated financially but not administratively by Durant, who was a master promoter and astute salesperson, but a poor manager. As a result of the loose controls exercised by GM's management, the Durant auto empire soon ran into some heavy fiscal seas. Caught with a large inventory on his hands when sales turned down, Durant was forced to surrender direction of General Motors between 1910 and 1916, first to a group of Boston and New York bankers and then, after he regained control briefly, to a group headed by Pierre S. Du Pont in 1920.

With Du Pont support, Alfred P. Sloan, a master administrator, brought order in the 1920s to GM's complex array of separate companies. Under Sloan, GM turned its vertical integration to full advantage by developing a flexible and systematic style of administration. The GM management program featured an elaborate forecasting system that enabled the business to keep inventory balanced with national demand and a cost accounting and reporting system that allowed the firm's managers to focus attention on those parts of the operation that most needed to improve productivity. By the

end of the twenties, so effective was the GM administration that the
business could manage annual style changes in its several automobiles without losing operating efficiency. Along the way, GM replaced Ford as the nation's—and the world's—premier automobile
manufacturer. Such were the rewards for achieving the proper balance between innovation and corporate efficiency.

At GM, Ford, and most other major corporations in the early
decades of this century, particular CEOs put a personal stamp on
their organizations' styles, but to run effectively such corporations had to have the active, vigorous leadership of hundreds of
other managers. One of the most important means of achieving
the full support of middle managers was through the committee
system, which brought managers up and down the line together
to work out problems and make plans for their particular departments. In the entrepreneurial firm such formal planning and consensus building had been unnecessary; there had been no layers
of executives between the top and bottom of the firm, so consul-
tation was direct and unstructured. But in the large twentieth-
century corporation, with its army of administrators, the committee system provided an essential means of building a compelling
corporate culture, of achieving full understanding and cooperation down the line, and of exploiting the innovative ideas of middle managers. Despite the well-known frustrations of committee
work, the giant business enterprise of this century could not do
without this means of using the managerial resources of the firm
to the fullest extent.

U.S. corporations employed this technique only for managers,
however. The large corporation did no better than the small firm in
making use of the innovative skills of its labor force on the shop or
factory floor. Indeed, innovations such as the assembly line moved
in the opposite direction, replacing labor with capital and reducing
the worker's role to that of an adjunct to a dominant machine
process. Both the assembly line and systematic management were
means of improving operating efficiency, cutting labor costs, and
reducing the unit costs of production. Both means worked. But as
implemented in American corporations in the years 1901–1930,
these new ways of doing business made it even more difficult for
labor to identify with the firm and its success than had been the case

in the nineteenth-century business. Even more responsibility for improving operations was shifted to management and away from labor. Workers were not encouraged to be innovators in most U.S. firms, and the nineteenth-century adversarial tradition of labor-management relations (see chapter 2, pp. 21–22) was actually strengthened in the mass-production era.

Using immigrant labor and mechanized factories, American mass-production firms were able to fend off labor unions and keep control of the shop floor and its work rules. In the early 1920s they joined hands with small and medium-sized businesses to mount a campaign for the so-called "American Plan," the open, nonunion shop. The political environment in the aftermath of the First World War was favorable for such an effort. Employers in a number of industries went to battle with the craft unions of the AFL and won. They used the carrot as well as the stick, developing various benefit plans, including health-care and retirement programs, that helped to shift workers' loyalties from their union to the corporation. Many firms also organized "company unions" that provided the form but not the substance of independent union representation. The company unions were, nevertheless, very successful in a number of industries. From management's point of view they were effective, because they undercut the craft unions and left the firm in sole control of the production process. In search of a reliable work force, managers were also often willing to buy labor peace during the prosperous twenties by making wage concessions to their employees. The cumulative impact of all these programs was a decided drop in union membership and a shift in power back toward management. This trend was especially pronounced in businesses characterized by large companies and mass production, businesses in which the adversarial traditions of labor relations had put down deep roots.

In the mass-production, mass-distribution industries the vertically integrated, administratively consolidated combine was a highly efficient style of business. Cutting costs and achieving tight control of their diverse operations, these businesses became a major factor in the fastest-growing sectors of the American economy. Wherever an advanced technology was being applied, wherever heavy capitalization was needed, wherever standardized goods or services were being produced for U.S. markets—the largest single

market area in the world—the highly centralized corporation established a secure position in the 1920s.


## THE BEGINNINGS OF RESEARCH AND DEVELOPMENT

While these sorts of corporate giants could master the problems of
routine, standardized production, it was less clear even as late as
1920 that they could do an equally good job as innovators. Unlike
the entrepreneurial firm, the large corporation suffered from some
of the same internal, bureaucratic problems that have plagued large-
scale public administrations throughout the world. In the course of
developing administrative controls and the committee system for
managing the modern corporation, businessmen had in effect built
into the firm impediments to rapid change. The line-staff system
ensured that major decisions were based upon careful staff studies,
which took time to conduct. Decisions that filtered through committees were routinely robbed of their most radical elements. Con-
sensus-building was an intricate process that was inherently anti-
thetical to rapid, decisive innovation.

Each of these giant corporations was somewhat like a federation
of separate political entities. Instead of being named Ohio or West-
chester, these subdivisions were named manufacturing, sales,
finance, or development. Each bargained for a share of the corporation's resources and its power. The line officers who headed these
departments spoke not only for themselves but also for the interests
of their managers and other employees down the departmental line.
Having acquired powerful positions within the firm, department
heads could often find a reason to be suspicious of innovations that
seemed to threaten their power base and the operations they had
mastered. As a result, the business was inherently easier to keep on
track than it was to switch onto a new approach, new product, or
new style of enterprise.

The CEO and the executive committee provided counterweights
to these internal forces of conservatism. In a crisis, the board of
directors might intervene, although if a problem had to be decided
by the board, it usually meant that the company's top managers

were likely to be changed in the near future. Power was hierarchical and highly centralized in these private bureaucracies. Responsibility was more focused than it was in public administration, and the profit and loss statement applied an immediate and powerful prod to executives unwilling to change their company's course of action. To implement a new program, however, they needed more than obedience; they needed the enthusiastic support of several layers of managers down the line. Thus innovation involved leadership and persuasion, as well as good decision-making. That alone ensured that the corporation would innovate at a more stately pace than the entrepreneurial firm.

The CEOs of early twentieth-century corporations were also handicapped by the fact that they could not be as directly involved in the process of innovation as they would have been in a smaller enterprise. They were, after all, full-time administrators. What they needed within the corporation was an institution that would encourage change, especially technological innovation. But before 1900, no such institution existed in American business. In the case of many industries, this entity would have to be capable of enabling the firm to draw upon and develop the scientific and technical theories and empirical studies being worked out in the academic disciplines thriving in turn-of-the-century America. A great expansion of science and engineering was taking place. The firm needed employees trained in mathematics, attuned to current theoretical developments, and willing to work in an organized setting where they would share responsibility for the innovative process. Standard Oil had earlier created a proto-laboratory in its efforts to learn how to refine Lima crude but had then disbanded its ad hoc research operation once it had succeeded (see chapter 2, p. 35). What a corporation needed now was a regular means of staying in touch with relevant developments, whether they were in particular branches of electrical engineering and physics, in chemistry and chemical engineering, or in other scientific and technical disciplines. It also needed effective means of developing its own scientific and engineering concepts that had specific business applications and then tailoring the resulting innovations to existing markets and processes of production.

Out of these needs grew the modern industrial laboratory. One of the earliest was organized by the General Electric Company, a Morgan-sponsored combination of the Edison and Thomson-Houston interests in electric lighting and power. In 1900 GE established its lab under the immediate direction of Dr. Willis R. Whitney, a faculty member at MIT who had the necessary scientific training to direct sophisticated, systematic research on the kinds of problems that GE needed to solve. Typical of the research Whitney carried forward was an effort to improve the electric lightbulbs GE was selling. To do so, he had to develop a lighting filament that would last longer, be less subject to breakage, and use less electricity than the carbon filaments in use at that time. The lab at GE mounted a well-organized assault on this problem, drawing upon scientific resources in the United States and abroad and using as many as forty researchers and assistants and an annual budget of close to $100,000. After a number of false starts and failures, this effort yielded an effective tungsten filament that could be mass-produced and was more durable and more efficient than any other lamp on the market. By 1914 General Electric lamps had over 70 percent of the market, and during the 1920s profits from incandescent lamps were over $30 million a year.

Behind the scenes of this success story was another narrative, one involving the problems of managing a successful research and development (R&D) operation in a large corporate setting. To be successful, the lab had to have resources: money, equipment, and men and women with special kinds of training and scientific skills. It had to acquire and maintain those resources over a long period when it could not always be producing immediate and obvious returns on GE's investment in research. One of Willis Whitney's most important tasks was to speak for the lab in dealing with the company's top leadership. He frequently had to justify large expenditures for work that might yield no returns in the short run, and maybe never at all. Other inventors might beat GE to the punch, as they sometimes did. Corporate leaders unaccustomed to this kind of indeterminate situation found investing in R&D difficult to justify. During the early years at the lab, Whitney was always under intense pressure to produce immediate results that would warrant continued support. When he could point to a successful innovation such as the tungsten filament lamp, he could at last argue effectively for the long-term support of an institution that only gradually became an accepted part of the corporation at GE and at a few other large American companies prior to the First World War. Once it had produced some winning products or processes, the industrial lab could be put (as it was at GE) on a longer corporate leash, but the leash was always there.

Two basic kinds of industrial labs emerged. One, typified by GE's laboratory, evolved into an institution that engaged in a wide variety of studies, many of which seemed to have only a vague relationship to the company's immediate needs. This type of organization generated new products and services that eventually carried the firm into entirely new areas of business activity. At GE that meant radio and X-ray lamps, which took the corporation down new paths with a common technological starting point. At Du Pont, the firm's lucrative business in agricultural chemicals grew out of a similar style of laboratory activity.

A second approach to R&D emerged at the American Telephone and Telegraph Company, where Frank Jewett, chief engineer, and J. J. Carty, chief engineer and then vice president for development, focused the lab's very considerable scientific resources on a smaller range of major problems in telecommunications technology. Here the lab was less important for generating new corporate directions than for solving discrete problems in the nation's emerging telephone network. Early on, improvement in long distance transmission was at the top of AT&T's list of objectives. This goal was important strategically because the company's long distance network provided the main advantage it had over other, independent telephone companies. It was also important symbolically, because AT&T's president, Theodore Vail, had publicly promised to have transcontinental transmission by the time the Panama-Pacific Exposition opened in January 1915. Under Jewett's direction, AT&T pushed into the relatively new science of radio transmission, purchasing the patents for and then greatly improving the three-element vacuum tube. The firm's large and talented research team drove the processes of invention and application of the innovation through to completion by the deadline. Coast-to-coast telephone service using the AT&T-devised electronic amplifier was launched in January 1915, and with it rode the reputation of what would eventually become the premier industrial research laboratory in the nation.

At both AT&T and GE, laboratories had proven their worth by the time the United States entered the First World War in 1917. During the war, the federal government vigorously promoted research in its own labs and in businesses such as chemicals and metallurgy that were vital to the mobilization effort. The wartime emergency also popularized scientific and technological accomplishment in a manner that encouraged many other corporations to invest in R & D during the 1920s. The general prosperity of the decade made it easier for managers to look with favor on R&D as a means of keeping the corporation innovative over the long term. By the end of the decade, the modern industrial lab—with its team of Ph.D. scientists and engineers, its library of technical publications, and its crew of research managers—was an established part of the large corporate enterprise. By that time, too, it had become evident that such labs were far more than conduits for technological and scientific knowledge; they were also contributing significantly to advances on both of these fronts.

As the industrial laboratories illustrated, the combines were not quick on their feet, but they were learning how to innovate in ways that were simply beyond the capabilities of small firms. The giant corporations could sustain large-scale research organizations over the long term. They could afford teams of specialists and expensive equipment. They could muster the engineering and managerial resources to ensure that inventions were efficiently transformed into practical innovations and brought into production in a timely way. Even the elaborate committee structures and bureaucratic hierarchies that slowed the process of innovation had one outstanding advantage: they reduced the risks of corporate entrepreneurship. The nineteenth-century firm was more agile than the combine but far more likely to end up in bankruptcy court. Corporate R&D has thus played a decisive role in the progress of American business from the First World War to the present day.

## NEW MODES OF MARKET CONTROL

To sustain large-scale R&D operations, managers had to take a long-range view of the company's strategy, to conceive of the business in terms that would justify large investments that might not pay off for many years. In order to adopt that perspective (as the leaders of such enterprises well knew), the firms had to be insulated in the short term from extreme fluctuations in prices and demand. Indeed, the initial impetus to combination had in most cases been a desire to dampen the intense competitive pressure that had weakened or driven into bankruptcy so many businesses in the major depression of the 1890s. As corporate executives learned, adequate control of the market could usually be achieved once a single combine or a few major firms were responsible for somewhat more than half of the industry's output; such oligopolies were normally characterized by a tolerable degree of stability of prices and of market shares. In the corporate economy, the dominant combines were no longer price takers; they could administer prices in the short term and could influence them over the long term as well.

Of course complete stability could never be achieved in a dynamic setting like the one that existed in the United States. Too much was changing. Even in an industry like iron and steel—where after 1901 U.S. Steel was the largest producer, with 50 to 70 percent of the market, depending on the products involved—it proved difficult at times to keep price competition from erupting. Judge Gary, U.S. Steel's CEO, tried to cool the competition by holding the famous Gary Dinners, beginning in 1907. At these pleasant evening meetings, each corporate CEO (acting individually, of course—there was an antitrust law to bear in mind) proclaimed what his company intended to do in regard to prices for basic products. The intent was to create pressure to hold the line on prices and follow the leadership of the largest company, U.S. Steel. Like other such loose associations of competitors, the Gary Dinners provided only a temporary respite from market pressure. But the dinners, the threat of competitive retaliation by U.S. Steel, and the growing recognition in the industry that intense price competition would leave all the steel businesses weaker, gradually brought steel executives in the 1920s to adopt a cooperative attitude toward their erstwhile competitors. By that time cutthroat competition had given way to oligopolistic price and production behavior.

The twenties indeed witnessed the flowering of interfirm cooperation in the United States. Encouraged by Herbert Hoover's Department of Commerce and tolerated to an increasing degree by the

Federal Trade Commission and the Department of Justice, trade associations developed elaborate codes of business ethics and complex cooperative programs in research, advertising, and the shaping of business-government relations. The associations also developed a wide variety of programs that were formal variants on the Gary Dinners, efforts to stabilize prices and market shares at profitable levels for all but the weakest of the industry's firms. The best of these programs skirted close to violating the antitrust laws, and the worst clearly broke the law. As substitutes for oligopoly they failed to achieve their major goal, price and market-share stability; as ancillaries to the large corporation in oligopolistic industries, they appear to have met with a measure of success.

As the development of these new business institutions and practices suggests, in the years immediately following the great merger movement many of America's corporate combines were still on somewhat shaky legs. The failure rate before 1920 was relatively high, and even some of J. P. Morgan's impressive corporate creations slid into bankruptcy. Unable to achieve a dominant position in their markets, unable to block the entry of more efficient competitors, unable to consolidate their own operations, such combines as the National Starch Manufacturing Company, the Mercantile Corporation, and several combines in textiles went bankrupt. Even such successful companies as the vertically integrated meat packers, the so-called Big Four—Armour, Schwarzchild and Sulzberger, Cudahy, and Swift—found themselves hard-pressed to keep profits at a satisfactory level in the early 1900s. Such businesses at times turned to government for help in stabilizing their markets, although an appeal for political assistance was the exception and not the rule in the United States. Most companies tried to solve their competitive problems in the private sector, even in the 1920s, when a series of Republican administrations in Washington, D.C., sought to sustain the nation's prosperity by keeping business happy.

The firms that were most successful in using the government to stabilize markets were in industries that were closely regulated by the state or federal governments.* The utilities described in the

*Paradoxically, these businesses had seldom sought closer ties to the government in the first instance; in most cases, regulation was initially forced on them by their political opponents. Once regulated, however, many of these firms adapted creatively to their new political environments and used the regulatory system, as best they could, to achieve their own objectives.

previous chapter were able to work with state regulatory agencies to maintain controls on entry and prices, controls that ensured an adequate level of profits in the industry. With rate-of-return regulation, private interests traded freedom of action for a relatively secure future. At the federal level, the U.S. ocean shipping firms, which had been unable to achieve successful consolidation around J. P. Morgan's combine, were able to achieve the same end through the U.S. Maritime Commission, which dampened the fires of competition among American companies and shielded part of their market from foreign ships.

As the railroads illustrated, even a regulatory system attuned to the needs of the regulated companies could not protect those businesses from every potential hazard. The ICC ended rate wars and in setting rates adopted the type of cost accounting that the railroad corporations had devised. But the ICC could not ignore the shippers and farmers; they were too well organized, too well represented for any government agency to neglect. Nor could the ICC permanently forestall those technological changes (automobiles, trucks, and airlines) that eventually eroded the railroads' markets in passenger and freight traffic. In these circumstances neither the ICC nor railroad managers were able to transform the roads into efficient, innovative businesses, and the result in this industry was a long painful decline for most of the leading companies.

Far more successful in this regard was the Bell System, which had a particularly elaborate relationship to local, state, and federal authority. In its early years (1876–1894) the Bell System (for which the American Telephone and Telegraph Company later became the parent company) had been protected from competition by its patents. After the patents expired, however, a rush of new independent firms came into the industry, especially in the Midwest and South, where the Bell interests were not providing service to many rural areas. By 1907, when J. P. Morgan became involved in the reorganization of AT&T and set Theodore Vail to work revitalizing the system, Bell provided only about half the phones in the United States.

Vail quickly reorganized and reenergized the Bell System. He adopted the customary Morgan policy of consolidating the firm's market position by acquiring many of the independent firms that were competing with Bell. Behind his leadership, AT&T also pushed forward vigorously with the program of industrial research described earlier in this chapter; these research operations were consolidated in 1925 under Bell Labs. Vail restructured the entire system along functional lines and centralized authority over the technical integration of the emerging national telephone network. The result was a technologically driven corporation in which the successful operation of the network became a mystique as much as a business policy. Vail's motto, "One System, One Policy, Universal Service," epitomized AT&T's corporate strategy for the next fifty years.

While he centralized authority over technology, Vail left corporate governance far more decentralized than was the case in most U.S. combines during the early 1900s. In part this was an accommodation to the phone company's great size and in part a consequence of the political situation Vail faced. A vigorous regulatory movement was underway, and AT&T's chief executive officer was ready to accept the authority of the states rather than be regulated by municipalities or by the federal government. Consequently, he left the several Bell operating companies (the horizontal element in the combine) to function as relatively autonomous parts of the system, so that they could each make their peace, as they did, with their respective state regulators. That protected one flank of the system from political attack.

Vail had meanwhile settled out of court a federal antitrust suit prompted by AT&T's acquisition policy. The price of settlement included an agreement to interconnect its long distance and local lines with noncompeting independent companies, a policy that indeed gave America "One System."* By the end of the 1920s, AT&T had a virtual monopoly of long-distance telephone service; its manufacturing subsidiary, Western Electric—which, along with Bell Labs, was a vertical component of the combine—made most of the nation's telephone equipment. All this had been achieved by a thoroughly regulated business. By 1925, AT&T was the nation's largest corporation. It had traded away the right to make unusually high profits (as had most public utilities) to protect its monopoly

---

*AT&T also divested its holdings in the Western Union company and agreed not to acquire any more independent telephone companies without the permission of the federal government.

and to make peace with public authority. It had achieved as well a particularly successful balance between efficiency and continuing technological innovation. As a result, the United States had the world's best telephone system.

Other businesses—even those in regulated industries—were generally less successful in promoting innovation and in protecting their turf. The problem was, in part, like that of the Roman Empire, whose frontiers always seemed to need more pacification. In a fast-growing, technologically advanced economy, even industry-wide controls could not prevent new goods and services from invading a market, as the truckers did in transportation during the 1920s. Similarly, the iron and steel firms had only just pacified competition among themselves before an aggressive new aluminum producer, Alcoa, began to shove its way into the markets for structural materials. For most executives, control of the market was thus an elusive goal, but one they could not afford to ignore.

## THE ROLE OF SMALL BUSINESS

In a capitalist system one business's problem was another's opportunity. Where big business faltered or settled down to enjoy its profits without remaining innovative, where there were opportunities for innovation that large firms were not exploiting, small businesses usually came along to challenge the giant corporations. Thus the entrepreneurial firm continued to play a crucial role in the new corporate economy. By the 1920s most of the nation's goods and a growing share of its services were provided by large centralized corporations (see figure 4.2). But many of the business system's innovations came from small and medium-sized firms, which eventually either sold out to their larger brethren or themselves grew to be large companies.

One such midget was Armco, a tiny steel producer centered in Middletown, Ohio. Its history is instructive. This entrepreneurial firm was like a seed planted in the shadow of a giant oak tree because Armco started operations in 1901, the same year that U.S. Steel was organized. Wisely Armco did not go head to head against

FIGURE 4.2

Concentration

in the U.S. Economy, 1929

a.  Percentage of the Total Assets in Their Respective Groups Held by Large Corporations, 1929

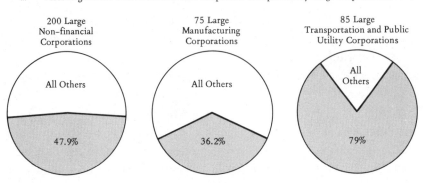

| 200 Large Non-financial Corporations | 75 Large Manufacturing Corporations | 85 Large Transportation and Public Utility Corporations |
|---|---|---|
| All Others | All Others | All Others |
| 47.9% | 36.2% | 79% |

b.  Percentage of Total Value of Manufactured Goods Produced by Largest Firms, 1929

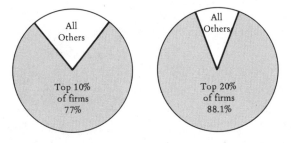

| All Others | All Others |
|---|---|
| Top 10% of firms 77% | Top 20% of firms 88.1% |

SOURCES: a. M.A. Adelman, "The Measurement of Industrial Concentration," *The Review of Economics and Statistics* 33 (1951): 286; b. G. Warren Nutter, *The Extent of Enterprise Monopoly in the United States, 1899–1939* (Chicago: University of Chicago Press, 1951): 34.

Morgan's behemoth. Instead, George M. Verity, its astute CEO, guided his enterprise into a niche in specialty steels, unusually pure metals that were used in other industrial products. He devised a new process for producing these steels, and in the years that followed the company grew until by 1930 it was the country's largest manufacturer of high-grade steel products. By that time Armco had vertically integrated from production of its basic metal into finished goods, but unlike U.S. Steel it still did not control its own coal or ore supplies or run its own railroad or shipping lines. It was nevertheless a highly successful company, whose early history reminds us that while American business has changed dramatically in this century, small enterprises still play a vital role in keeping that system innovative.

Otto Haas played that role by transferring new technology from Germany to the United States in the business of industrial chemicals. In the years before the First World War, Germany was far ahead of the United States in chemical research. As we have seen, the first modern industrial laboratories in this country were not established until 1900; by that time similar research organizations had been active in Germany for several decades. When Otto Haas immigrated to the United States in 1908 and went into business in Philadelphia the following year, he launched his small endeavor with a specific innovation in hand, a chemical for tanning leather. He also had the advantage of strong personal and professional ties to the German industry, especially by way of his partner, Otto Röhm. Over the years Haas built up a successful enterprise that stressed salesmanship by technically qualified employees who could help their customers devise the best ways to use Rohm and Haas chemicals in their production processes. Haas continued to draw most of his innovative ideas from abroad, while he held the Rohm and Haas Company tightly on course as a manufacturer of producer's goods—that is, goods used to manufacture other products, as opposed to consumer goods, which go directly into wholesale and retail distribution. By 1929 Haas's formula had built the Rohm and Haas firm into a substantial business with sales of $4.2 million.

In addition to transferring or generating innovations, small businesses continued to offer services where economies of scale or system could not be achieved. In that sector of the business system the small firm's flexibility continued to give it an edge. The personal attention of the entrepreneur-owner was vital in retail food services, in the growing market for repair work on consumer durables, and in businesses in which fashion was an important factor.* Failure rates continued to be high, but there was apparently an inexhaustible supply of new entrepreneurs eager to take the places

---

*This would include many grades of women's clothing and jewelry, for example.

of those who failed. While large enterprises were in general stabilizing their positions in the economy by the 1920s, small business continued to churn ahead, generating new ideas, filling the interstices between the great corporations, and providing opportunities for Americans who were willing to take high risks in the hope of establishing a successful business that would bear their personal imprint.

## PUBLIC RELATIONS AND PUBLIC AFFAIRS
## IN THE ASSOCIATIVE STATE

These small businesses as well as the country's large corporations were challenged during the years 1900 to 1930 to bring under control their social and political environments as well as their markets and internal activities. As we saw in the previous chapter, the political economy of the United States was beginning to change in the Progressive Era in ways that gave business leaders pause, if not reason to fear for their future. As single-industry regulation became more prevalent, as cross-industry policies were implemented, as government-directed activities increased, executives sensed that they were losing contact with and control over their political and social environments. Big business had never enjoyed the public good will that the entrepreneurial firm generally had on the local community level in the previous century. After 1900, enterprises of all sizes shared the hostility toward business generated by liberal reform and radical critiques of capitalism in this country. Sparks were struck, and managers quite naturally feared the fire that might follow. The United States was beginning to develop a new type of political system, one in which individual influence and a local power base were becoming less important than effective lobbying on the state and national levels. Effective legal representation on a continuous basis and effective media campaigns were necessary to build public understanding and confidence. In 1900 U.S. businesses were not well equipped to perform any of these functions. They had to develop new organizations to enable them to preserve the influence they had and, as far as possible, to regain the position business had lost.

The initial effort to build institutions capable of coordinating the activities of an industry, including business-government relations, was usually mounted through trade associations. These privately financed and managed organizations—many of which were launched or reorganized before the First World War—took the lead in forging in the 1920s a more cooperative form of capitalism, one that historians have since labeled "the associative state." At first glance, this approach to cooperation and greater coordination in a maturing industrial nation seems unfamiliar and certainly out of touch with American society since the New Deal. Yet associationalism had strong roots in the nation's past, and it held considerable appeal as a means of shaping political behavior and a way of coordinating an increasingly complex economy without heavy reliance on direct government control.

The activities of the American Petroleum Institute (API) in the 1920s suggest both the strengths and weaknesses of associationalism. The API was the trade association most representative of all segments of the industry, and it included all the major oil companies active in the United States. It was created after the First World War from the organizational structure and the membership lists of the National Petroleum War Service Committee, the oil industry committee that had helped manage the war mobilization. Staffed by a small group of administrative officers, it began its operations originally in New York but later moved to Washington.

Like many trade associations in the 1920s, the API proved particularly adept at coordinating industry-wide activities aimed at fostering greater cooperation among firms and between the industry and government. The API took the lead, for example, in organizing an industry-wide crusade for uniform standards in many areas of operation, especially oil drilling. These "API standards" were defined by experts from the various branches of the industry with the assistance of Herbert Hoover's Department of Commerce. The API organized a similarly successful drive to establish uniform accounting standards. Standardization required the joint action of many individual oil firms, and the trade association's success in these previously neglected areas of business development doubtless enhanced the efficiency of the industry as a whole.

In addition to handling technical questions, the API focused its resources on public relations, the collection of statistics on basic conditions in the industry, and lobbying. Its broad, well-financed campaign to improve the public image of the oil business helped counteract the popular concept of "Big Oil" or "Standard Oil" inherited from the days of John D. Rockefeller. Its timely expert testimony before Congress helped the industry gain a variety of favorable laws—notably the oil depletion allowance*—while helping to repulse several legislative threats to the industry, including an effort to increase the gasoline tax. The API was adept at this new style of lobbying, a form of highly-organized, well-funded activity that replaced the old personal mode of lobbying characteristic of the entrepreneurial firm.

The backbone of the institute's effective lobbying and public relations was the aggregate statistics on conditions in the oil business that it compiled from data provided by individual companies. Many firms initially were hesitant to provide figures on operations, because they might be of use to competitors. But by guaranteeing the confidentiality of statistical reports by individual concerns, the API gradually developed accurate, timely information about conditions in all branches of the business. These statistics proved quite valuable to the industry and government officials involved in oil policies.

In several other areas, however, the API's efforts to coordinate the activities of individual oil companies came into conflict with the realities of a competitive marketplace. In the early 1920s, the API set forth on an ambitious attempt to create an organization capable of conducting research and development—a cooperative form of industrial lab. The aged John D. Rockefeller stepped forward with seed money for this endeavor, which was placed under the leadership of a former head of the U.S. Bureau of Mines. But the effort quickly bogged down in a dispute over the focus of API-sponsored R&D. Several of the large oil companies adamantly opposed collective research on problems of applied technology that their newly created company labs had already begun to study. The result was a narrowing of the focus of the API's efforts, to fundamental re-

---

*The oil depletion allowance was a tax break given to the oil firms to help them sustain the high costs of exploring and drilling for new oil.

search on such questions as the chemical composition of oil. Neither the API nor other associations could move ahead when they encountered determined opposition from within the industry. In this case what was lost was a very promising program of cooperative, industry-wide research and development.*

Conflicts within the industry also hampered the API's efforts to develop workable, durable solutions to two controversial problems of the 1920s: oil pollution control, and regulation of the supply of oil. These two issues illustrated the great difficulties in reaching associative solutions to problems about which there was no clear consensus within an industry. The first was particularly unfortunate, because oil pollution of America's waterways had reached alarming levels during and after the First World War. Congress responded with a variety of strong proposals for regulation, but the API coordinated an intensive lobbying campaign to pull the teeth out of the new regulations. The heart of its lobbying effort was a national survey of conditions done in cooperation with the Bureau of Mines. The survey's conclusions that conditions were already improving and the industry's assurances that it would attack this problem cooperatively helped limit the Oil Pollution Control Act of 1924 to the regulation of discharges of oil from ships in harbors.

With the legislative crisis passed, the API moved to clean up pollution through the work of committees of engineers from all branches of the industry. These API study groups published valuable materials suggesting how individual oil producers might clean up their operations and at the same time save oil and money. But at this point, the associative program hit a roadblock. Several of the leaders of the API's antipollution work suggested that the API hire a small group of engineers to monitor the industry's efforts in controlling pollution. But the president of the API responded that the organization was not going to be a "policeman." Unfortunately, a policeman was needed. Suggestions and voluntary compliance with the new standards did not solve the pollution problem. The API's program illustrated the limits to the associational approach and to self-regulation in general. The pollution problem would become

---

*Today some U.S. business leaders and public officials are interested in promoting cooperative R&D as a means of meeting international competition.

worse in the years to follow, and eventually business would find itself in the position of having a federal solution forced on it, despite the API's resistance.

The API was even more limited in its ability to confront the key issue in the industry in the late 1920s, the glut of oil. The discoveries of new oil fields in this era placed more and more crude oil on the market, pushing down prices. But the API could not persuade the various segments of the industry to reach a common ground on how to bring production under control. Particularly intense were the tensions between the smaller domestic producers and the major, vertically integrated companies, which were increasingly importing foreign oil into the United States. For a time, most oil producers seemed to agree that self-regulation, not government regulation, was the answer, but the result of ineffective self-regulation was a distressing price decline that created a sense of crisis in every phase of the oil business in the late 1920s. Through effective associational activity, the oil firms had acquired a powerful influence on public policy, but they were still unable to use that power to bring production and hence the market for oil under control.

Within businesses, as well as among them, efforts were made to deal more effectively with problems of public relations and public affairs. While many nineteenth-century firms had sought to influence public opinion toward business, in the twentieth century this effort was institutionalized in permanent corporate staff functions and new professional consultants to service the business system. The foundations of the new public relations and public affairs departments and consulting organizations were laid in the turmoil of the progressive era between the 1890s and 1917. The First World War witnessed rapid additions to this structure of new institutions and the popularization of the idea. The twenties saw both developments achieve a maturity that assured their place in the modern American business system.

Public relations grew directly out of the perception on the part of business managers, especially corporate officers, that liberal or progressive political campaigns were generating an intensely negative concept of business and threatening to create an ever more restrictive political economy. Admittedly many of these apprehensions were exaggerated, suggesting a threat of radicalism in a nation dedicated to moderate reform. But businesses actually had good reason to fear that the business image was suffering among the public during the years 1900 through 1916, and their new public relations departments labored hard to alter a negative public concept of the corporation. Public relations departments also began to provide input to corporate decision-making, reporting on public perceptions and advising how business might avoid antagonizing its several publics. In the 1920s, this function was popularized as the "two-way street," with influence flowing out of the company to the public and back as well, all by way of the conduit provided by the public relations department. While the popular literature over-estimated the impact public relations officers had on most corporate CEOs, there was no question that by the 1920s most businesses were in better touch with their social environment than they had been since the rise of the large corporation. While some business leaders may still have privately embraced the late-nineteenth-century sentiment "The public be damned," they now knew enough not to say it in public, and public relations had something to do with that change.

Similarly, public affairs departments helped larger enterprises cope with the more active state and federal governments that were increasingly interested in business activities. They kept businesses in touch with legislative developments and agency actions on an ongoing basis. Constant surveillance was needed. Good legal talent had to be deployed where the company's vital interests were at stake. To a considerable extent the business-oriented politics of the 1920s was a result of the manner in which business had—both within and among firms—reorganized in an effort to project a new public image and shape a new brand of politics.

Small firms could not afford full-time public affairs departments, but they came to support interfirm associations that supplied many of the same services. The resurgence of the National Association of Manufacturers was in part related to this sort of effort, as was the rise of the Chamber of Commerce. The latter organization came to be a leading advocate for business (for large businesses as well as small) in Washington, D.C. The activities of the Chamber, the NAM, and the thousands of new industry and commercial associations represented a revolutionary change in business's means of controlling its social and political relations.

The combined impact of these organizational developments and

TABLE 4.1

Measures of U.S. Business Progress, 1900–1930

| Year | GNP Billions (1958 prices) | GNP per capita in dollars (1958 prices) | Growth Rate of GNP* (%) | Productivity Index† (1958= 100) | Manufacturing‡ (1929=100) | |
|------|------|------|------|------|------|------|
| | | | | | Output | Productivity |
| 1900 | 76.9 | 1,011 | 2.7 | 38.0 | 27.7 | 46.2 |
| 1901 | 85.7 | 1,105 | 11.5 | 40.3 | 30.9 | 49.1 |
| 1902 | 86.5 | 1,093 | .9 | 38.6 | 35.5 | 51.4 |
| 1903 | 90.8 | 1,126 | 5.0 | 39.1 | 35.4 | 49.6 |
| 1904 | 89.7 | 1,092 | −1.2 | 38.8 | 34.2 | 52.1 |
| 1905 | 96.3 | 1,149 | 7.5 | 39.8 | 39.0 | 52.1 |
| 1906 | 107.5 | 1,258 | 11.6 | 42.5 | 41.6 | 52.7 |
| 1907 | 109.2 | 1,255 | 1.5 | 42.0 | 42.1 | 50.8 |
| 1908 | 100.2 | 1,130 | −8.1 | 39.4 | 33.7 | 47.4 |
| 1909 | 116.8 | 1,290 | 12.2 | 42.4 | 43.4 | 53.5 |
| 1910 | 120.1 | 1,299 | 2.8 | 41.4 | 45.1 | 52.7 |
| 1911 | 123.2 | 1,313 | 2.6 | 42.0 | 42.7 | 50.2 |
| 1912 | 130.2 | 1,366 | 5.7 | 42.6 | 51.3 | 57.5 |
| 1913 | 131.4 | 1,351 | .9 | 43.7 | 53.8 | 60.0 |
| 1914 | 125.6 | 1,267 | −4.3 | 40.6 | 51.1 | 60.0 |
| 1915 | 124.5 | 1,238 | −.8 | 41.6 | 59.9 | 67.6 |
| 1916 | 134.3 | 1,317 | 7.9 | 44.7 | 71.2 | 66.2 |
| 1917 | 135.2 | 1,310 | .7 | 42.2 | 70.6 | 61.4 |
| 1918 | 151.8 | 1,471 | 12.3 | 45.1 | 69.8 | 61.1 |
| 1919 | 146.4 | 1,401 | −3.5 | 47.5 | 61.0 | 58.0 |
| 1920 | 140.0 | 1,315 | −4.3 | 46.9 | 66.0 | 61.5 |
| 1921 | 127.8 | 1,177 | −8.6 | 49.2 | 53.5 | 71.0 |
| 1922 | 148.0 | 1,345 | 15.8 | 49.2 | 68.1 | 80.4 |
| 1923 | 165.9 | 1,482 | 12.1 | 52.1 | 76.9 | 77.4 |
| 1924 | 165.5 | 1,450 | −.2 | 54.1 | 73.4 | 82.3 |
| 1925 | 179.4 | 1,549 | 8.4 | 54.1 | 81.9 | 87.7 |
| 1926 | 190.0 | 1,619 | 5.9 | 55.3 | 86.2 | 89.4 |
| 1927 | 189.8 | 1,594 | .0 | 55.5 | 87.1 | 91.5 |
| 1928 | 190.9 | 1,584 | .6 | 55.5 | 90.1 | 95.6 |
| 1929 | 203.6 | 1,671 | 6.7 | 57.8 | 100.0 | 100.0 |
| 1930 | 183.5 | 1,490 | −9.8 | 55.1 | 85.6 | 100.6 |

*source: U.S. Bureau of Economic Analysis, *Long Term Economic Growth, 1860–1970*, p. 105.
†Productivity is a measure of efficiency—in this case total factor productivity for the U.S. economy.
‡source: John W. Kendrick, *Productivity Trends in the United States* (New York: National Bureau of Economic Research, 1961), 465–66. In this case, productivity is the output per unit of labor input. Note in particular the changes between 1919 and 1929.

prosperity was felt throughout America during the 1920s (see Table 4.1). As a more probusiness social environment developed, many firms became increasingly strident and successful in defeating the labor unions seeking to organize their workers. Benefit programs and company unions were popular; antiunion campaigns were successful. As firms prospered and the unions grew weaker, more and more support developed for the idea that a new "corporate-liberal commonwealth" under business control was here to stay. The new commonwealth was to replace dog-eat-dog competition with associational cooperation and business-government strife with the new "associative" state. For the first time the government had begun through programs such as those involving standardization to provide significant support for firms seeking to enhance their efficiency. Industrial labs were generating corporate innovations. These threads drew together with the election in 1928 of Herbert Hoover, the progressive-conservative "Engineer in the White House." Seldom has private enterprise enjoyed a more secure and prosperous position than it did in 1928. The economy was growing. The stock market was booming. Business was becoming more efficient. It appeared that nothing could disrupt the steady progress of the new commonwealth.

But then suddenly—with warning signs detected by only a few—the corporate commonwealth of the 1920s came crashing down with the stock market. As the economy sagged into the first stages of the Great Depression, companies went into bankruptcy, utility giants collapsed, unemployment mounted; President Hoover's reassurances became ever more hollow, and the fragile nature of the public consensus about the corporate commonwealth was revealed. Trust turned to bitter opposition that neither the public relations departments nor public affairs officers could effectively counter. The reputation of American business plunged. The accomplishments of giant enterprise were forgotten as Americans began in the early thirties to look for new leaders and government programs that could do what the marketplace and the leaders of capitalism had not been able to accomplish.

CHAPTER 5

# The First Crisis
# of the New Corporate
# Commonwealth

T he year 1930 was not a good
one for business. America's corporate commonwealth, recently so
self-assured and prosperous, was suddenly reeling about without
direction. Business leaders whose speeches about the "new era" of
perpetual prosperity had previously won them appreciative respect
now evoked sneers of cynicism. The quest for greater corporate
control, efficiency, and innovation—a quest that had seemed to be
progressing quite well before 1929—was now subordinated to a
more immediate need for national recovery. As the gross national
product (GNP) plunged dramatically downward, economic distress
fed a sense of crisis and prompted a reassessment of the American
business system (see table 5.1).

As the depression made clear, neither the nation's businesses nor
its government had developed any suitable means of controlling
aggregate demand. Large corporations in oligopolistic industries
such as chemicals, automobiles, and iron and steel, had learned how
to contain the forces of price competition in the short term, but they

TABLE 5.1

The Economic Impact of the Great Depression

| Year | Unemployed | | GNP | | Business Failures per 10,000 businesses | Bank Failures |
|------|------------|------------|---------|----------|--------------|--------|
| | Total (in thousands) | As % of civilian labor force | Billions (1958 prices) | Annual % Growth Rate | | |
| 1929 | 1,550 | 3.2 | 203.6 | 6.7 | 104 | 659 |
| 1930 | 4,340 | 8.9 | 183.5 | −9.8 | 122 | 1,352 |
| 1931 | 8,020 | 16.3 | 169.3 | −7.6 | 133 | 2,294 |
| 1932 | 12,060 | 24.1 | 144.2 | −14.7 | 154 | 1,456 |
| 1933 | 12,830 | 25.2 | 141.5 | −1.8 | 100 | 4,004 |
| 1934 | 11,340 | 22.0 | 154.3 | 9.1 | 61 | 61 |
| 1935 | 10,610 | 20.3 | 169.5 | 9.9 | 62 | 32 |
| 1936 | 9,030 | 17.0 | 193.0 | 13.9 | 48 | 72 |
| 1937 | 7,700 | 14.3 | 203.2 | 5.3 | 46 | 83 |
| 1938 | 10,390 | 19.1 | 192.9 | −5.0 | 61 | 80 |
| 1939 | 9,480 | 17.2 | 209.4 | 8.6 | 70 | 72 |
| 1940 | 8,120 | 14.6 | 227.2 | 8.5 | 63 | 48 |
| 1941 | 5,560 | 9.9 | 263.7 | 16.1 | 55 | 16 |

could do nothing to prevent the collapse that took place in the thirties. Indeed, insofar as the combines cut back quickly on output and employment in an effort to stabilize prices, they probably accelerated the downturn. Through single-industry regulation, government had brought the markets of particular industries under control, but the regulatory agencies could do nothing to stop the sharp declines in demand and in expenditures on new plant that took place after 1929. The Federal Reserve Board could of course use monetary policy to loosen credit and encourage a higher level of investment in the private sector. But as prices, wages, investment, and gross national product spiralled downward in the early thirties, the dismayed leaders in both the private and the public sectors were uncertain what policies might stem the powerful tide of the Great Depression.*

*Even today the causes of the Great Depression are poorly understood. Similar severe downturns had occurred in the 1870s and 1890s. In this case the length and depth of the depression were probably a result of demographic factors, the collapse of the banking system, and structural changes taking place in the industrial sector. Moreover, the depression was a worldwide phenomenon, and American developments were to some extent affected by the collapse abroad.

In a charged political climate in which few traditional assumptions were left unchallenged, all sorts of solutions for the nation's economic ills were considered. Those finally adopted generally embodied trade-offs among a variety of interest groups, including a chastened business community. Responses to the economic crisis of the 1930s brought significant departures in public control over a variety of economic functions previously managed by corporations or left to the control of the market. By the time the Second World War finally eased the economic, social, and political tensions of the Great Depression, the foundation had been laid for a modern administrative state, the vastly enlarged public component of the American system of political economy.

## REGULATION OF THE SECURITIES INDUSTRY

Nowhere did the old foundation appear to be in greater need of repair after 1929 than on Wall Street. Before the stock market crash, self-regulation by the securities industry had been accepted as a sufficient means of ensuring a smoothly operating marketplace. State regulation had been used in an effort to eliminate flagrant abuses, but weaknesses in the statutes and the reluctance of regulators in New York State (the home of the most important financial center) to challenge the major exchanges left the industry largely free to make its own rules. When the nation sought to place blame for the calamity of 1929, the securities business was an obvious candidate for criticism and increased government regulation. Given the political vulnerability of the industry, the only real surprise was that the regulations ultimately passed left considerable authority in private hands.

During the 1930s investors asked what had changed since the days when control over financial institutions had seemed secure in the hands of big bankers such as J. P. Morgan. Congressional hearings in the aftermath of the crash suggested an answer: a new generation of bankers lacking Morgan's personal integrity had manipulated the financial system in the interest of insiders. The presidents of the largest New York banks were held up for special scorn. In retrospect these men seem to have been oblivious to the distinction between their personal aspirations and their obligations to their shareholders and to the society as a whole.

The symbol of the decade was Albert Wiggin, former president of the nation's second largest commercial bank, Chase National of New York. This much-praised banker had placed himself in the awkward—if at the time legal—position in 1929 of selling stock in his own bank short.* Wiggin therefore had a strong personal incentive to see that the value of his own company's stock declined. This behavior was not what most Americans expected of their bankers. The sensational revelation of such questionable practices helped convince the public that "self-regulation" had been a smokescreen behind which Wall Street manipulators had built their own fortunes at the expense of the public.

Despite the inevitability of government regulation, the old guard on Wall Street resisted. Led by Richard Whitney, the president of the New York Stock Exchange (NYSE) and the brother of a partner at J.P. Morgan & Co., the exchange reformed its internal rules. It required greater disclosure of information, while limiting the amount of stock that could be bought on margin. Whitney then went to Washington to proclaim that the NYSE was "a perfect institution" that should no longer be a legitimate concern of government. He went so far as to threaten a "strike of capital" if the government imposed unreasonable regulations.

But President Franklin D. Roosevelt (1933–1945) and the Democratic majority in Congress held the upper hand. Seldom has a business been as vulnerable to public control as was the securities industry in the early 1930s. From 1933 to 1938 Congress passed a series of new regulations giving the federal government a strong presence in the securities markets. The thrust of reform was simple and direct: a Securities and Exchange Commission (SEC) was given the power to require disclosure of financial information and to regulate the performance of securities traders. Thus reforms that

*Selling short or taking a short position is a stock market transaction in which you borrow securities from a third party and sell them immediately for cash. You anticipate that the market price of the stock will fall in the near future so that you can buy back substitute shares at a lower price and return them to the lender; the price difference creates your profit margin. If the price of the stock rises, however, you would be forced to cover the original sale at an even higher price and thereby suffer a loss.

business leaders had chosen not to implement in the 1920s became the responsibility of government in the 1930s.

The regulators wisely decided, however, to use as much of the old system of self-regulation as could be salvaged. James Landis, a Harvard professor whose work on various regulatory problems earned him the label "dean of American regulators," helped design a regulatory agency capable of securing the public goals of equity and security while working largely through existing private organizations. Landis's theoretical understanding of regulation blended nicely with the practical orientation of the first head of the SEC, Joseph Kennedy, a former "insider" on Wall Street who knew where the skeletons were buried. This sort of effective leadership continued in the late 1930s under William O. Douglas, a strong-willed Western reformer. Throughout its formative years, the SEC had unusually capable direction, an asset as important to public as it is to private administration.

Central to the regulatory strategy these leaders chose was the use of the accounting profession as a neutral third party to assure the accuracy of the financial information needed from business. By using independent accountants, the SEC avoided the need for a large public bureaucracy. In trading some part of its traditional standing as the employee of business for the status of a detached third party, the accounting profession enhanced its prestige and also created new jobs for its members. The investing public was the big winner. It gained more reliable data about potential investments and could compare opportunities more accurately.

The SEC also encouraged the major exchanges to institute reforms that would make self-regulation more effective. In implementing that part of its program, the SEC benefited both from the wisdom of its leaders and from a stroke of fate worthy of a Greek tragedy. Reform of the rules was not likely so long as the old guard at the NYSE, led by Richard Whitney, held sway. But in 1937 and 1938, revelations about Whitney's personal financial affairs suddenly toppled his faction and opened the way for a new generation of leaders. Whitney, newspaper readers learned, had been leading an increasingly tense double life. His public persona was that of a solid and confident pillar of the financial community. But incredibly, this insider had been drawn into numerous get-rich-quick schemes that pushed him deeper and deeper into debt. His downfall came as he tried to obtain money to support a losing gamble that "Jersey Lightning"—an alcoholic beverage containing cider—would sweep the nation. Whitney bet his personal fortune that he would emerge as the Jersey Lightning magnate, and lost. His brother at J.P. Morgan & Co. proved more than patient in lending him money, but when this source of funds proved insufficient, Whitney began borrowing from members of the exchange. Finally he turned to embezzlement, taking money from clients and even from the Gratuity Fund of the NYSE. In late 1937 Whitney's house of cards finally collapsed, and as he entered Sing Sing prison, the exchange's new leaders joined hands with the SEC to overhaul the rules of the NYSE. No longer would social constraints be depended on to preserve order. The new regime used a novel blend of private and public power to regulate the complex securities business.

## BANKING REFORM UNDER THE NEW DEAL

If Whitney symbolized the end of the old order, Franklin D. Roosevelt was the symbol of the emerging American state. Many business leaders saw every New Deal reform that impinged on their industry as clear evidence that FDR was driving the nation steadily down the path to socialism. In the heat of battle, business leaders were understandably concerned about their base of authority and prestige as well. But if they had watched more closely what FDR did, rather than what he said, they might not have felt so threatened by the New Deal. For what evolved was a set of new public institutions that created a more stable capitalist economy and ultimately a more predictable and profitable environment for business.

One of the first orders of the day was to revamp the country's financial institutions. About the need for this, there was little debate. By 1933 most Americans seemed convinced that the banking system had failed. There was little agreement as to what should be done, but out of the ensuing political bargaining there emerged three far-reaching laws: the Banking Act of 1933 (known as the Glass-Steagall Act), the Securities and Exchange Act of 1934, and the Banking Act of 1935. These statutes transformed the business of banking, constructing what has been labeled a "segmented and sedated" system. In the wake of the near-total collapse of the nation's banking system, the elected representatives of a shaken society were happy to settle for a system that was "segmented and sedated" so long as it was safe.

Commercial banks—that is, those that take deposits and make loans to individuals and businesses—seemed the most in need of attention in the winter of 1933. After many states and ultimately the federal government created breathing space by declaring bank holidays, the newly inaugurated president and Congress moved rapidly to meet the crisis. The creation of the Federal Deposit Insurance Corporation (FDIC) in 1933 reflected Congress's commitment to the protection of small depositors. Initially, federal insurance paid for by levies on banks protected individual accounts up to $2,500 (a limit that rose steadily in subsequent decades). To make these institutions appear less risky to the general public, Congress drew distinct boundaries between various banking functions. The Banking Act of 1933 mandated the separation of the commercial and investment banking functions, giving each bank twelve months to choose its new identity. No other major industrial nation chose this particular form of segmentation. But then again, no other nation's banking system had become so enmeshed in stock speculation.

Geographical segmentation reenforced the functional divisions. For most of America's history, unit banking had been the norm, as local banks had served local needs under local ownership and control. But in the 1920s, several large banks had pressed against the traditional restrictions on geographical expansion across state lines. The reforms of the 1930s stopped such expansion by explicitly forbidding interstate branch banking. On the issue of branch banking within a single state, the new law was less strict; it allowed individual states to govern the structure of their banks, stipulating that the same rules must apply to both national and state-chartered institutions. Geographical segmentation along these lines left much of the regulatory power over commercial banks in the hands of state officials. Along with the separation of commercial and investment banking, this move reflected a strong desire for a simplified system broken down into manageable geographical and functional units capable of being regulated.

The commercial banks were "sedated" by "Regulation Q," which granted the Federal Reserve Board the power to set ceilings on interest rates payable on time and savings deposits. Again, Congress chose security over market-induced efficiency, reasoning that competition for funds in the 1920s had led to excessive speculation. Speculative behavior could not be tolerated in the more stable, more predictable system that was being constructed in the thirties. Congress also gave new powers to the Fed to regulate the creation of banks, conduct more frequent examinations, and adjust reserve requirements. Tighter margin requirements on loans for which securities provided collateral also strengthened the Fed's hand in restraining speculation. All in all, the Banking Acts of 1933 and 1935 produced results worthy of a health club advertisement: the Fed, a weakling before the crash, had been given the muscles it needed to manage effectively the nation's currency and credit and to control its lending institutions.*

## THE NATIONAL RECOVERY ADMINISTRATION

Like many of the New Deal measures, the reforms in banking blended single-industry regulation with an effort to develop new capabilities in macroeconomic planning. The two activities were combined largely because neither public officials nor business leaders had a clear, workable plan for national recovery. Nor did the mainline economic theory of that day provide much help. As a result, the planners experimented as they muddled along, adopting several—sometimes conflicting—policies at the same time.

That was the history of one of the most publicized and least significant of the programs, the National Recovery Administration (NRA), a two-year effort to foster recovery through government-sanctioned, industry-wide cartels. The NRA, which generated considerable fanfare during its brief existence, used as planning agencies public-sanctioned variants on the trade associations that had enjoyed such a vogue in the 1920s. The association for each industry, now wielding federal authority, developed a code designed to regulate various aspects of the industry's labor-management rela-

*To some extent the Fed shared this power with the Office of the Comptroller of Currency and the FDIC.

tions and its market behavior. Most of the codes sought to stabilize prices and production. Even armed with coercive powers, however, the associations and their codes could not promote recovery, and the NRA was little mourned when it was buried by the Supreme Court in 1935.

The basic concept of the NRA had seemed simple enough. The antitrust laws were suspended, and representatives of industries were encouraged to form committees (usually through trade associations) to manage wages, hours, output, and other aspects of the industry. In theory, workers as well as managers were given a voice in the "code of competition" for each industry. The operations of these codes were monitored by government officials, who were supposed to ensure that they stressed equity as well as profitability. Consumers were encouraged to show their patriotism by buying from businesses that had codes and could thus proudly display the Blue Eagle of the NRA. As recovery began, the theory suggested, the restrictions of the codes could be eased gradually. Soon the experiment would be over. Competition would be restored.

In practice, however, no aspect of the NRA proved simple. Even in the depths of the depression, numerous businesses had serious problems in agreeing to a code. Small and large firms disagreed, as did those in different parts of the country. Only in a few industries with weak associations and strong labor unions—as was the case, for example, in soft coal—did workers manage to play a decisive role in the code process. The government was unable to fit the plans of each industry committee into an overall plan for recovery. All too often the cooperative spirit proved too weak and the competitive spirit too strong to sustain this New Deal variation on Hoover's "associative state." In the end, even the plan's strongest advocates could not explain where the additional investment needed to spur the economy ahead would come from under the NRA program.

## THE RECONSTRUCTION FINANCE CORPORATION

To those concerned primarily about investment, an institution more promising than the NRA was the Reconstruction Finance Corporation (RFC), which had been created when Herbert Hoover was still president in 1932. In its heyday, the RFC served as a national recovery bank, targeting government loans for businesses in need of capital not readily available through traditional channels of credit. The RFC stabilized important sectors of the business system at relatively little cost to taxpayers, since its assistance was primarily in the form of loans that ultimately were repaid. It helped start money flowing again, restoring a pinch of confidence and a dash of optimism at a time when both were in very short supply.

The leader of the RFC was Jesse Jones, a Houston banker and builder. One of the few businessmen with a prominent position in the New Deal, Jones served as a banker of last resort for many businesses hard hit by the depression. He was a tall Texan with a horse trader's mentality, and he happily used his control of credit as leverage to persuade businesses to make adjustments in their methods of management. He tirelessly exhorted his fellow executives to join him in supporting the New Deal's experiment in achieving recovery. On this front he had limited success. He was much more successful in identifying fundamentally sound businesses and helping them adjust to the competitive conditions of the 1930s.

The RFC was designed along the lines of the War Finance Corporation, which had been used to strengthen capital markets and to provide credit for defense industries during the First World War. The RFC's proclaimed function was "to stop deflation in agriculture and industry and thus to increase employment by the restoration of men to their normal jobs." To achieve that objective, between 1932 and 1935 it distributed approximately $2 billion per year in credit borrowed from the public, primarily through the Treasury. From its headquarters in Washington and thirty-one loan offices throughout the nation, the RFC extended credit to businesses (and other organizations) that were basically sound but temporarily troubled because of the overall decline of economic activity. Its loans primarily supported projects that were potentially self-financing, and under adverse circumstances the RFC compiled an impressive record of repayment. By helping individual banks, it cushioned the impact of the depression on the regions they served. It also came to the aid of another vital sector of the economy, transportation. By Jones's estimate, companies owning fully one-third of the nation's railroad tracks were in receivership or bankruptcy in the 1930s. Another one-third might have followed without RFC loans, which in this industry alone ultimately totaled more than a billion dollars, spread among eighty-nine corporations. These funds helped keep the nation's transportation system functioning while protecting the interests of the many individual and institutional investors who had favored railroad securities.

The RFC's initial success prompted Congress to expand both its funding and its discretion and powers. Farm loans were politically popular, and the RFC established several important agricultural institutions, notably the Commodity Credit Corporation. It also served as the primary funding vehicle for the Rural Electrification Administration, which supported power projects in rural areas not easily serviced by private companies. After 1934 the RFC had the authority to make loans to any business that could not obtain credit from a commercial lender. Such loans initially were limited to $500,000 per borrower for a maximum of five years, but these limits were gradually extended. The businesses received excellent credit terms. More importantly, they found that the RFC would make loans that many private banks had grown too timid to advance. Small businesses were favored clients of the RFC, which saw itself as a special defender of this vulnerable sector of American capitalism.

One distressed business that touched many Americans directly was the home mortgage industry. Drastic measures were needed to restore confidence in this crippled sector of the business system, and the RFC sought to revive the market by making loans for home mortgages, by subscribing to the capital stock of mortgage loan companies, and by establishing two mortgage subsidiaries, the RFC Mortgage Company and the Federal National Mortgage Association. In doing so, the agency helped redefine the country's assumptions about home ownership by bolstering the market for long-term mortgages. During and after the 1930s, private lenders followed the RFC's lead by extending the length of mortgages and reducing the percentage required for the down payment. In years to come this financial innovation would open the possibility of home ownership to broader segments of American society and spur the construction business.

As even this brief review of the agency's functions makes clear, the RFC was not a carefully designed recovery bank that could systematically target industries for government assistance on the basis of some clearly defined overview of the nation's needs. It was what it had to be: a jerry-built mechanism to respond to some of the most pressing problems of the New Deal era. Despite Jesse Jones's stated preference for operating the agency in a "business-like" way, it responded to these problems in an ad hoc manner, having neither the time nor the inclination to worry much about the long-term implications of its actions. The depression had dried up the flow of credit, and the RFC tried with some success to prime whatever pump seemed to be in close to working condition, using all the credit Congress would give it. On balance, the agency played a positive role in cushioning the immediate impact of the depression. But like the NRA, it was locked on a firm-by-firm, industry-by-industry course for stimulating recovery. By the late 1930s, many Americans began to realize that a new course was needed if the problem of massive unemployment was ever to be solved.

## FEDERAL JOBS PROGRAMS

When the unemployment rate first ballooned in the early years of the depression, the problem quickly overwhelmed local and state relief programs. Unemployment in massive proportions led to an irrepressible political impulse for new federal policies to provide both relief and work. Never before had federal jobs programs been used to supplement the "natural" market of private hirings. Yet never before had the nation faced an economic crisis of such magnitude. The result was a federal jobs program that was modest in comparison to the total number of persons out of work but significant because it represented an innovation in the functions of the U.S. government. The New Deal experiment with jobs in public works established a precedent for using the federal government as the employer of last resort in times of severe unemployment.

Many at first found this idea difficult to accept, but President Roosevelt instinctively embraced both direct federal relief and public works jobs as practical necessities. The first major New Deal program was intended to get the nation through the difficult winter of 1933–34. With unemployment rates surpassing 25 percent, the federal government moved forcefully to create temporary jobs. The Civil Works Administration, under the direction of Harry Hopkins, drew workers from the relief rolls and from the ranks of the needy not on relief and placed them on the federal government's payroll. They worked primarily on labor-intensive projects for pay averaging about $15 a week. In a matter of months, Hopkins had mobilized a work force of more than 4.2 million men and women— roughly the number of persons who had served in the armed forces during the First World War. Hopkins spent little time responding to critics who decried "make work"; he was too busy creating jobs as fast as he could. By the end of the winter, the CWA had spent an estimated one billion dollars building roads, schools, playgrounds, and airports. It had hired teachers to keep rural schools open while also finding work for artists, writers, and opera singers. Through a long cold winter, the CWA provided visible evidence that the nation's political leaders would no longer passively accept the human suffering of the depression.

But the end of winter brought the end of the CWA, and even Roosevelt was hesitant to push forward with another similar plan. Like Herbert Hoover, he feared the creation of a permanent class of citizens dependent on government jobs. Fortunately some of the slack was taken up by the Federal Emergency Relief Administration (FERA), which had been created in the first days of the Roosevelt administration to use federal money to augment state and local relief efforts. Using RFC funds, the FERA provided both direct relief and work relief to the unemployed.

As the welfare rolls grew, the opposition to jobs programs began to wane. Work relief seemed superior to the dole. Jobs offered dignity to the individual while repaying something to the nation in the form of permanent improvements in such public goods as roads and parks. The Emergency Relief Appropriation Act of 1935 embodied this sentiment. Its $5 billion appropriation for work relief was the largest single sum ever spent by Congress up to that time. The money went primarily to the newly created Works Progress Administration—an agency in the tradition of the CWA and headed by its former director, Harry Hopkins—and the Public Works Administration, which directed large-scale construction projects under the leadership of Harold Ickes, Secretary of the Interior. The WPA made work in hundreds of ways. It succeeded admirably in its goal of getting as much of its appropriation as possible into the pockets of the needy. While roads and parks proved ideal projects for Hopkins' purposes, the WPA also embarked on a variety of creative programs to make work for artists and writers as well as laborers. The PWA focused on bigger, more permanent projects employing skilled labor and engineers. Schools, bridges, hospitals, court houses, and city halls around the nation eventually had the imprint of the PWA on their cornerstones. While Ickes thus created jobs more slowly than Hopkins, both men ran programs that helped alleviate the nation's worst unemployment crisis.

In certain respects, the Tennessee Valley Authority (TVA) was the ultimate PWA-like project. Created in 1935, the TVA sought to control floods and produce electric power in one of the most impoverished sections of the country. In the process, it put people to work building dams and other construction projects required in the development of the Tennessee River Valley. This was public works on a scale that even Harold Ickes could not match. Unlike Ickes' agency, the TVA had a permanent administration with a mandate to assure that its individual projects fitted into an overall scheme of regional development. This was the high-water mark of planning and direct government ownership in the New Deal. The Great Depression encouraged Americans to make broader use of their federal government than had previously been the case. But even the widespread perception that the TVA was a successful experiment did not persuade Congress to approve other plans for TVA-like agencies.

Actually the New Deal's employment policies revealed as clearly as did the investment and banking programs just how deep set were American concepts of a limited federal state. The Great Depression was an unprecedented economic crisis, but even that disaster could not convince most Americans of the need for an administrative state that planned and controlled business activity on a national basis. The result was a series of half-measures that softened the impact of the depression without fully committing the government to large-scale permanent jobs programs or to a direct role in macroeconomic planning. In the name of economic recovery, one TVA was acceptable, but not other similar agencies. Temporary jobs programs could be justified, but not permanent government job guarantees or public jobs that competed directly with private employers. The RFC might target ailing businesses for special assistance, but it granted this support on a businesslike basis while making every effort to restore to working order a privately controlled economy. In most instances, the government worked with and favored those groups that were best organized to represent their interests. The agricultural programs, for example, helped farmers who owned their property and supported the agricultural associations but hurt the interests of sharecroppers. Thus in one sense the New Deal was in practice—although not in rhetoric—a conservative political movement.

## LABOR POLICIES OF THE NEW DEAL

One area of policy that seemed at first to involve radical change disturbing to businesses was the New Deal's labor program. New policies had to be developed and implemented as often-violent confrontations between industrial workers and corporate managers wracked American society. The struggle was fierce, because the creation of industrial unions in the manufacturing heart of the economy represented a direct challenge to the autonomy of managers on the shop floors of their own plants. In the fight for control over wages and the conditions of labor in large factories, management traditionally had been able to rely on the support or at least the nonintervention of government. But in the changed political climate of the 1930s, the federal government intervened decisively to help define a new accommodation between labor and management. The National Labor Relations Board, a powerful new regulatory agency established in 1935, acquired a leading role in the political economy of labor relations. As the arbitrator of disputes between labor and management, the NLRB hastened the emergence of "big labor" in the United States.

Business skepticism about FDR began to increase in 1933 with the passage of the labor provisions of the NRA, but the National

Labor Relations Act of 1935 turned many skeptics into active Roosevelt-baiters. The specter of a powerful, government-sponsored labor movement sent many business leaders to the legal barricades and inspired many ardent speeches proclaiming the end of the free enterprise system. The gradual realization in the late 1930s that they were fighting a losing battle brought a frenzied tone to these efforts.

The National Labor Relations Act—commonly known as the Wagner Act—significantly strengthened the power of organized labor to bargain with management on such issues as wages, hours, and conditions of labor. The law established the National Labor Relations Board, a five-member independent regulatory commission responsible for guaranteeing the freedom of workers to select the bargaining agent of their choice, without interference from their employers. Defining and preventing "unfair labor practices" and conducting elections in which the workers selected the union to represent them became the dominant tasks of the NLRB. In its earliest years the NLRB was sometimes neutral, more often pro-labor in the performance of its duties.

The NLRB challenged methods long used by management to block the growth of independent unions. Firing and blacklisting workers for union activities, for example, now brought reinstatement by the NLRB. The agency was particularly effective in disbanding company-controlled unions. Included were numerous employee-representation plans originally established in the 1920s, as well as company unions hastily organized to block the rise of independent unions under the NRA. Once a company union had been removed, the NLRB called and conducted a representation election. Instead of striking for union recognition, workers could now vote, with the NLRB certifying the organization chosen by the workers as the legal bargaining agent. This change in the legal and political setting fundamentally altered the historical balance of power in labor-management relations in the United States.

When the craft unions that dominated the American Federation of Labor were slow to take advantage of these conditions, John L. Lewis, the head of the United Mine Workers, led a group favoring industrial organization out of the AFL. The industrial labor unions organized all the workers in a particular industry (automobiles, for instance) without regard for their varying levels of skill. Lewis and his supporters formed the Committee for Industrial Organization (later called the Congress of Industrial Organizations; CIO in either case) and set out to organize workers along these lines in steel, automobiles, oil, and other major industries. The period from the creation of the CIO in 1935 to the end of the Second World War was one of the most active and eventful decades in the history of organized labor in the United States. The CIO launched a series of dramatic challenges to many of the nation's largest corporations. During the winter of 1936–37, the union won a climactic victory over General Motors. This confrontation had begun as a protest against layoffs and wage cutbacks at General Motors' Fisher Body plant in Cleveland. As the protests spread to other GM plants in Flint, Michigan, the CIO—which at the time was preparing for an organizing drive in the steel industry—came to the support of the United Auto Workers (UAW). At Flint, strikers sat down in the factory and refused to leave, making it impossible for GM to operate a vital part of its manufacturing. The burden of choice was placed on management: how far was GM willing to go to remove the workers and reopen the plant?

Management responded with a variety of tactics that traditionally had succeeded in this type of situation, but to no avail. Neither injunctions nor a company union nor violence by local officials nor appeals to the governor and to the president of the United States sufficed to free GM's property from the sit-down strike. When the company's management realized that the National Guard would not be used, it had little choice but to recognize the union. Later in 1937 business suffered another setback when the Supreme Court held the Wagner Act to be constitutional.

Business leaders in all the country's major industries now faced a harsh reality. They would have to learn to live with a new and potentially powerful outside force in managing their industrial work forces. The extent of change was brought home dramatically by the action of U.S. Steel, long considered the bastion of anti-unionism among large manufacturing companies. In the aftermath of the UAW's victory over GM, the president of U.S. Steel, Myron Taylor, reversed fifty years of history by agreeing to recognize the CIO without a strike. As the CIO proved itself in the automobile and steel industries, the AFL became more aggressive and more flexible about what constituted a craft or skill. As a result it too began to acquire new members at a rapid pace.

Some companies still chose to resist, and others tried with better results to twist the new institutional setting in their favor. Perhaps the most successful in adjusting to the new situation was Standard Oil of New Jersey, which transformed an existing company union into a more independent workers' organization. As a leading advocate of welfare capitalism in the 1920s, Jersey Standard (now Exxon) had pioneered in creating benefit programs and in implementing an employee representation plan. In the late 1930s, the company responded to a determined organizing drive by the CIO's Oil Workers International Union (now the Oil, Chemical, and Atomic Workers) with a combination of old-style intimidation and a new round of benefits for the "inside" Employee Federation. In essence, the federation became something more than a company union, while it remained something less than an AFL- or CIO-affiliated organization. By expanding the workers' control of the Employee Federation, Standard gave its industrial work force a greater voice in determining the conditions of labor in the company's refineries. By paying wages and benefits roughly equivalent to those won from other oil companies by the Oil Workers' International Union, the company neutralized one of the most important appeals the outside unions had. Until the 1960s Standard's labor strategy proved successful in blocking the acceptance of the CIO into its major plants.

Standard was the exception; the labor relations of most large and medium-sized manufacturing concerns in the United States now involved a complicated bargaining process between management and strong unions, with the oversight of a powerful regulatory agency. In manufacturing industries employing large industrial work forces, the rise of big labor forced fundamental adjustments in managerial decision-making. Managers had to learn how to mediate instead of dictate. For their part, millions of workers used the organizational clout of national unions to regain, increase, and protect the sorts of benefits that some of the country's leading corporations had begun to provide under welfare capitalism. In addition, the unions gave workers new powers to shape the conditions of labor within their factories and a new freedom to determine democratically who would speak for their interests. The unions paid a price for these changes: they were now part of a government-controlled system that limited their freedom of action and made the general welfare the guiding goal of public policy. But few organized workers in 1940 would have considered that to be a bad trade.

In sectors of the business system not directly affected by the expansion of industrial or trade unions, government shaped the conditions of labor with the Fair Labor Standards Act of 1938. This statute, which was the last major legislative enactment of the New Deal, established minimum wages and maximum hours for companies engaged in interstate commerce. It forbade the employment of child labor, thus finally writing into federal law a ban sought by reformers for decades. The initial minimum wage of 40 cents per hour was indeed minimal, and Congress provided significant exemptions from the measure. But in subsequent years, the coverage would be expanded, and the minimum wage increased.

One other federal program affecting the management of labor was the unemployment compensation provision of the Social Security Act of 1935. In the late 1920s, a few corporations had experimented with private insurance systems designed to cushion the impact of temporary unemployment for their workers. In the Great Depression, however, the funds in such programs had been quickly exhausted and the debate had turned from private schemes to government-sponsored unemployment compensation. Before the passage of the Social Security Act, several states had sought to put together systems of temporary assistance for the unemployed. To assure the continuation of these state systems and foster their adoption by other states, the federal government tied their funding to the payroll tax used to finance social security. All employers, not just the "progressive" companies that had experimented with private plans, now contributed along with their workers to the unemployment compensation fund. Control over disbursements moved from the hands of private companies to state employment offices, with the federal government collecting the funds and establishing basic guidelines for the states. The new system represented a marked departure from the method of dealing with temporary unemployment before the Great Depression.

As with other cross-industry regulations, the redefinition of the government's role in regulating labor had taken place amid substantial social tension. Because the policies cut across most of the business system, they generated intense discussion and conflicts that at times became violent. In the 1930s, most managers resisted this challenge to their autonomy with every means at their disposal. By the end of the decade, however, it was becoming evident to the most perceptive business leaders that the essential fabric of America's corporate capitalist system remained intact. The government was not marching ever faster toward socialism. The rules of labor-management relations had changed, and the balance of power had shifted. But having assured the workers of a new measure of security, the NLRB actually served the national interest in preserving a more peaceful, effective business system—a new brand of mixed capitalism that would, above all, provide the products, services, and jobs the public wanted.

## SINGLE-INDUSTRY REGULATION

Often obscured by the high human drama of the struggles between management and the unions were important changes in single-industry regulation. Many of these developments proved far-reaching. In transportation and communications, in energy and power, and in financial services these measures would have a decisive impact on business behavior for at least the next four decades.

The depression heightened the problems that had long plagued the railroads. In the wake of mass bankruptcies, continued private ownership was by no means a foregone conclusion—at least not until the Reconstruction Finance Corporation rushed to the rescue, providing much-needed capital. In the short term, this infusion of public dollars facilitated the recovery of the strongest roads. But as events revealed, the problems of the railroads were long-term. Government assistance bought time, but it did not buy economically viable railroad corporations or an efficient national transportation system.

Regulation had been introduced when the railroads dominated

the nation's transportation system. A basic assumption of the regulators had been that the railroads held a near-monopoly on ground transportation, but in the twentieth century a series of competing carriers had entered this market. First came pipelines, and then trucking. As a result, the Interstate Commerce Commission confronted the classic problem that all regulatory agencies face when the technological or economic landscape changes: should the agency extend its control to the new competitors so that it can preserve the stable prices it has created by rate-of-return regulations? Or should it retreat, allowing market forces to dictate prices and the growth of the new competitors? The ICC's response to pipelines had been to cast its regulatory net over the new businesses. In the 1930s the agency and Congress had to decide what to do about trucking and similar competitors.

The exigencies of the Great Depression dictated the government's choices. Widespread unemployment and financial chaos made it difficult to opt for market forces, especially since they seemed likely to push the already beleaguered railroad businesses into total collapse. The overriding mandate was stabilization, not competition. As alternative modes of transport—including water carriers, trucking, and airlines—cut into the railroad's markets, Congress responded with a wave of single-industry regulation that covered the competing firms and shored up the railroads. Control was in the saddle. Little regard was given to innovation or economic efficiency.

Trucking was the most significant threat to the railroads, and the government responded with the passage of the Motor Carrier Act of 1935, which gave the ICC substantial powers to shape business behavior in this emerging industry. The new regulations largely ignored fundamental differences between trucks and railroads. Unlike its older rival, the trucking business was carried on by numerous small companies with relatively low capital costs. Entry was easier. Competition was intense. Because government essentially paid for the highway system, trucking companies did not incur the long-term financial burdens the railroads had accumulated when they borrowed to build and maintain their roadbeds. The taxes the truckers paid provided only a fraction of the funds needed to maintain the highway system. Railroad executives and regulators focused on the fact that rail companies and trucking firms sought many of the same markets, but they tended to ignore the dissimilarities that made the new business an unlikely candidate for the ICC's approach to regulation. The agency simply crammed trucking into its traditional regulatory structure, making it a privately owned, government-regulated cartel, with the ICC wielding the power to determine both the players and the rules of competition.

The same thing happened to the airlines, although in this case Congress gave a new single-industry agency control in the name of orderly development. Air transport had grown rapidly after the First World War, and by the thirties an important industry was clearly on the horizon. Numerous peculiarities of the business argued for some sort of regulation. The government was providing most of the funds needed for the construction and maintenance of airports. Safety considerations—the potential problems of applying a relatively new technology to passenger transportation—also clearly called for public oversight, as did concerns for national security (the airline industry would be important in the event of another war). All these factors supported government regulation, but none dictated the type of regulation that should be applied.

History ruled: the choices mirrored those the government had made decades earlier in railroad regulation. In 1938 Congress created the Civil Aeronautics Board (CAB), a clone of the ICC. The CAB approach encompassed the basic "railroad" techniques of rate regulation backed by control of entry. The special safety problems of the airline industry ultimately led to the creation of a separate agency responsible for air safety, the Federal Aviation Authority (FAA). But the similarities between the airline regulations of the 1930s and those governing overland transportation far exceeded the differences. In both areas, the potential for innovation was sacrificed to a search for stability that produced single-industry regulation committed to predictable operations.

Before the Second World War, Congress made one attempt to unify the various transportation-related regulations. The Transportation Act of 1940 placed water carriers under the supervision of the ICC, but the main thrust of the Act was to define a general national policy. Having blurred industry boundaries, Congress now tried to give the ICC guidance in separating the different technologies and in managing long-run technological change. The results were the same as they had been in 1920. The ICC rolled up its sleeves and continued doing exactly what it had been doing, determining rates and routes on a case-by-case basis as they affected individual companies. The job of forging a unified, flexible national policy was left untouched.

In the vital area of energy policy there was not even a pretense of a unified program. Policies for the oil, coal, natural gas, and electric power businesses were developed separately, under the authority of different regulatory agencies. Each of these agencies sought to address the short-term problems of a single energy industry. None sought to understand how these separate industries fitted together and influenced the nation's production or use of energy. If there was a central theme to their efforts, it was the predisposition of all parties involved to look to government control for stability.

In the petroleum industry a deepening glut threatened to sink the existing businesses in a flood of cheap oil. Although most segments of the business had known in the late 1920s that something had to be done, the discovery of new oil fields and the declining demand for petroleum products produced a heightened sense of crisis in the early 1930s. The outpouring of extraordinary quantities of oil from the giant new East Texas field after 1930 finally forced oil producers and government officials to forge a consensus in support of a new system to control production. After the repeated failure of self-regulation, many oil producers came to view government involvement as a necessary evil. The plan they helped to devise involved regulation through the Texas Railroad Commission (TRRC) and similar regulatory agencies in the major producing states in the Southwest. The TRRC was not as unlikely a candidate for this job as its name implied. Although created in the late nineteenth century to regulate the railroads, the commission had gradually become involved in oil industry affairs through the regulation of tank car shipments and later through the control of oil pollution caused by the runoff from producing fields. Still, the move to prorationing, as price and production controls are known in the oil industry, was a giant step in the history of the commission.

Under the joint federal-state system established in 1935, the Texas Railroad Commission stood at the center of a complicated web of controls over the production and shipment of oil. An interstate oil compact had established a cooperative system in which state agencies agreed to limit production to the total amount of oil that could be absorbed by the market at an agreed-upon target price. Assistance in determining market demand and in allocating this demand among the producing states came from the U.S. Bureau of Mines (in the Department of the Interior), which collected statistics on conditions in the industry with the cooperation of the American Petroleum Institute. Within each state, the prorationing agency had the power to allocate production among existing fields and to determine how best to phase in new producers. Holding this complex system together was a federal law forbidding the shipment across state lines of oil produced in violation of state regulations.

Curiously, the politics of oil prorationing proved manageable. The Texas Railroad Commission (an elected body) shared many of the goals of the industry it regulated and seldom pursued policies deemed detrimental to its major constituency, the producers of petroleum. It balanced the needs of large, vertically integrated companies and independent producers (at least those strong enough to survive prorationing), keeping both groups happy by maintaining prices at a level higher than would have been the case in an unregulated market. In the process, it clearly served the nation's long-term interest by reducing the waste of oil stemming from unregulated production. Oil producers came to regard prorationing through the TRRC as a natural part of their world. So long as the industry's major problem was a surplus of oil, the TRRC proved to be an effective institution for imposing control over prices and production.*

In energy, as in transportation, New Deal regulations were developed in an ad hoc, piecemeal fashion. They stressed control, often at the expense of efficiency and innovation. The regulatory agencies commonly ended up protecting the interests of the businesses involved more than they did those of consumers. Business executives upset by the new labor or welfare laws of the New Deal should have looked to the regulatory agencies for some solace. The record there indicated very clearly how conservative the New Deal was; the search for stability had overridden the concern for equity. The

---

*The industry would eventually swing from surplus to shortage, and the regulatory system would experience great difficulty in making this transition. See chapters 8, "Tensions at Home and Abroad," and 9, "New Directions and Misdirections in the Public Sector."

overriding interest in the New Deal was economic recovery, and the most popular mechanism for achieving it was some form of control of prices and production by blending public and private power. For those well enough organized to take advantage of this new environment, the changes in the national political economy proved in the long run to be highly beneficial. Business was of course very well organized. It was not able to prevent other groups—labor in particular—from organizing and gaining power. Nor could it stop the growth of an administrative state (see table 5.2) that took an active interest in business affairs. But business generally was able to protect its interests through a difficult decade of change in the corporate commonwealth.

## THE IMPACT OF THE GREAT DEPRESSION
## AND THE NEW DEAL

The businesses that suffered most in the Great Depression were small and medium-sized firms, as well as those large corporations

TABLE 5.2

The Expansion of Government in the United States, 1920–1985

| Year | Federal Civilian Employees | Federal Budget Expenditures ($1,000) | Surplus or Deficit ($1,000) | Federal Expenditures as % of GNP |
|------|------|------|------|------|
| 1920 | 655,265 | 6,357,677 | 291,000 | 6.9 |
| 1925 | 553,045 | 2,923,762 | 717,000 | 3.1 |
| 1930 | 601,319 | 3,320,211 | 900,000 | 3.7 |
| 1935 | 780,582 | 6,497,008 | −2,400,000 | 9.0 |
| 1940 | 1,042,420 | 9,055,269 | −2,700,000 | 9.9 |
| 1945 | 3,816,310 | 98,302,937 | −45,000,000 | 43.6 |
| 1950 | 1,960,708 | 39,544,037 | −2,200,000 | 15.9 |
| 1955 | 2,397,309 | 68,509,184 | −300,000 | 17.7 |
| 1960 | 2,398,704 | 92,223,354 | 300,000 | 18.2 |
| 1965 | 2,527,915 | 118,429,745 | −1,600,000 | 17.6 |
| 1970 | 2,981,574 | 196,587,786 | −2,800,000 | 19.8 |
| 1975 | 2,882,000 | 332,300,000 | −53,200,000 | 21.8 |
| 1980 | 2,987,000 | 590,900,000 | −73,800,000 | 22.2 |
| 1985 | 3,001,000 | 946,300,000 | −212,300,000 | 24.0 |

that had incurred heavy debts. Many large utility companies and, as we have seen, many of the nation's railroads went into bankruptcy. The failure rate for banks was high as well. But the full weight of the depression fell hardest upon those smaller enterprises that had slim resources and could least afford the higher costs associated with the new labor policies, the wage and hour laws, and social security. Not strong enough to seek the help of the RFC and not capable of withstanding sharp decreases in demand and price cuts over a long period, they went under in record numbers. Venture capital dried up. New undertakings found credit hard to obtain, and in the wake of the stock market collapse, equities became almost impossible to sell on reasonable terms. Insofar as the vitality of the American business system stemmed from the continued process of innovation sparked by small entrepreneurs and new enterprises, the Great Depression was a sharp setback for the nation's business.

Large corporations, by contrast, were generally better situated to ride out the price cuts and declines in demand during the thirties. Most were forced to retrench, cutting staffs and reducing expenditures for research and development. In the early thirties even Du-Pont, a corporation uniquely dedicated to R&D, could not resist the pressure to shave its laboratory budgets and reduce its large force of researchers. But the best financed and most efficient American corporations soon rode out the worst effects of the downturn and began to turn a profit again, although at reduced rates of return. By the mid-thirties, GM was doing quite well. It had sharply cut its work force and output, but like many such giant firms, it had enough influence on prices to shelter its markets from the worst effects of the prolonged depression. By the latter part of the decade, GM and similar firms were again increasing output and beginning to look to the war-induced demand from abroad for the additional orders that would put their operations at full capacity again.

The New Deal clearly complicated the lives of corporate CEOs attempting to set a business strategy that would strike a profitable balance between efficiency, innovation, and control. By the end of the 1930s the federal government was larger than it had been, much more complex, and more difficult for any interest group, firm, or political faction to influence. The government now intruded more on business decision-making than it had before 1933. In labor-management relations in particular, the governmental role was now of overwhelming importance. As a result, labor unions shared with management control over wages, hours, and work rules in many industries. Managers perforce had to negotiate about some of the technological and organizational innovations that they had once implemented by command. Some of the changes that might have been introduced could no longer be made as a result of new single-industry or cross-industry controls. A society with an overwhelming interest in economic security had created a more elaborate system of governmental controls that constrained management's efforts to achieve higher levels of innovation and efficiency. But of course the opposite side of that coin was the economic stability that the new system promised to deliver.

Although managers of individual firms initially decried many of these changes in the economic functions of government, most would gradually adapt to them and discover that there were in fact many advantages to a corporate commonwealth that was more stable economically. The operating adjustments required to absorb the "Roosevelt Revolution" would prove much easier to make than many business executives thought possible, once a new era of growth pushed the nation out of its economic doldrums.

# Part Three

## THE AMERICAN ERA,

# 1940–1969

AMERICAN BUSINESS in 1940 was deeply scarred by the trauma of the Great Depression, and despite the many New Deal innovations in the public sector, confidence in the corporate commonwealth would not be easy to restore. Attitudes in the United States toward business enterprise had never been so favorable in the twentieth century as they had in the nineteenth. The giant corporation had decisively altered the sociopolitical context in which business was conducted in this country. Even during the First World War and the 1920s, there had been an underlying tension, an uneasy suspicion about the giant firm and the nature of its leaders. The panic and depression had confirmed those suspicions for many Americans, and the political rhetoric of the New Deal had provided the slogans that would shape the thinking of a generation: "economic oligarchy," "unjust concentration of wealth and economic power," "economic royalists."

During the 1940s it would be impossible to erase those epithets entirely, but the Second World War—like the First—would start a process of reconciliation between business and American society. War-induced prosperity would ease political tensions while focusing attention on the need for efficiency in mass production, large enterprise's strongest suit. In the thriving postwar economy the corporate style of control would appear to be more of a boon than a social problem. This was especially true in the 1950s, when so many government agencies would recruit businesspeople for their staffs, making good use, it appeared, of their experience and administrative ability. President Dwight D. Eisenhower set the tone for what would become an era of good feelings toward business akin to the 1920s.

The postwar years were by no means entirely devoid of conflict. Struggles between business, government, and labor were particularly intense during the late 1940s, when the peacetime power relationships within the corporate commonwealth were being established, and the late 1960s, when these relationships began to break down. Yet for most of the intervening years, the business system was not the main focal point of public concern. The cold war and the civil rights movement held center stage in the politics of this era; for the first time in more than half a century, "Big Business" was a secondary issue in electoral politics.

Against this backdrop, with its strong elements of public acceptance, U.S. business enjoyed a long phase of sustained expansion and international preeminence. This was truly the American Era. The keynote of the national experience was measured growth. As potential foreign competitors struggled to rebuild their war-ravaged economies, the dynamic American business system established a position of world leadership; business and business values played major roles at home and abroad. By the mid-fifties, certainly, the bitter memories of the great crisis of the 1930s were fading, losing their hold on a society intrigued by the prosperity, the power, and the promise of the American Era.

CHAPTER 6

# Redefining
# the Public Sector

A REFURBISHED corporate commonwealth provided a framework for the orderly growth that enabled the United States to lead the way in supplying the Allied forces during the Second World War and in rehabilitating the international economy after the war was won. During the two decades that followed, U.S. business became the international symbol for efficiency and managerial innovation. Once the tensions of the immediate postwar years had subsided, a successful and durable accommodation between business, government, and labor promoted a long era of sustained expansion of the American business system. The strength of U.S. business combined with the wartime devastation suffered by most of the other major industrial nations seemed to herald the beginning of an "American Century"—an era in which the United States would dominate international trade as Great Britain had at the height of its imperial power in the nineteenth century.

Several significant developments fostered the improved performance of U.S. business: the widespread adoption of managerial innovations, the expansion of many leading firms into international markets, and the harnessing of science and high technology to business endeavors.* Furthermore, the society now had a significantly larger public sector that helped to shape a more stable, relatively predictable environment for business activity. In this setting, big business and big labor were gradually able to forge a workable relationship that banished some of the uncertainties and tensions that had distressed the political economy of the 1930s and the immediate postwar years.

This reconstruction of the American system went smoothly, in large part because of uniquely favorable international conditions. The United States emerged from four years of global war as the world's unchallenged economic leader. The industrial capacities of the major European nations, the Soviet Union, and Japan had been devastated by the war, but U.S. business had been strengthened. As America assisted in rebuilding the war-ravaged economies of its postwar allies, American corporations enjoyed an unprecedented opportunity to share in this process and to dominate international trade. They had access on excellent terms to natural resources from much of the world and business institutions in this country began to play a central role in international finance.

Not all the events of these years were peaceful and cooperative. The international tensions generated by the cold war between the United States and the Soviet Union had a substantial impact on the evolution of America's corporate commonwealth. The desire to foster the growth of capitalism in developing nations as a bulwark against the spread of communism led the U.S. government to encourage expansion of American corporations abroad. At the same time, the quest for national security prompted peacetime defense budgets of a size unprecedented in America's past. Defense spending spawned a significant new government-directed sector that functioned under rules unlike those governing business activity in the rest of the economy. In other sectors as well, the federal government came to play a far more direct, far more significant part in the development of business and of the context in which business operated.

---

*These developments are described in detail in chapter 7, "The Modern Firm in Triumph."

Missing from the political discourse of this period was sustained discussion of the long-run implications for business of these momentous changes in the federal government's role in the economy. The single-industry regulatory agencies; macroeconomic planning; defense spending; government support for science and engineering, highways, social benefits, and space were all necessarily interrelated, and their total impact on business was significant. But in this era of good feelings most Americans dealt with these issues separately, and as the political passions of the New Deal subsided, they came to accept government's broad involvement in the economy. For business managers, for labor, and for middle-class consumers alike, the commonwealth was producing ample opportunities to take advantage of a new style of orderly growth that dampened tensions and fed consensus.

## GOVERNMENT CONTROL OF THE ECONOMY

After 1940 the most significant changes in the role the federal government played in the private sector came in government-directed activities. The Great Depression had prompted a decade of political debate over the proper role of government in managing the economy. The Second World War temporarily suspended this discussion while placing effective control over many business activities in the hands of public officials. During the mobilization, government controlled most of the important sectors of the economy, with the assistance of business committees. The overriding goal of victory in a worldwide struggle against powerful adversaries provided the glue that held together a hastily conceived planning system coordinated through the War Production Board. The mobilization effort attempted to fill the needs of the military with the minimum of disruption to business and the lowest possible level of inflation. Rationing, the allocation of scarce materials, and the targeting of public and private investments into the factories required to supply the war machine generally went forward in a climate of cooperation between business, government, labor, and consumers.

The War Production Board, the Office of Price Administration, the Office of Science and Technology, and the Reconstruction Finance Corporation all played significant, often overlapping roles in the mobilization. In general, rigid and highly formal controls were not required, in part because the largest and most significant war-related businesses readily cooperated with the government. Critics cited the considerable organizational confusion and the bureaucratic infighting that accompanied those controls that were established. But the mobilization planning was manifestly a great advance over the plans implemented in the First World War, and besides, it worked. Astonishing quantities of war materials were produced, prices and wages were kept in line, and essential civilian needs were met. The nation's giant corporations had a great deal to do with those accomplishments.

As the nation prepared to return to peace, the debate over controls started anew, but the dialogue lacked the fire and force of the New Deal years. Reformers who had railed against big business in the 1930s were less vociferous in their attacks after the long experience with war-induced cooperation. Business leaders accustomed to griping about government bureaucrats were somewhat more subdued after working closely with government officials in the successful war effort. Now the discussions centered on what the government's specific goals should be, what kinds of institutions would help achieve those goals, and who should control those institutions. Most of the participants in the controversy assumed that the federal government should and would be responsible for the overall performance of the economy. There was, in fact, substantial business support for the creation of a new institutional base in Washington, D.C., for controlling the economy.

In 1946 the debate over planning came to focus on a bill in Congress originally entitled the Full Employment Act. As first drafted, the bill asserted that Americans able to work and seeking jobs had a right to employment. The government had the responsibility to provide the volume of federal investment and expenditure "needed to assure continuing full employment." Each year the president would submit to Congress national employment and production projections, accompanied by policy recommendations for achieving the nation's goals. This early draft of the bill reflected the experience and the fears of the 1930s. To many observers, it called up the image of jobs programs and large appropriations to fight unemployment. It forced Americans to consider anew which of the

New Deal programs affecting employment should be permanent and which should be temporary.

As the debate over the bill revealed, there was no consensus on these specific issues. The business community reflected the splits within the broader public. Some vocal business groups supported government efforts to achieve the goals set forth in the original bill, but most staunchly defended a free market approach to employment problems. Practical considerations intruded: government spending would require either increased taxation or an unbalanced budget, neither of which was attractive to most business executives. Nor was it at all clear how extensive government jobs programs would affect private investment in specific industries. Government-built housing, for example, might threaten the well-being of private construction and real estate companies. As the debate over the bill developed, such practical concerns gradually came to outweigh the sentiment in favor of a full-employment measure.

Attitudes toward macroeconomic planning were also influenced by the surprising surge of economic growth that America enjoyed. The anticipated postwar slump did not take place. The gross national product (GNP) had risen from about $227 billion in 1940 to $355 billion in 1945; in 1947 it dipped to $310 billion but was back up to $355 billion by 1950 (see table 6.1). Prosperity moderated the passion for the original bill, and Congress passed the retitled Employment Act in 1946. This law now embodied not one but many goals, several of which reflected business concerns about controlling inflation and maintaining a high level of demand. The wording of the act was a masterpiece of legislative compromise or evasion, depending on what kind of a bill you favored:

> The Congress hereby declares that it is the continuing policy and responsibility of the federal government to use all practicable means consistent with its needs and obligations . . . to coordinate and utilize all its plans, functions and resources for the purpose of creating and maintaining, in a manner calculated to foster and promote free competitive enterprise and the general welfare, conditions under which there will be afforded useful employment, for those able, willing, and seeking to work, and to promote maximum employment, production, and purchasing power.

Exactly what constituted cause for government action or what steps were to be taken by government were left unclear. Nevertheless, by

TABLE 6.1

## Measures of U.S. Business Progress, 1940–1969

| Year | GNP in Billions (1958 prices) | GNP/ per capita Dollars (1958 prices) | % Growth Rate of GNP | Productivity* 1958 = 100 | Manufacturing† Output Index | Productivity |
|------|------|------|------|------|------|------|
| 1940 | 227.2 | 1,720 | 8.5 | 69.3 | 47.5 | 68.7 |
| 1941 | 263.7 | 1,977 | 16.1 | 72.0 | 63.2 | 71.2 |
| 1942 | 297.8 | 2,208 | 12.9 | 72.3 | 78.9 | 72.4 |
| 1943 | 337.1 | 2,465 | 13.2 | 73.1 | 95.3 | 73.4 |
| 1944 | 361.3 | 2,611 | 7.2 | 77.8 | 93.0 | 72.5 |
| 1945 | 355.2 | 2,538 | −1.7 | 81.3 | 78.6 | 71.5 |
| 1946 | 312.6 | 2,211 | −11.9 | 78.4 | 64.3 | 65.8 |
| 1947 | 309.9 | 2,150 | −.9 | 77.2 | 71.3 | 69.6 |
| 1948 | 323.7 | 2,208 | 4.5 | 79.5 | 73.7 | 72.1 |
| 1949 | 324.1 | 2,172 | .1 | 81.5 | 69.6 | 74.9 |
| 1950 | 355.3 | 2,342 | 9.6 | 87.1 | 81.1 | 81.4 |
| 1951 | 383.4 | 2,485 | 7.9 | 87.8 | 87.6 | 81.3 |
| 1952 | 395.1 | 2,517 | 3.1 | 87.9 | 91.1 | 83.0 |
| 1953 | 412.8 | 2,587 | 4.5 | 90.8 | 99.1 | 86.9 |
| 1954 | 407.0 | 2,506 | −1.3 | 92.8 | 92.3 | 88.3 |
| 1955 | 438.0 | 2,650 | 7.6 | 97.0 | 104.1 | 94.9 |
| 1956 | 446.1 | 2,652 | 1.9 | 96.6 | 107.3 | 96.5 |
| 1957 | 452.5 | 2,642 | 1.4 | 97.8 | 108.1 | 98.8 |
| 1958 | 447.3 | 2,569 | −1.1 | 100.0 | 100.0 | 100.0 |
| 1959 | 475.9 | 2,688 | 6.4 | 103.3 | 113.7 | 106.2 |
| 1960 | 487.7 | 2,699 | 2.5 | 104.4 | 116.7 | 108.8 |
| 1961 | 497.2 | 2,706 | 2.0 | 106.8 | 117.4 | 112.6 |
| 1962 | 529.8 | 2,840 | 6.6 | 111.4 | 127.1 | 116.6 |
| 1963 | 551.0 | 2,912 | 4.0 | 114.2 | 133.7 | 121.5 |
| 1964 | 581.1 | 3,028 | 5.5 | 117.7 | 142.5 | 125.6 |
| 1965 | 617.8 | 3,180 | 6.3 | 121.0 | 155.2 | 131.0 |
| 1966 | 658.1 | 3,348 | 6.5 | 123.2 | 169.9 | 134.2 |
| 1967 | 675.2 | 3,398 | 2.6 | 123.8 | 169.8 | 135.0 |
| 1968 | 706.6 | 3,521 | 4.7 | 126.9 | 182.2 | 142.0 |
| 1969 | 725.6 | 3,580 | 2.6 | 127.3 | 189.5 | 145.7 |

*Total factor productivity for the entire economy. U.S. Bureau of Economic Analysis, *Long Term Economic Growth, 1860–1970,* pp. 208–209.
†1958 = 100.0. See *ibid.,* pp. 184–5 and 210–11. Productivity in manufacturing is output per man-hour.

creating the Council of Economic Advisors (CEA), the Employment Act augmented the ability of the president to understand and analyze economic trends, and by establishing a Joint Committee on the Economic Report in Congress, it assured that the legislature would regularly study national economic conditions. The act formally acknowledged the federal government's responsibility for the overall performance of the economy.

The precise implications of the Employment Act, however, remained to be defined in practice. Beyond the general consensus that strong new initiatives of some sort would be justified by the threatened recurrence of a severe depression, little else was certain. The goal of providing a stable economic environment often seemed in practice to mean policies designed to avoid a major recession—especially on the eve of an important election. The standards for acceptable economic performance would be shaped in the short term by the political tolerance for changes in the level of unemployment, business activity, and inflation. Given the frequent elections that are of central importance to American democracy, this was probably the best the nation could do in the planning process.

A few years after Congress passed the Employment Act, the Korean War temporarily preempted concern about macroeconomic management. But with the end of hostilities, newly elected President Dwight Eisenhower (1953–1961) faced an important crossroads. As a Republican predisposed to fear the growing powers of the central government, Eisenhower seemed likely to abandon the cause of planning. Yet the political logic of countercyclical measures proved irresistible. During his first administration, he cut spending and reduced the rate of inflation at the price of somewhat higher unemployment. When the economy became sluggish in 1957–1958, the administration responded with a package of initiatives that increased government expenditures for defense, highways, and the postal system, encouraging a spurt of growth on the eve of the 1958 elections. Eisenhower in a sense legitimized the planning function in fiscal policy (the use of government expenditures and taxation to affect the economy). Meanwhile the Federal Reserve Board, which was learning to use the purchase and sale of government bonds and the setting of the rediscount rate to stabilize the economy, strengthened the element of planning in monetary policy (the use of programs that affect the supply of money and credit in the economy).

The Democratic administrations of John F. Kennedy (1961–1963) and Lyndon B. Johnson (1963–1969) embraced macroeconomic planning as an integral part of modern policy. The "new economics" had arrived, and economists in the government attempted in the 1960s to design packages of monetary and fiscal policies capable of stabilizing and sustaining business growth while maintaining politically acceptable levels of unemployment and inflation. In 1963 and 1964 the administration considered using a tax cut to stimulate growth. The progressive income tax in force in the United States generated increased revenues for government during periods of economic expansion. Such revenues presented a potential threat to continued growth unless the funds were pumped back into the economy, either through increases in government spending or through tax cuts. A thorough analysis by the Council of Economic Advisors of the probable impact of a reduction in taxes helped prepare the way for legislative action. In 1964 Congress approved a $12 billion tax cut. As predicted by the CEA, this cut spurred impressive increases in private investment, laying the groundwork for a new surge of economic growth.

The tax cut of 1964 marked the highpoint of Keynesian countercyclical fiscal policy.* By that time the federal government's new role in macroeconomic planning had won the frank approval of a widening range of business organizations. There was still intense debate over specific goals—especially the trade-offs between inflation and unemployment—but few Americans questioned the means used to achieve such goals. Enthusiasm over Keynesian policies actually led to exaggeration of their accomplishments. It is important to bear in mind that the 1964 tax cut involved only 2 percent of the GNP of that year. (By contrast, the Emergency Relief Appropriations Act of 1935 had committed $5 billion—or 7 percent of the GNP—to jobs programs.) The policy of 1964 was one of "fine-tuning," of attempting to counter the fluctuations of the business

---

*The "new economics" of the postwar era was based largely on the theories developed in the 1930s by the English economist John Maynard Keynes. In the Keynesian formulation, government should use fiscal policy to counter recessions and to dampen periods of rapid expansion.

cycle. It succeeded in part because the government had become a permanent employer of millions and a purchaser of significant amounts of goods and services. These and other innovations since the 1930s—including Social Security—acted as built-in stabilizers. But the enthusiastic supporters of Keynesian policies ignored these qualifications and applauded the simple fact that the 1964 tax cut had achieved its immediate goals.

## GOVERNMENT SPENDING FOR NATIONAL SECURITY

In three areas of particular importance—defense, highway building, and the space program—government spending shaped the expansion of entire sectors of the economy. Much of this spending took the form of purchases from private corporations. Although these orders were seldom considered as jobs programs, they nonetheless produced jobs in numbers that would have been the envy of such New Dealers as Harry Hopkins and Harold Ickes. Government spending in these three areas helped keep unemployment at tolerable levels and encouraged the development of new industries and advanced technologies. High levels of public spending allowed macroeconomic planners to focus on the impact of relatively modest changes in monetary and fiscal policies; in the absence of such spending, aggregate investment would probably have been insufficient to sustain anything approaching full employment. It was a pleasant bonus for politicians that the increased expenditures for defense, highways, and space did not displace existing private investment (as had been the concern about many of the jobs programs of the 1930s). Moreover, these expenditures could be justified by reference to the cold war threat to national security, without discussing the need for jobs and investment.

National defense accounted for the bulk of the government's new spending from 1940 to 1969 (see figure 6.1). The Second World War forcefully demonstrated the potent economic impact of war. It was, after all, wartime expenditures and not the New Deal's programs that at last pulled the nation out of the Great Depression. The cold war that followed taught a similar lesson. Mobilization could

FIGURE 6.1

Expenditures for
National Defense, 1940–1985
(In Millions of Current Dollars)

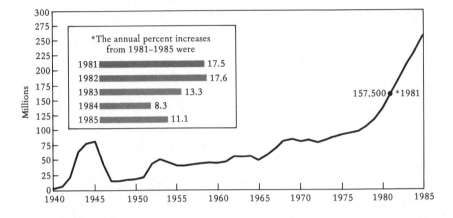

be economically advantageous, and defense expenditures were almost always politically feasible. Most Americans supported the
arms race with the Soviet Union on the grounds that it was necessary to defend America against the threat of communism. From the
late 1940s, peacetime defense spending grew steadily for the first
time in American history, creating a permanent new sector of the
economy that by the 1950s amounted to approximately 10 percent
of the GNP. The debate over the required level of defense spending
focused not on the need for investment and jobs, but rather on
strategic necessities in a worldwide struggle. Nonetheless, the expenditures had far-reaching impacts on the level of aggregate business activity and the patterns of investment within various sectors
of the corporate economy.

Defense alone accounted for almost one trillion dollars in spending from 1946 through 1969.* In addition to those employed in
building military hardware, the defense establishment supported a
large standing army and navy that directly reduced unemployment.

*One trillion dollars is equal to the total cash payouts for Social Security from 1937 to
1981.

The armed forces removed on the order of three million job-seekers from the market while paying them far higher wages and benefits than had been paid to Harry Hopkins' "army" of WPA workers in the 1930s. The services also provided job training that could be of value to military personnel upon their discharge (and to their potential employers). Moreover, the peacetime army of the cold war era—unlike Hopkins' forces—was generally acknowledged to be a permanent part of the American system.

There were numerous other ways to spend federal dollars, ranging from education to welfare. Indeed, the government increased its involvement in these and other areas. But increases in defense spending engendered much less political controversy than most alternative expenditures. Although in theory other types of spending might have produced greater benefits for society or a greater multiplier effect in the economy, these possibilities did not sway America's political leaders, the corporations responsible for supplying the goods and services demanded by the military, or, for the most part, the public itself. Most American citizens looked upon large defense budgets as an absolute necessity in a dangerous age.

Defense businesses operated under rules different from those governing the remainder of the corporate commonwealth. Government officials contracted with private companies for most of the goods and services needed for national security. Cost-plus contracts—that is, contracts under which business received its costs plus a negotiated rate of profit—took much of the risk out of this sort of production. Political lobbying for advantage in the procurement process often supplemented considerations of quality and cost in determining which companies would produce particular defense systems. The defense industry was as closely linked to the Congressional appropriations process as other businesses were to their markets. Once budgets were set, officials from the Department of Defense let contracts and supervised the completion of work. Under these unusual conditions, privately owned and managed corporations operated under the scrutiny of the government on a wide variety of projects that together made up far-and-away the largest "industry" in America.

Several large corporations, notably those active in the aircraft industry, became highly dependent on military projects; others, such as the major automobile companies, augmented their traditional markets with military contracts. Defense spending reached deeply into the heart of American business. In his farewell speech to the nation in 1961, President Eisenhower warned of the possible ramifications of the continued growth of the "military-industrial complex." He pointed out that "we annually spend on military security more than the net income of all United States corporations." There was certainly cause for concern. While the national security was being safeguarded, this goal was being achieved at considerable cost. In the years after 1940, the defense industries absorbed large amounts of capital and large numbers of highly trained technicians at the expense of such basic industries as steel, automobiles, and oil. Defense employed a significant amount of the nation's creativity and resources in activities that contributed only marginally to the efficiency or innovativeness of its core businesses.

The quest for national security also affected the growth of two other areas of government investment: highway building and the space program. Traditionally, the construction of highways had been a concern primarily of state and local governments. After decades of discussion, however, the federal government in 1956 became more directly involved in financing highway construction with a commitment to shoulder 90 percent of the cost of 41,000 miles of "interstate and defense highways." The federal government projected expenditures of $27 billion on federal aid to highways from 1956 to 1971, and ultimately the national network of four-lane highways would be completed at a cost estimated at $100 billion. These highways were available for the use not only of the country's truckers but of all Americans; they constituted a valuable extension of the nation's transportation system. But the expenditures could not have been made (especially under a Republican administration) had they not been justified in terms of their contribution to the nation's cold war defense.

The space program had a similar history. After the Soviet Union's success in launching Sputnik, its first satellite, in 1957, the desire to "close the gap" in space exploration between the United States and its cold war adversary gave the program an irresistible appeal. NASA's budget was not large in comparison to that of the Defense Department, but it was nevertheless a strategic program because of the high level of technology concentrated on one set of tasks. Government direction of the space program took on many of the same characteristics as its handling of defense spending. Public officials defined broad goals and contracted out much of the work on specific programs to private companies. Major firms in the evolving aerospace industry often worked for both NASA and the Defense Department under arrangements that insulated them from many of the risks of competition.

Of similar importance were the new federal outlays to support training and advanced research in science and engineering. Prior to 1940, most of the financial support for the scientific and engineering disciplines had come from state governments through their educational institutions or from private foundations, schools, individuals, and businesses. These sources had sufficed to build an elaborate network of professional disciplines, associations, publications, and research organizations in this country. America's early industrial labs (discussed in chapter 4) had been built on and had contributed to this framework of science-related organizations. During the years 1900–1940, American science and engineering had as a result achieved high international stature for the first time in the nation's history. Business benefited from this growing network of institutions, from which it obtained trained personnel and scientific and technical knowledge. Seldom did business managers acknowledge the important support they received from educational institutions when they discussed business-government relations. They should, however, have added that support to the balance sheet when they evaluated the emerging administrative state, especially after 1940.*

During the war, the federal government pumped large sums of money into and recruited talented personnel for military projects, many of which achieved impressive technical and scientific results. Large-scale efforts such as the one that produced the atomic bomb and those that developed advanced radar systems were extremely successful, as were a large number of smaller ventures funded by the government. This successful experience led in the late forties to a substantial federal investment in science and engineering, largely

---

*The obligations flowed both ways: state and local educational institutions received income from the taxes paid by business, and private universities, in particular, were dependent upon contributions from businesspeople and the private foundations they had established. That support was reflected in the memberships of university boards of trustees.

channeled through existing academic and professional institutions. Once again the results were outstanding. The United States became the international leader in many of the most important disciplines, including physics and biology.

Business benefited directly and indirectly from the astonishing postwar expansion of the science-technology network in this country. Corporate research and development organizations could recruit trained personnel from schools and laboratories supported with state and federal funds. Ideas generated in the public sector could be used to commercial advantage. For instance, much of the early basic research on microwave transmission was sponsored by the government; in the postwar years microwave devices have revolutionized communications (as well as many of our kitchens), lowering costs and spawning entirely new industries using satellites to transmit television shows as well as business messages and data. The computer and numerically controlled machine tools had similar histories of public/private development.

While shaping the nature of substantial new segments of the American economy, large government expenditures gradually became vital to sustained growth. This marked a fundamental shift in the corporate commonwealth, one that was little debated because of the overriding concern with national security. The large government outlays supplemented those of the private sector, helping to assure a level of aggregate investment that generated a long era of relative prosperity, unmarred by serious depressions. Government spending combined with macroeconomic management to produce a healthy business environment in which neither inflation nor unemployment got out of hand—at least until the late 1960s.*

## THE PERFORMANCE OF THE REGULATED INDUSTRIES

The American Era also witnessed generally favorable results in regulated businesses deemed critical to the functioning of a modern economy. As we have seen, the reforms of the Progressive Era and

*The only exception was during the Korean War, when inflation reached serious levels. The government temporarily introduced price controls in an effort to keep prices under control.

the New Deal had resulted in an extensive array of regulatory authorities in transportation, communications, energy, banking, and finance. During the decades after the Second World War, there was little debate about whether that form of political control should continue to be exercised; the critical questions facing government regulators involved how they were to use their existing authority. From the late 1940s to the late 1960s, most of those in positions of authority in the single-industry regulatory agencies followed the same path: they pursued policies that fostered growth along familiar, predictable lines.

Because the regulated businesses broadly influenced most other areas of the economy, the stability that flowed from regulatory supervision contributed to the smooth operations of the business system as a whole. Admittedly, stability was often achieved at the expense of innovation. Management in the regulated companies became more averse to risk. Yet societal benefits from this bargain were evident in the era of prosperity after the war, and at that time few critics attacked the policies of the single-industry regulatory agencies. Together with the companies they regulated, the agencies fashioned a durable accommodation that fostered orderly expansion. The ability of the businesses to expand their services to new markets at rates attractive to many more consumers made an important contribution to the nation's growth in the postwar era.

The accomplishments of the regulated sector were impressive. Under the guidance of the CAB after the Second World War, a modern American airline industry emerged whose service and prices were the envy of the industrial world. In the same era AT&T, a technologically oriented monopoly regulated by state utility commissions and the FCC, promoted the work of a system of laboratories generally acknowledged to be the best in the world. Working within the framework of regulatory policies, the Bell System spread telephone service to the masses throughout the nation. The FCC also supervised the extension of television to a mass audience. Under rules enforced by several regulatory agencies, most notably the Texas Railroad Commission, the petroleum industry fueled the nation's growth with cheap, abundant energy. At the same time, utility companies throughout the nation not only kept pace with dramatic increases in the demand for electricity but also steadily lowered their unit costs. Finally, the banking industry (which is now remembered as "stodgy and conservative") facilitated in these years the flow of credit needed to sustain investments while making financial services such as checking accounts available to much broader segments of the population. Taken as a whole, the performances of these regulated businesses were excellent. The industries that consumed the goods or services they provided came to rely on steady improvements in quality and to expect steady expansion of sales. In this half-forgotten era, most American companies did not have serious concerns about transportation, communications, energy, or finance.

The airlines provide an excellent example of both the short-term successes and the long-term costs of single-industry regulation in the postwar style. The Civil Aeronautics Act of 1938 had established a government agency with a mandate to regulate the young airline companies and to foster their development. The Second World War emphasized the importance of air transport, demonstrating its reliability and stimulating technical improvements. After the war, the CAB began in earnest to oversee the creation of a modern system of civilian airlines. With only the vaguest of guidance from Congress and with no previous experience to draw upon (other than that of the railroads and the ICC), the CAB managed to create a government-sponsored cartel whose primary goals were the extension of airline service and the protection of the economic health of the existing carriers.

The CAB played a variety of important roles in maintaining this cartel. It strictly governed the entry of new airlines. A carrier could neither establish nor abandon a route without the approval of the government. Rates were also subject to its approval, as were mergers between airlines. The CAB thus tightly controlled the market structure of the industry. Under this control, the number of carriers on trunklines shrank to eleven by the 1960s. On occasion, the CAB encouraged competition among the various carriers through its decisions on rates and routes, but, all in all, expansion of service along familiar lines was valued over competition.

One of the prerequisites for growth was the construction of airports throughout the nation. Here the airlines enjoyed a significant historical advantage over the railroads. Whereas the cost of track construction had pushed many railroads deeply into debt, airports were constructed with public funds, and public employees operated the air terminals. Airlines paid fees for usage, of course, but these were small relative to the costs of constructing airports. Most of the nation's major airports were owned by municipalities, but federal assistance for construction was available if the plans for a new airport complied with the overall program developed by the Federal Aviation Authority (FAA) for the expansion of the nation's aviation system. Under this blanket of public control and financing, the nation's system of airports steadily spread.

The CAB joined in the effort to assure the broadest possible extension of airline service through temporary subsidies on feeder routes that promised to become economical but initially could not support the full cost of airline service. The agency also gave indirect subsidies to feeder lines by allowing the airlines to charge high rates on the more profitable routes between major cities and by directing them to use the resulting revenues to subsidize traffic on less profitable routes. Such policies did not make sense from a strictly microeconomic perspective, but they hastened the geographical expansion of the industry while serving the useful political purpose of giving much of the nation a stake in the continued growth of air transportation.

The CAB's approach to regulation and the FAA's policies on long-term growth and safety fitted the needs of this formative era of airline expansion. The creation of a national system of airline transportation was an expensive proposition that could be undertaken only with large public investments in airports. Under the CAB's direction and with FAA support, airline firms avoided the sort of unrestrained competition, with large investments in parallel lines, that had plagued the railroads during their formative years and that remained at the heart of the railroad problem well into the twentieth century. The expansion of air service was not hampered by mass bankruptcies and disruption of service. The results were generally favorable by any international comparison. In pursuing predictable, orderly expansion of service, the CAB and FAA probably slowed the pace of the airline industry's growth and certainly raised the total costs to consumers. But the balance struck between the goals of orderly expansion and low-cost operation seems to have been acceptable to most Americans at the time.

The future problems of the CAB could be seen, however, reflected in the much different history of the ICC in these decades. The long-term costs of insulating a mature industry from competitive pressures were evident in the case of the railroads, which stagnated under the supervision of the ICC. Nevertheless, the Transportation Act of 1940 gave the ICC an ambitious mandate to extend its regulation of the railroads to other forms of ground transportation. Thus an agency that had not proven capable of effective regulation of the railroad industry after more than fifty years of effort was instructed to take on the burden of supervising the development of the nation's entire ground transportation system, including rail, water, and highway transport. Not surprisingly, the ICC failed to balance the competing demands of the various transportation businesses or to coordinate their activities into an efficient, integrated system. Shackled by the complexities of its task, by the practical difficulties of deciding whether the nation could best be served by its traditional clients in the railroad industry or their upstart rivals in trucking, and by the crushing work load generated by its case-by-case approach, the ICC deservedly became the target of much criticism by the mid-1950s.

The growing perception that something was deeply wrong led Congress to reopen discussion of the powers of the ICC. As the debate proceeded, several prominent academic economists suggested that what was needed was greater competition within and among the different modes of transportation. But these early calls for deregulation went unheeded. Congress passed the Transportation Act of 1958, which kept the regulatory system largely intact while authorizing the ICC to guarantee loans of up to $500 million to railroad companies to upgrade their equipment and service. This law also gave the ICC the power to suspend unprofitable passenger service.

Critics attacked these policies as a classic case of the rigidities produced by a "triocracy" or "iron triangle" of regulators, members of Congress, and interest groups with a stake in preserving the status quo.* For the most part, they were right. The ICC, unlike the

*These three-sided alliances of interest groups, legislators, and federal bureaucrats became one of the most significant aspects of American government in the postwar era.

CAB, was not serving the nation well; it had failed to come to grips with the rise of interstate trucking. Unable to exploit the potential strengths of a new technology, the Commission became a barrier to innovation. Although trucking and railroads were dissimilar in several fundamental ways, the ICC encased the trucking firms in the same sort of rigid regulatory structure—controlling entry and rates—that it had used for the railroads. Its controls lacked the flexibility of an unregulated market, and it offered few obvious benefits to compensate for this rigidity. The ICC experience suggested that government regulators could not afford to ignore long-term changes in basic technological and economic conditions any more than could corporate managers.

More successful in this regard were the FCC and the telecommunications companies, most prominently AT&T. The telephone company was shielded from criticism in large part by its high level of performance and its unusual record of technical innovation. Challenged by the Department of Justice in 1949, AT&T had in 1956 successfully concluded an out-of-court settlement that kept the monopoly intact. During these years the public as well as the Eisenhower administration had good cause to favor Ma Bell. The Bell System greatly extended and improved the communications system of a booming nation. Although its rates were thoroughly regulated and its overall performance overseen by the FCC, AT&T enjoyed an impressive era of expansion (see figure 6.2). Americans from all walks of life and in all geographical areas became accustomed to high quality telephone service at affordable rates. So well did AT&T perform its basic function that it was largely ignored by most Americans (with the exception of those who had used the telecommunications systems in other countries, and thus understood how good the Bell System's service was).

But potential competitors certainly saw opportunities in the system of nationwide rate averaging and of setting long distance rates high to subsidize local service—if only they could crack the regulatory barrier to entry. Meanwhile firms wanting to sell telecommunications equipment in competition with the Bell System had begun to press the FCC to allow them into the business. The FCC had been more responsive to these pleas than the ICC had been to the changes taking place in transportation. As late as 1969, however, the Bell

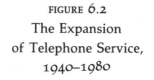

FIGURE 6.2

The Expansion
of Telephone Service,
1940–1980

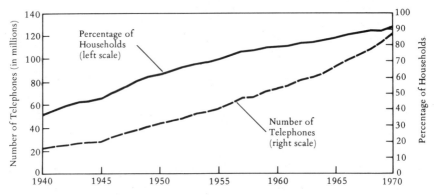

In 1970, the Bell System provided 99,903,000 of these phones, and independent companies the remaining 20,315,000.

System's near monopoly was still intact, and the public, the regulators, and Congress were generally pleased with the performance of this unusual regulated enterprise.

Energy businesses were not subject to rate regulation of the sort prevalent in transportation and communications, but the regulatory powers of government were nonetheless important in shaping an era of energy abundance after the Second World War. As private petroleum companies developed new sources of oil and gas and new markets for their products, government regulation provided a stable context in which expansion could take place. For three decades, cheap, abundant energy fueled economic expansion, shaping America's postwar prosperity.

The prorationing system put in place in response to the oil glut of the early 1930s became the industry's all-important balance wheel. By correlating production with estimated demand, state regulatory commissions in cooperation with the Bureau of Mines fostered an era of price stability unprecedented since the days of John D. Rockefeller. From 1945 through the late 1960s, the price of oil remained relatively constant, declining slightly in real terms.

Predictability encouraged careful planning of investments and exploration and a growing sense of professionalism in the industry. Prorationing also eased the orderly flow of credit to companies with growing needs for capital. Conservative lenders, notably commercial banks, made substantial loans secured by oil in the ground, an arrangement little used before prorationing.

Predictability and price stability were achieved at the expense of competition. Small producers traditionally had been able to survive by aggressively seeking new sources of oil and then rapidly developing and selling their product at whatever price the market would bring. Under prorationing, however, this strategy was closed off to marginal producers, and the search for stability through regulation ultimately led to a decline in the number of independent producing companies. Since such firms played a large role in the discovery of new sources of oil, the decline in their numbers did not bode well for the future of domestic oil exploration.

Domestic producers also had reason to be concerned about the growth of imports. The large international companies were able to obtain access to foreign oil that was much less expensive to produce than oil from the older, less prolific fields in the United States. As imports mounted in the 1950s, domestic producers turned to government for assistance in protecting their traditional markets. They mustered potent political arguments: the growth of imports threatened the national security, they said, by undermining the domestic production that would be vital in any future wars. The international companies countered with their own version of a national security rationale: every barrel of domestic oil saved by using imports would be available for use in a future emergency. The government considered these arguments and then responded to the political pressure of the numerous small domestic producers with a quota on imports.

In this aspect of the oil business, as in railroads, the attempt to use political controls to counter dramatic shifts in the economic or technological setting would eventually create more problems than it solved. The quota program temporarily delayed the long-term adjustments that inevitably would accompany the introduction of less expensive imports into U.S. markets. At a cost estimated to have reached approximately $50 billion to U.S. consumers, quotas on imported oil remained in effect from 1959 until 1973, slowing the flow of imported oil while encouraging the consumption of increasingly scarce domestic fuel.

Regulation of the price of natural gas in the 1950s and 1960s also created problems for the future. In this case, the Federal Power Commission's policy of holding the price of natural gas low relative to that of competing fuels fostered an era of extraordinary expansion in this industry. Indeed, natural gas became the fuel of choice for many purposes, from home heating to manufacturing. The increase in natural gas use was a source of dynamism for the economy as a whole, as was the expanding use of oil. These fuels were cheaper, cleaner, and more efficient than the coal they replaced. As the natural gas businesses strove to keep up with the growing demand for their product, however, they confronted regulated prices too low to encourage replacement of reserves. As was the case in the oil industry, the short-term benefits of regulation postponed the long-term adjustments that would be forced on the regulators and the entire nation by the impending scarcity of natural gas.

In this era of energy innocence before the 1970s, the long-term implications of the depletion of reserves were neglected in part because of the promise of nuclear power. Nuclear advocates proclaimed it the power of the future. Its most optimistic proponents foresaw a time when nuclear reactors would supply almost costless power. As a bonus, these enthusiasts promised, nuclear power would also solve growing problems with air pollution, for nuclear energy did not yield the emissions that plagued coal-burning industries. The Atomic Energy Commission, which was arguably the most powerful single-industry regulatory agency in U.S. history, sought to foster the growth of an industry capable of fulfilling this starry vision of a nuclear future.

Congress created the AEC in 1946 to regulate the development and application of the technology produced by the Manhattan Project during the Second World War. From its early years through its absorption into other agencies in 1974, the AEC had to perform a difficult juggling act. It had a legislative mandate to serve as both the promoter and the regulator of nuclear power. Whereas airline regulation had sought to minimize potential conflicts by separating the promotional (CAB) from the safety (FAA) functions, the AEC was made responsible for both activities. Predictably, the agency exhibited more interest in hastening the development of nuclear power than in assuring its safety. The nuclear "club" of regulators, reactor manufacturers, scientists, and utilities enthusiastically embraced this new and complex technology, assuring the public that any existing health, safety, or waste disposal problems could be solved as the business developed.

The apogee of nuclear enthusiasm came in 1961, when Consolidated Edison of New York, one of the largest utilities in the nation, announced that it would seek permission from the AEC to construct a full-scale nuclear power plant at a site in Queens, just across the East River from densely populated Manhattan. Con Edison's chairman, Harlan C. Forbes, based his decision strictly on economic considerations. Asserting that it was the AEC's responsibility to determine the acceptability of sites, he argued that if nuclear power plants were safe enough to build, then his company should get on with the task of constructing them as close to existing markets as possible. Amid a chorus of questions and complaints, Con Edison subsequently revised its plans. But the entire episode aptly captured the tone of nuclear excitement in this era. By pushing the implementation of the new technology before problems of health, safety, and waste disposal had been addressed and by underestimating the difficulties that would arise, those in control of the business helped foster a growing skepticism about nuclear power.

While the utilities planned for their nuclear futures, they went forward with aggressive expansion of electric power production using coal, oil, and natural gas generators. The regulation of the utility industry in the postwar era in many ways epitomized the best of the history of single-industry political control in these years. After the turmoil of the 1930s, utility regulators, owners, managers, and consumers welcomed orderly expansion and consolidation. Underlying the harmony of the era was a steady decline in electric rates as a result of economies of scale in the production of electricity. As long as cheap fuel, improvement in existing technologies, and growing markets were available to the utilities, they eagerly built new plants. Larger, more efficient plants lowered their unit costs. Regulators had a relatively easy, undemanding job: they gradually passed on decreases in rates to consumers, who came to take inexpensive electricity for granted and seldom questioned the workings of the system as a whole. Like the telephone company's managers, utility executives enjoyed considerable autonomy as they went about their engineering tasks largely out of the public eye. As long as the conditions underlying the trend toward lower rates remained unchanged, sustained expansion was assured.

A final and critical sector of the American business system in which single-industry regulation fostered stable patterns of growth was finance. The strict regulations imposed on financial institutions during the 1930s left commercial bankers with little incentive or leeway to innovate or to compete aggressively. Chastened by the banking crises of the 1930s, most professional bankers made security of deposits, not profitability or innovation, their primary goal. The result—largely the intended one—was a conservative industry, which critics claimed operated by a "3–6–3 rule: pay depositors 3 percent, lend money at 6 percent, and tee off at the golf course by 3 P.M."

But despite these attitudes and barriers to change, commercial banking was deceptively dynamic. In the twenty years after the Second World War, the assets of commercial banks in the United States increased by 250 percent; a steadily growing stream of credit flowed from these security-conscious banks, providing financing for a new array of business activities. For almost a quarter of a century, the commercial banking industry provided a solid foundation for the expansion of American business. After the turmoil of the 1930s, security in banking institutions was welcomed by business executives and small depositors alike.

In banking, as in transportation, communications, and energy, regulators traded innovation for stability. These choices reflected the lingering impact of the Great Depression, but they also matched the mood and the needs of the time. All these businesses were vital to the health of the economy as a whole, and their steady growth made an important contribution to the impressive economic performance of America's corporate commonwealth. For most of these enterprises, stability did not mean stagnation but rather orderly expansion. For a quarter of a century regulated industries were thus able to deliver at reasonable prices the vital goods and services needed in the rest of the economy. Single-industry regulation, as well as government spending and macroeconomic planning, contributed to the stable business environment that made possible this era of growth.

## POLITICAL STABILITY AND BUSINESS EXPANSION

What the government did not do was also important in fostering orderly expansion. Unlike the period of almost perpetual crisis from the Progressive Era through the Second World War, the years after 1945 witnessed no fundamental changes in the rules governing business decision-making. Traditionally, cross-industry regulatory initiatives had embodied the new demands society made on private enterprise. During most of the period from 1940 to 1969, there were few new demands expressed through cross-industry regulations. This is not to suggest that the system was humming along perfectly. There were, for instance, growing problems with air and water pollution, problems that were slighted by business and government during the postwar era. But in general during these years controversy and tension between business and government yielded to consensus.

The pressures on business managers from cross-industry regulations passed by previous generations also subsided during the heyday of the corporate commonwealth. The antitrust movement had been a political passion during the Progressive Era, but by the 1950s it had become primarily a series of rules enforced by several loosely coordinated bureaucracies. GM, Ford, and Chrysler steadily increased their dominance of the U.S. automobile industry largely free from threats of antitrust action. The major international ore companies were encouraged by government to consolidate their control in international markets. Indeed, in much of the industrial heart of the American economy, oligopolistic control was strengthened as antitrust officials looked elsewhere—particularly to smaller, less concentrated industries—for cases that might be less important but could be more easily won.

Even the "landmark" antitrust case of the 1950s, the DuPont-GM case, illustrated the increasing irrelevance of antitrust sentiments in shaping competitive forces in the business system. As a result of this case, DuPont was forced to sell its stock in GM because that equity position gave the chemical firm an advantage in selling goods to the nation's leading automobile company. But the decision did not fundamentally challenge the existing highly concentrated market structures in either the chemicals or the automobile industry. These oligopolistic structures were by this time largely beyond question.*

Outcomes such as these accurately reflected the tone of the corporate commonwealth in the American Era. Government was more likely to be a partner or helpmate than an opponent of the modern corporation. Executives remained wary of antitrust action, but programs put in place during earlier periods of political tension had been largely absorbed and their sharp edges rounded by administrative compromise. There were still conflicts, and shortly after the war and during the late 1960s, sharp struggles disturbed the peace of the commonwealth. But this era of consensus greased the wheels of a smoothly functioning business system. After experiencing two world wars and the Great Depression during the previous quarter-century, most Americans were content to overlook any shortcomings of the new corporate order as long as prosperity continued.

For business executives the American Era was a relief, in part because the problems of controlling the political environment were no longer so complex or so threatening. The government had always to be taken into consideration, but instead of new forms of regulation, it was experimenting with new ways to encourage innovation by American businesses. The rules were fixed and known to all. Opportunities for profits were great, and stability was the keynote of national fiscal and regulatory policy. It was a good time to be in business in the United States, an era when American efficiency and entrepreneurship were the wonder of the world.

*An exception to the rule was provided by the government's 1957-1958 suit against the Radio Corporation of America (RCA) to break up the patent monopoly in that industry. There was also a suit against the electrical manufacturers, but it involved price fixing, the kind of loose combination that had been a prime target for antitrust action since the 1890s.

CHAPTER 7

# The Modern Firm
# in Triumph

DURING THE 1940s and the following two decades, corporate executives and business associations played a leading role in the successful effort to redefine the public sector. Their willingness to mount such an effort is not difficult to explain: many of them had emerged from the cauldron of the Great Depression chastened, somewhat uncertain about the future, and determined to do everything possible to ensure that America would never again suffer such a long and painful collapse. Actually, small and middle-sized firms had suffered the most. But the 1930s had been harrowing for most corporations and large financial institutions as well, and the officers of these companies played a significant role in formulating the public policies that provided the setting for orderly growth in the postwar era.

## RECOVERY FROM THE DEPRESSION

Before any campaign for change could get underway, however, the business system had to escape from the hammerlock of the Great

155

Depression and start running at profitable levels again. All the planning and experimenting of the New Deal years, the subsidies and loans, the manipulation of the currency, and the controls on output, wages, and prices had failed to put the corporate commonwealth solidly on its feet again. As late as 1938, America's businesses were still operating well below normal capacity, and more than nine million persons were unemployed.

The onset of war in Europe soon changed those conditions, however, and following America's entry into the war in 1941, the nation's businesses were hard-pressed to produce all the goods and services needed by the military and by the civilian population. Profits were high. Many government contracts were written on a cost-plus basis, which ensured that the firms could not, whatever their problems, suffer a loss. In a number of businesses, including steel and aluminum, the government encouraged rapid expansion of capacity either directly by financing the growth or indirectly by allowing the firms to write off their investments over a few years. For a company such as U.S. Steel, the latter advantage was a far more significant source of funds for expansion than retained earnings, which also increased during the war.

Even in these favorable conditions the problems of business were not negligible. Firms had difficulties keeping an adequate supply of labor when the military was drawing off millions of workers. By 1942 and 1943, U.S. companies were employing virtually all the readily available men and women and in some areas were beginning to offer special inducements such as day-care centers in an effort to bring more mothers into the plants. In addition to labor shortages, companies had to cope with the government's elaborate program of price and production controls. The mobilization in the 1940s was far more complex and complete than it had been during the First World War. Even when business managers familiar with industrial problems were in charge of it, the controls they set up were bound to chafe against businesses striving to make up for the ground they had lost in the previous decade. Shortages of materials used in the war effort and transportation problems created further difficulties for business in the prosperous forties.

Balanced against the problems of operating in a control-laden context were some obvious and some not-so-obvious advantages of the wartime business environment. One was the basic shift in orientation on the part of the government: the New Deal's antibusiness sentiment gave way to a cooperative approach stressing the positive contributions business was making to the war effort. This transformation was symbolized when the Office of Price Administration changed leadership, from New Deal–oriented economists like John Kenneth Galbraith to businessmen like Chester Bowles, a car salesman. Antitrust activity was placed on hold throughout the war. Labor relations too were altered in basic ways as unions focused their concerns on Congress and the federal bureaucracy, not on management itself.

Critical businesses like the nation's large steel producers prospered during the war. As late as 1938, steel firms had been using only about 40 percent of the existing capacity in the United States. By 1943 U.S. Steel and its erstwhile competitors were using over 98 percent of their expanded facilities and were posting substantial profits. Management used these favorable conditions to position their firms for the postwar economy. For one thing, they reduced their fixed obligations to an all-time low for the modern industry. At the same time they replaced their oldest and least efficient plants with modern units. During the war they spent over $2.6 billion to boost output (half provided by the federal government). Larger, more cost-effective blast and open hearth furnaces were built, and with them came better auxiliary equipment and instruments. While this new plant was not state-of-the-art, it was more efficient than the mills it replaced. Man hours per ton dropped. Increased productivity and larger retained earnings placed such top steel manufacturers as U.S. Steel, Bethlehem, and Republic in the front row as the race for postwar markets at home and abroad began after 1945.

In a context of growth and a common national purpose, many business managers came to accept the larger role that the political system had come to play in the country's economic life. The war thus eased business toward accommodation with the newly enlarged national state. This was especially true of the heads of very large corporations, who took the leadership in the Committee for Economic Development and the Business Advisory Council in looking for ways to protect the United States from a postwar economic collapse. There was a deepset fear that once the stimulus of wartime demand was gone, once the troops returned to civilian life, the business system would sag back into the sort of depression that had plagued the 1930s. Business leaders like Paul Hoffman, president of Studebaker, and Jesse Jones thought the answer was for the federal government to play a larger role in controlling aggregate demand. According to Hoffman, "Private business had little to do with maintaining high levels of employment, and . . . there is little that local government can do. It follows, therefore, that the [federal] government must take certain steps if we are to achieve high levels of employment." Peacetime price controls were not needed. The answer was monetary and fiscal policy employed in a sensible, noninflationary, countercyclical manner. These were the sorts of attitudes that came to be expressed in statutory form in the Employment Act of 1946, as we have seen, and this measure as much as any reflected the new and positive role that business leaders were to play in the nation's postwar version of the corporate commonwealth.

Actually, business fears about the postwar economy turned out to be exaggerated. There were problems of adjustment. Labor strife in the forties reached alarming proportions. When price controls ended—and most businesses were happy to see them go—the economy began to experience a sharply increased rate of inflation. Women who had begun to work outside the home in record numbers were in many cases squeezed out of their jobs and replaced by men. But despite these tensions and a precipitous decline in government expenditures, the economy stayed afloat and actually grew. Pent-up demand, fueled by wartime savings, kept the business system prosperous. Americans wanted homes, cars, and other consumer goods, and they had jobs and the money to pay for them. In the late forties all you had to do to sell an automobile was smile.

## DIVERSIFICATION AND DECENTRALIZATION

In this favorable context, many U.S. firms were encouraged to expand their operations, even to look beyond the industries in which they were established for opportunities elsewhere. Diversification into related products and services—often linked by a common technology or by common forms of marketing—became a popular corporate strategy. A few leading firms had already explored this territory before the Second World War. One of the first had been Du Pont, which had developed substantial research and development capabilities and used its technical skills to produce and market products significantly different from its basic line of explosives: artificial leather, for instance, and later paints and paint products as well as plastics. Until that time, most U.S. businesses had stuck to one basic set of traditional products. A firm in the iron and steel industry, for example, might venture to control the railroad over which it shipped its raw materials. U.S. Steel had from its inception owned a large part of the stock of several railroads, steamship lines, and dock companies, and National Steel and others had adopted a similar strategy. A company might also begin to sell finished products as well as plate steel or ingots. During the Great Depression and the 1940s, most of the country's steel manufacturers acquired a stake in fabricating. Bethlehem, for instance, bought several firms that made structural steel, oil field equipment, and welded products like drums and tanks. But a steel company seldom branched out into the businesses that used its products—the oil industry, for instance. Businesses stayed in and sought to control one basic set of products in a well-defined market.

But Du Pont and other firms, including General Electric, began gradually to explore a new kind of corporate strategy: diversification along a path dictated by the technological capabilities and market opportunities of the business. This strategy was only possible in the new age of the large corporation. The entrepreneurial firm of the nineteenth century had depended for its technological inputs on a single businessman or on the partners who ran the enterprise. Du Pont and other centralized corporations had, by contrast, large and varied research organizations that could easily add new personnel to look into promising technologies. They also had the financial resources to buy into new lines of business.

As it turned out, diversification offered several advantages to the large firm. It enabled the corporation to make full use of its technological and financial resources. Demand in any market had a natural tendency to level off as the products matured. This tendency imposed a constraint—often labeled the "product cycle"—on the firm's growth. It also left the business vulnerable to price competition when, for instance, its patent protection expired (after seventeen years) or when competitors managed to achieve locational or other advantages in the production process. Through diversification the large firm could repeat over and over again its initial growth phase.

But to do so effectively, Du Pont and other companies had to abandon a centralized style of organization and develop a new form of business corporation, the decentralized firm. In a centralized business, each basic function of the firm—marketing, for instance—had been performed in one department. But what Du Pont learned (by losing large amounts of money) was that one marketing department could not effectively distribute highly varied products. Nor could one manufacturing department handle the problems of producing both gunpowder and artificial leather. The solution was separate functional departments organized into divisions handling related product lines. Over all these divisional lines of business was a central office that performed the basic functions of allocating the firm's resources and supervising in a general way the performance of the divisions (see figure 7.1). Day-to-day operations were left in the hands of the divisions; power was clearly decentralized. While major entrepreneurial decisions were made by the CEO and executive committee, maintenance of efficiency and a good profit performance were largely divisional responsibilities.

The decentralized firm organized along these lines also turned out to be effective where businesses operated over very wide geographical areas. Companies that were truly national—Sears Roebuck, for instance—found regional divisions an efficient way of controlling and directing their operations. In the 1930s, Standard Oil found the new structure useful for directing its worldwide activities.

Before 1940, however, most U.S. corporations had not diversified or entered international markets, and they kept the centralized structure. During the depression, most businesses were less concerned with growth and innovation than with survival. Cutting costs and holding on to existing customers were more important than investing in entirely new lines of products or services. American corporations had hunkered down to wait out the storm. In the 1940s, however, wartime profits left many companies looking for new opportunities to exploit, new and promising places to invest their capital and use their talents. Expansion during and after the war strained the centralized administrations of these firms. More and more companies began to invest in overseas operations, which were especially difficult to control in a highly centralized corporation. Communications overseas were rapidly improving in the postwar years, but quick responses to local conditions could be made only if the head of the business in that country had the authority to act.

Problems such as these prompted a sweeping reorganization movement in the 1940s, and by the end of the decade most large, innovative U.S. industrial corporations had adopted the decentralized mode of organization. Many had also begun to diversify their operations. This was the case at General Electric and other electrical manufacturers. At GE, thoroughgoing decentralization paved the way for further expansion abroad as well as for further diversification into computers and industrial automation systems. Others in the electrical and electronics field followed suit, as did such leading heavy-machinery manufacturers as International Harvester, Allis-Chalmers, and Borg-Warner. In chemicals the Du Pont story was repeated at Allied Chemical, the Celanese Corporation, and Union Carbide. Mass distributors as well as manufacturers charted a similar course, using territorial instead of product divisions, as Sears Roebuck had done before the Second World War. By the end of the 1950s, this phase of the managerial revolution had reached deeply into the business system, remaking the firm along multidivisional, decentralized lines.

Decentralization and diversification basically transformed the American business setting. They were as revolutionary as the transition from the entrepreneurial firm to the centralized corporate combine at the beginning of the century. They freed the corporation from the limits of a single industry's growth path—the seemingly inevitable curve or product cycle. Now a corporation could renew itself by edging into entirely new industries or new market areas around the nation or, for that matter, around the world. The limits upon corporate expansion—the point at which growth would become dysfunctional because the managers could no longer cope with the degree of complexity and amount of information in-

FIGURE 7.1

## The Decentralized Structure at Du Pont

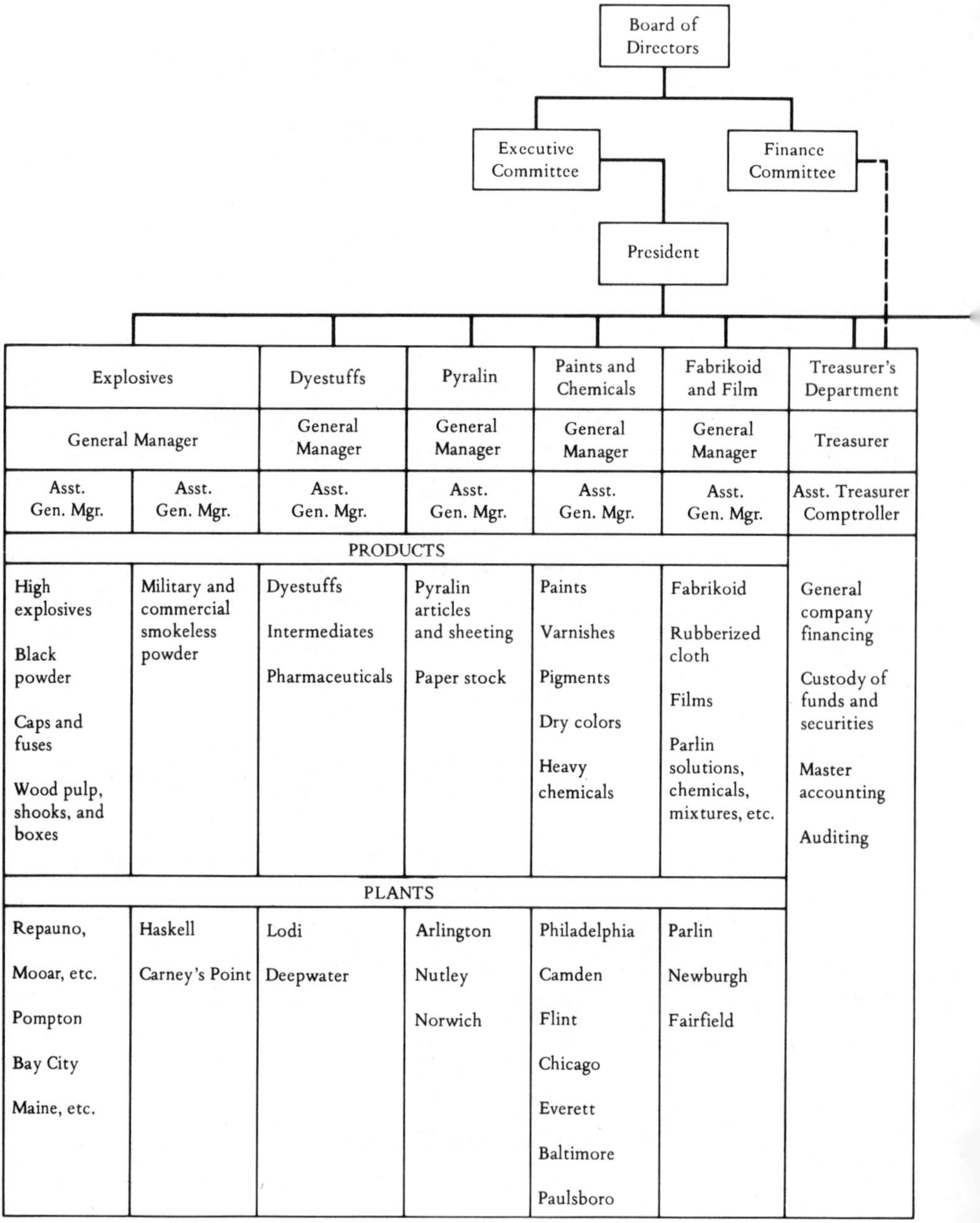

```
                          Board of
                          Directors
                              |
           +------------------+------------------+
           |                                     |
      Executive                             Finance
      Committee                             Committee ----+
           |                                              :
       President                                          :
           |                                              :
```

| Explosives | | Dyestuffs | Pyralin | Paints and Chemicals | Fabrikoid and Film | Treasurer's Department |
|---|---|---|---|---|---|---|
| General Manager | | General Manager | General Manager | General Manager | General Manager | Treasurer |
| Asst. Gen. Mgr. | Asst. Gen. Mgr. | Asst. Gen. Mgr. | Asst. Gen. Mgr. | Asst. Gen. Mgr. | Asst. Gen. Mgr. | Asst. Treasurer Comptroller |
| **PRODUCTS** | | | | | | |
| High explosives<br><br>Black powder<br><br>Caps and fuses<br><br>Wood pulp, shooks, and boxes | Military and commercial smokeless powder | Dyestuffs<br><br>Intermediates<br><br>Pharmaceuticals | Pyralin articles and sheeting<br><br>Paper stock | Paints<br><br>Varnishes<br><br>Pigments<br><br>Dry colors<br><br>Heavy chemicals | Fabrikoid<br><br>Rubberized cloth<br><br>Films<br><br>Parlin solutions, chemicals, mixtures, etc. | General company financing<br><br>Custody of funds and securities<br><br>Master accounting<br><br>Auditing |
| **PLANTS** | | | | | | |
| Repauno,<br><br>Mooar, etc.<br><br>Pompton<br><br>Bay City<br><br>Maine, etc. | Haskell<br><br>Carney's Point | Lodi<br><br>Deepwater | Arlington<br><br>Nutley<br><br>Norwich | Philadelphia<br><br>Camden<br><br>Flint<br><br>Chicago<br><br>Everett<br><br>Baltimore<br><br>Paulsboro | Parlin<br><br>Newburgh<br><br>Fairfield | |

SOURCE: Alfred D. Chandler, *Strategy and Structure: Chapters in the History of the Industrial Enterprise* (Cambridge: MIT Press, 1962), 108–109.

AUXILIARY DEPARTMENTS

| Legal | Purchasing | Development | Engineering | Chemical | Services | Traffic | Advertising |
|-------|-----------|-------------|-------------|----------|----------|---------|-------------|
| Chief Counsel | Director of Purchasing | Director | Chief Engineer | Director | Director | Director | Director |
| Legal and legislative matters | Major purchases and those not special or routine within industrial departments | Expansion and development studies | Major construction and engineering in the experimental and operative activities | Research laboratory and consulting chemical in the operative and experimental lines | Medical<br><br>Welfare<br><br>Real Estate<br><br>Protection<br><br>Publicity<br><br>Salvage and recovery<br><br>Safety<br><br>Fire protection<br><br>General inspection<br><br>Stationery and printing<br><br>Mailing | Traffic activities, rate adjustment not carried out within the departments | Advertising |

volved—had been pushed back significantly. Now it was not clear that there was any such internal limit upon size and power.

The entrepreneurial horizon of the corporation thus began to push out toward infinity. Managers of this type of firm could no longer imagine that there would ever be a point where the company would go out of business, for whatever reason. The decentralized structure enabled U.S. managers to strike a new balance between the three major functions of innovating, achieving efficiency, and maintaining control of the firm's external environments (see figure 7.2). The decentralized firm was an essential element in the business expansion that highlighted the American Era.

The business managers of this era had ample cause to be optimistic. Cheap energy—especially oil and natural gas—encouraged sus-

FIGURE 7.2

The Three Major Business Functions
and the Decentralized Firm

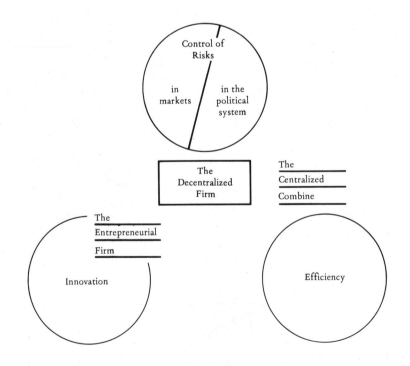

tained business expansion. The financial system, buttressed by a new regulatory framework, also favored measured growth on the basis of long-range goals and expectations. American capitalism seemed to have solved the problem of major depressions like those of the 1930s and 1890s. The American Era would, it seemed, be long and fruitful for those who worked for the corporation as well as for those who owned or managed it.

The managers of some firms also began to assume that they could efficiently supervise almost any sort of business that promised to turn a profit, even in the short term. They began to abandon the idea that corporate activities should be technologically related or linked by common markets. The conglomerate acquired various unrelated types of businesses, even those that might be profitable only because they had certain tax advantages. This latter approach was adopted by Textron, a corporation that started from an ailing industry by taking advantage of the unique tax breaks provided to firms that had accumulated deductible losses. From this shaky base, the Textron CEO, Royal Little, guided the business through some seventy acquisitions of unrelated businesses. Like many other conglomerate entrepreneurs, Little was essentially a financial manager; he looked for a "better cumulative growth rate on capital than can be obtained in any normal, single-industry operation." By the late 1960s he had steered his hodge-podge of enterprises into the top one hundred American corporations.

Others, including James J. Ling of Ling-Temco-Vought and Charles Bluhdorn of Gulf and Western, adopted similar strategies. During the rush of mergers in the sixties, Gulf and Western spread by acquisition into such diverse undertakings as publishing, zinc production, cigars, motion pictures, insurance, and musical instruments—to mention a few. By 1968 it ranked thirty-fourth in *Fortune's* list of the largest businesses in the nation. Clearly the conglomerate movement had begun by that time to have a significant impact on many of the nation's largest, most important corporations. By the end of the sixties, acquisitions involving diversification accounted for over 80 percent of the large mergers among U.S. corporations.

With the conglomerates came a new attitude toward management. No longer was management industry-specific. Top managers did not reach their positions by working their way up through manufacturing or marketing, learning a single business from the ground up. Instead, they approached the business as a packet of diversified assets that they directed by allocating or cutting off capital and by supporting or changing the managers of the various lines of business. In the subsidiaries owned by the conglomerates, the traditional management concept of adding value through more efficient organization, better marketing, or technological improvements in a single industry or a cluster of closely related ones remained of central importance. But top managers of the conglomerate focused on the quite different tasks of choosing the most profitable acquisitions and interpreting financial data on the performance of the subsidiaries and their managers. They embraced the concept of "synergy"—the idea that wise investments and good controls could make the overall performance of the conglomerate greater than the sum of its parts. In the growing economy of the postwar years, many of the conglomerates seemed to have found the managerial secret to generating corporate synergies.

## THE MULTINATIONAL FIRM

Another important development in U.S. business was the rapid growth of multinational operations. U.S. businesses had unique opportunities to expand overseas in the postwar era, and a substantial number of corporations took advantage of those conditions. This was a significant transition for the American firm. During the previous century and a half, U.S. businesses had been overwhelmingly occupied with the domestic market—long the largest market in the world without internal barriers such as taxes and regulations that might have interfered with commerce. The United States had abundant natural resources and a large, rapidly growing population that provided all the opportunities needed by most domestic firms. Foreign resources and populations had been left to the attention of businessmen from other industrial countries, especially the English, German, and Dutch traders.

During the 1890s, when many U.S. industries faced problems of overproduction, the interest in overseas outlets for U.S. goods had increased. Some American businesses had also begun to control their own foreign sources of agricultural products and minerals, especially in Central and South America. From that time on, doing business abroad had been normal for a number of American corporations. But still, the overwhelming majority of large and small businesses continued to be preoccupied with the domestic scene, and during the 1930s and the Second World War, many companies that had previously gone overseas were forced to retrench to the domestic market.

In the aftermath of the war, however, the economies of the European countries were either so devastated or so far converted to wartime output that they could not quickly recover the markets they had been forced to abandon. U.S. corporations saw those opportunities, and structured as they now were along decentralized lines, they were well situated organizationally to take advantage of them. Moving into a foreign country was easier when it involved adding a semiautonomous geographical division than it had been when operations were highly centralized, controlled on a short-term basis out of corporate headquarters. In this case strategy flowed out of structure instead of the other way around.*

In this favorable setting, American businesses became multinational for a variety of specific reasons. In some cases they did so to bring under their direct control vital sources of raw materials, as had long been the case with the major oil companies. After the war, U.S. oil firms acquired a stake in the highly productive fields of the Middle East. In South America—especially in Venezuela, where Standard Oil of New Jersey was heavily involved—the American multinationals became an important presence in the postwar era. Companies in other industries moved toward sources of cheap labor and began low-cost production in overseas—now commonly called "offshore"—plants. Another compelling reason to look offshore was to avoid tariff and trade barriers and to penetrate foreign markets by producing within the host country. This

---

*The reference here is to Alfred D. Chandler's important book, *Strategy and Structure: Chapters in the History of the Industrial Enterprise* (Cambridge: MIT Press, 1962). As Chandler demonstrates, the normal relationship is for strategy to shape structure.

was the case in Europe, where U.S. firms invested heavily in the postwar years.

An especially interesting example of this latter type of development was provided by the Ford Motor Company. At war's end Ford was in solid financial shape, but it was an administrative nightmare. Henry Ford had long directed and dominated the firm, running it in a personal, idiosyncratic fashion according to his whims and those of his cronies. In the 1920s, when Alfred Sloan and Pierre S. Du Pont were introducing new administrative controls and the decentralized style of organization at GM, Ford had stubbornly clung to his own way of running an automobile company. That style of operation had of course produced a succession of triumphs before the First World War: the Model T, the original automobile assembly line, the five-dollar day, and a dominant position in the fast-growing domestic market for cars. But in the twenties, GM had supplanted Ford as the industry's leading firm. During the thirties, Ford had continued to slip behind, and when the U.S. entered the Second World War, it was only the third ranking company in the industry, behind both GM and Chrysler.

When Henry Ford died in 1947, control of the company went not to a professional manager like Sloan of GM but to the founder's grandson, Henry Ford II. In this case fortune smiled on the family. The new president quickly reorganized the firm, using some elements of the now-thoroughly-tested GM pattern. Assisted by the so-called "Whiz Kids"—ten wartime Air Force officers who had sold their knowledge of systems analysis and business controls to Ford as a package deal—the company's young CEO brought in new managers, introduced GM-type financial controls and business systems, sold off some of Ford's losing operations, and recast the firm in a divisional, decentralized structure.

In the course of reorganization, Henry Ford II also moved to improve his company's position in overseas markets. Before 1940 the Ford enterprise had established an elaborate, highly varied series of agencies, assembly plants, and (to a lesser extent) manufacturing operations overseas. The war had of course disrupted most of this network. Only in Latin America did the firm's interests abroad gain ground during the early forties. After 1945, Henry Ford II restored and reshaped the company's international subsidiaries. Inefficient operations—including its French plants and an abortive attempt to produce rubber for tires in Brazil—were chopped off and the central offices of Ford-U.S. began to move both investment capital and skilled personnel to the subsidiaries. Meanwhile, Ford bought the stock of the refurbished foreign operations, bringing the important German, English, and other affiliates under tighter control by the Dearborn offices of the U.S. company. Efficiency was improved. Output expanded. While there were formidable barriers (including labor strife and new political controls) to clear, Henry II managed to restructure the entire international division of his corporation, making it a highly profitable part of Ford's operations. As foreign countries raised new barriers to imported cars and parts, Ford increased its overseas manufacturing. New plants were built in Argentina, Brazil, Mexico, and Australia. By the end of the 1960s, the Ford Motor Company was a thriving multinational with successful operations on six continents.

The Ford story was repeated by a growing number of large firms in the years following 1945, and it was no coincidence that this turn toward international operations accompanied the expansion of America's political involvement abroad. In the cold war years the United States forged a worldwide network of military bases and political alliances directed primarily at containing Russian military power and preserving as far as possible the status quo overseas. At times these new international ties directly assisted U.S. businesses, as they did under the Marshall Plan.* A substantial part of the Marshall Plan aid was spent in the United States for the purchase of products supplied by American businesses. In most other instances the assistance was indirect, as, for instance, when nations militarily allied with the United States were encouraged to buy U.S. military hardware and to be accommodating to American multinationals. Business normally followed the flag.

So formidable was the American business expansion abroad that it aroused suspicion and hostile reactions in a number of foreign countries. In this era, other nations looked on U.S. management as the model for modern business. There was fear that U.S.

---

*Under this plan, which was named for Secretary of State George C. Marshall, the United States provided substantial amounts of economic aid to assist the postwar recovery of the Western European nations and Great Britain.

multinationals, using their technological advantages, their modern organizational techniques, and their abundant capital would simply squeeze out the significant indigenous producers. American values often rode with American products, and that too prompted concern overseas. There was also fear that political influence would inevitably flow toward business power, resulting in a loss of autonomy by the host country. Confronted by these concerns and by the regulations they prompted, American multinationals had to learn to accommodate to political and social pressures abroad, just as they had adjusted to a more active national government at home in the 1930s and early 1940s. In France, for instance, the postwar government became concerned that U.S. firms would come to control strategic sectors of the business system and thereby exert undue influence on the national economy. Takeovers of existing firms were frowned upon by the government, which for a time limited U.S. investment. IBM became tangled in a political thicket over the sale of a modern computer in France. Other U.S. multinationals, including General Electric, had similar problems.

American multinationals thus frequently found themselves treading a fine line overseas, but these problems did not deter them from continuing to seek and find opportunities to invest abroad. By the late 1960s, most of the largest American corporations had at least part of their operations overseas. Like the Ford Motor Company, many of these corporations were manufacturing abroad; unlike Ford, many were obtaining raw materials in less developed countries in Latin America, Africa, the Far East, and the Middle East. According to one study, there were 3,350 direct investors involved, and they controlled over 15,000 foreign businesses. These firms, some of the nation's most progressive in technological terms, were still primarily national insofar as their control was concerned. But increasingly their foreign divisions—in part because of political pressures such as those in France—were operated and in some cases partly owned by foreign nationals. In that sense American business was becoming more truly multinational, an astonishing transformation for a nation that as recently as the 1930s had turned its back, both politically and economically, on the rest of the world. No longer could America even consider that course, so deep were our diplomatic obligations and so firmly rooted in foreign soils were our multinational corporations.

## SCIENCE, TECHNOLOGY, AND THE MODERN CORPORATION

The multinationals and many other American businesses were able to maintain their innovative edge in the postwar years partly because of the amazing expansion of the nation's scientific and technological establishments. As we saw in the last chapter, this rapid growth had begun during the war, when the federal government supplanted higher education and private foundations as the prime financer of scientific and engineering research. In pursuit of the war effort, the government drew together large groups of talented scientists and provided them with substantial support—at MIT, for instance, and at Chicago, where the basic research for the atomic bomb was conducted. So successful were these efforts that during the early years of the cold war the federal government began to introduce similar programs. Large-scale federal financing became a feature of postwar science, especially in physics and biology, the glamour sciences of this era. Even the less popular sciences such as electrical engineering and other technical disciplines benefitted. Entirely new centers of scientific endeavor developed. One was at Stanford University, which became a leader in microwave research, a major element in the communications revolution of the postwar era. Transmission of messages by way of microwave towers and satellites was much cheaper than modes of communication using wires and more reliable than traditional radio transmission. A wide variety of new businesses sprang up to exploit the opportunities this new technology provided. Some of the entrepreneuers worked closely with researchers at universities that, like Stanford, were on the frontiers of research in this and other new fields.

There were in fact several scientific and technological revolutions, and one of the constituent elements in a number of them was the transistor developed at Bell Labs in 1947. The transistor made large, efficient computers feasible, and the computers in turn enabled technicians to make calculations and to control and manipulate bodies of data that had previously been too large and too unwieldy to handle. Now technicians could make accurate calculations that made possible the construction of commercial jet-propelled aircraft; they could develop new means of exploiting nuclear power and new means of controlling the nation's telecommunications network. Biological research, high energy physics, trips to the moon—all were beholden to the computer. During the Second World War, RCA was the leading firm in the business of developing and producing the early computers for the military and for defense-related academic projects. Later in the postwar era, IBM moved to the forefront in the commercial development of this new technology. It became the world's major producer of sophisticated mainframe computers for commercial and academic applications. Thomas K. Watson, IBM'S chief executive officer, drove his firm to this position of leadership by combining effective salesmanship with technological expertise.

The computer enabled businesses to process quickly large amounts of data: about customers, about divisional and departmental performance, about personnel, and about inventories in the United States and overseas. The computer complemented the multidivisional, decentralized structure in extending the reach of the large corporation, making it possible to maintain efficient operations on a much larger scale. This capability proved to be especially important in the postwar years, when mass retailing came into its own. The efficient chain stores squeezed small local retailers out of the major markets, just as mass production had earlier triumphed over small local and regionally oriented manufacturers.

In the country's largest companies during these years, organized research and development was an accepted—if not always well understood—part of the business. The laboratories in many firms reached very large proportions: at Du Pont by the end of the 1960s there were about 5,000 persons on the company's R&D staff; at Bell Labs there were three times that number, about two thousand of whom held the Ph.D. degree. RCA, another high-tech company, had centralized its research operations in Princeton, New Jersey, in the 1940s. Wartime contracts seeded this development, which was parlayed after the war into a dominant position in the new television industry and its related entertainment businesses. Through the late sixties, these and other large corporations led the way as expenditures for basic R&D in the private sector steadily increased, reaching almost $10 billion by 1969.

Two basic styles of organizing research emerged. One was to centralize a large part of the operation, as RCA, Bell Labs, and Du Pont did; in this case the main labs came to resemble university campuses, a feature that was part of their appeal and helped them recruit topflight scientists and technicians. Firms with centralized labs normally did a considerable amount of basic research, as well as applied research and development work on specific products and processes. Other companies were less interested in basic research and the prizes and publications that accompanied it. They decentralized their research operations and kept them closely tied to development, the actual implementation and engineering of the innovations that came out of the lab. At one time or another, most large corporations switched from one style to the other, trading part of their basic research program for an enhanced capability for developmental engineering, or vice versa. Some years later, they were likely to repeat the experience, as Du Pont did several times.

One of the most successful companies in exploiting its research potential was RCA, which had a central position in radio and then in TV broadcasting, as well as in the development and sale of electronic consumer durables. The company, with income of $300 million in 1947, was directed by its founder, David Sarnoff, a self-educated engineer. In these years Sarnoff provided the vital link between the Research Center in Princeton and RCA's engineers and factories around the country. Sarnoff, unlike some of those who would follow in his footsteps in RCA's top management, took a direct, active interest in the nuts and bolts of R&D. He personally made certain that the lab did not stray too far from the company's basic entrepreneurial path and that the path was realistic, given the company's technical capabilities. Under Sarnoff, RCA pioneered in the development first of black-and-white and then of color television. These were indeed triumphant years for RCA. In 1947 alone the company sold $40 million in TV-related products, and its lab was able to spend over $10 million on a successful crash program to develop color television.

This story of success through a combination of well-managed R&D, well-organized corporate production and distribution, and nationwide and then worldwide operations was duplicated many times over by America's postwar corporate giants. In the chemical business, the oil industry, automobiles, electronics, and business machines, U.S. businesses were experiencing growth and rapid technical change. The United States was a world leader in all these businesses, and part of the secret seemed to be the ability of the decentralized firm to manage its resources efficiently and to harness modern science and engineering to business endeavors. American firms experienced steady increases in efficiency during these years: between 1948 and 1966, the average annual increase in the efficiency of the business sector as a whole was 2.9 percent.*

In agriculture as well as in business, efficiency was increasing rapidly, and the gulf between these two sectors of the modern economy was narrowing markedly. The United States was experiencing an agricultural revolution. As farmers applied the knowledge accumulated over the previous half-century, frequently in public institutions, they were able to increase yields dramatically while cutting the amount of labor used. On the heels of these responses to a wartime market came the development of agribusiness, or corporate farming. In the vineyards and truck farms of California, in the chicken farms of the East Coast, and throughout the country in the production of beef and cotton and rice, the family farm began to give way to the corporate farm. Standard business techniques of accounting, financing operations, and managing the work force began to replace the traditional patterns of behavior associated with dirt farming (as opposed to what once was labled "book farming").

One of the most interesting examples of agribusiness was in poultry, where an agrarian form of the assembly line was introduced. No longer did chickens scurry about a farmyard looking for food. Corporate chickens in fact never touched the ground during their entire lives. They were comfortably housed in a controlled environment and stuffed with food carefully selected to yield just the sort of plump fowls needed in particular markets. Even color was carefully controlled to match tastes in, for instance, the large urban markets like New York. The new style of corporate farm was

---

*The figures used here and in statements concerning efficiency in the rest of the book are for productivity increases—that is, the ability to produce a larger output from the same inputs.

as unlike its predecessors as the giant multinational, decentralized corporations were unlike the nineteenth-century entrepreneurial firm.

## THE CONTINUING ROLE OF THE ENTREPRENEUR

The small, entrepreneurial enterprise had not disappeared, of course. Even in the age of corporate giants, there were several important roles for the small business to play. The individual proprietorship, the partnership, and the small corporation continued to perform their customary functions of experimenting with new techniques and products, of filling the niches which large producers eschewed or overlooked, and of facilitating transactions by way of financial brokerage and arbitrage activities. Very large companies moved slowly, especially where large risks were involved. Where entirely new products or services were being developed, where markets were ill defined, or where technologies were in a state of rapid flux, small business frequently controlled the terrain. In the early years of the electronics industry, for instance, large corporations were at a disadvantage. In California's Silicon Valley (so named because transistors were made with silicon), entrepreneurs who could quickly adopt the newest technology in small segments of the market were most successful. By the end of the 1960s many of these businesses had grown to formidable size, as did Hewlett-Packard. Many others had been absorbed by large companies or had failed. The failure rate for entrepreneurial firms continued to be high, even in a booming industry like electronics. But the examples that seemed relevant to the next wave of entreprenuers were not the bankrupt businesses but the companies like Hewlett-Packard and Texas Instruments.

In 1953, Texas Instruments (TI) was a small geophysical services company that ventured into transistor manufacturing. Its laboratory, headed by Gordon Tool (who had left Bell Labs), logged a series of startling innovations in semiconductor research, and by 1957 TI was producing one-fifth of the transistors in the United States. This initially small enterprise moved faster than most of its larger rivals. It pushed its products to the market quickly, solving production problems along the way. This was a risky business, but it succeeded. By 1959 the market price of shares in Texas Instruments had shot up from $5 in 1952 to $191. The company's assets by the mid-1960s were over $186 million—by 1969 over $336 million.

One sector of the economy where small business had a special role to play was in services. In providing repairs, personal services, food services, and financial services, businesses in these years were seldom able to achieve significant economies of scale or system. Frequently the services were site-specific, as in the restaurant or repair business. Normally the labor content of the work was high, and there were fewer opportunities than in manufacturing to substitute capital for labor. The service sector was thus the natural domain of small enterprise, and its share of the total amount of business done in the United States was growing. Actually, its relative position had been growing in importance since the previous century, but in the 1960s its role in the economy passed a milestone: in that decade service-oriented businesses provided more new jobs for Americans than did industrial production.

By that time not all the new jobs were in the kind of small firms that had populated America in the nineteenth century. There were, for instance, some very large financial institutions, such as Citibank and BankAmerica. They had began to push up against the regulatory boundaries containing commercial banking by offering an expanding array of financial services in broader markets. Large companies also developed franchise operations to blend the advantages of local entrepreneurial talent and capital with centralized purchasing, advertising, and standards generated by the parent firm. The example familiar to every American and to the citizens of many foreign countries is the franchise food business; McDonald's, first franchised by Ray Kroc in 1955, quickly became a familiar fixture in most towns and cities across the United States. By the end of the 1960s McDonald's had 1,500 outlets, each under the famed golden arches. Others in the fast-food business challenged the hold McDonald's had on the market, and there were soon hundreds of such chains selling fast food around the United States and abroad. The franchise style of operation was also used in motels (Holiday Inn), automobile repairs (AAMCO), tax preparation (H & R Block), and beauty salons (Cut & Curl). One estimate placed total franchise sales at $190 billion by the end of the 1960s.

The franchise operations and the vitality of small firms in such growth industries as electronics should have served to remind Americans that even in the corporate commonwealth there was a significant place for small business and the entrepreneur willing to face high risks, ready to work unreasonable hours, and able to promote a new idea. Small enterprise helped to keep the business system innovative. It also filled the niches between the nation's very large, vertically integrated corporations. In some cases small firms were protected from their giant corporate neighbors by public policy—antitrust, for instance—but for the most part the entrepreneurial firm kept an important position in the postwar business system because it performed significant functions for which it was uniquely qualified.

## MARKET STABILIZATION

While the major themes of U.S. business development in the postwar era were orderly growth and technological progress, American business executives never lost sight of the need to protect their investments, to reduce risk wherever possible, to control relevant parts of their economic environment, and thus to achieve a measure of security. The corporate commonwealth, both its private and its public wings, involved a series of compromises—trade-offs, if you prefer—between control, innovation, and efficiency.

Compared with the nineteenth-century firm, America's large corporations, whether centralized or decentralized, were long on the ability to control their markets and to achieve efficiency in mass production and distribution. As we have seen they were less quick to innovate than smaller firms. Nevertheless the decentralized corporation of the postwar era was clearly more flexible and more innovative than the centralized combine. The new form of business organization was itself an innovation. It was in its time a successful attempt to improve the corporation's ability to control diverse internal affairs effectively while implementing an innovative strategy over the long term. One of the constraints on management, however, continued to be the need to maintain stable market relationships. No corporate manager could afford to ignore that crucial goal for very long. In that sense corporate policy and public policy both favored orderly, sustained growth.

The single most important thing that can be said about this blend of goals in the years 1945 through 1969 was that it worked. On balance it seemed suited to the domestic and world economies, and it produced a long phase of sustained business expansion. Downturns were recessions—cyclical phenomena—and not the sort of deep depression that had weakened the business system, as well as the rest of society, in the 1930s.

In the private realm, oligopoly sufficed in most industries to produce relatively stable prices and market shares. The aluminum industry provides an interesting example of how the process worked. Before the war the market in this industry had been monopolized by Alcoa, which had initially enjoyed patent rights to the basic electrochemical process for recovering the metal from its bauxite ore. That patent had enabled the firm's founders to transform a $20,000 investment in 1888 into a corporation with gross earnings of over $34 million in 1929. Alcoa had subsequently used research and development,* as well as vertical integration into finished products, to promote increased demand, and to preserve its monopoly.† During the Second World War, however, the government had built its own production units, which were run by Alcoa, and after 1945 it had sold these plants to other firms to introduce a measure of competition in the industry. The result was an oligopoly, with Alcoa sharing the market with the Reynolds and Kaiser companies. All three came to have somewhat similar characteristics: vertical integration into end products such as aluminum foil, and multinational operations that were a result of their search for sources of cheap ores and the power needed to refine them.

Under oligopolistic conditions, market shares and prices stayed relatively stable, although Alcoa under threat of further antitrust

---

*In 1928 alone Alcoa spent $700,000 on R&D. The company's annual expenditures on research fell to $445,000 in 1932, but by 1940 they were back up to $868,000.

†Vertical integration enabled Alcoa to use its substantial resources to promote new uses for finished products. This was especially important because aluminum was a relatively new material that was replacing wood, other metals, and plastics in end uses; extensive promotion was frequently needed before potential buyers would make the switch.

action gradually yielded larger market shares to its rivals. Competition was primarily focused on new product development and on heavy advertising of end products. With demand growing, especially from industries like automobiles that were substituting aluminum for steel, there was no acute pressure on management to break the line on prices for such major products as ingot and rolled aluminum sheets. The same sort of uneasy truce existed in the automobile industry itself, where changes in basic prices were less of a competitive tool than style changes, advertising, credit terms, and other aspects of the sale of an automobile. The largest corporations were averse to price competition and inclined to favor policies that removed even the element of locational advantage and transport costs as competitive factors.*

Many other businesses achieved a similar measure of stability in these years by way of the government regulatory systems. In the airlines and in trucking, for example, the public regulators controlled entry and prices and generally favored stable relationships that promised to keep up the quality of service or to ensure that all customers would receive the same price (and hence that high-cost customers would be subsidized). The businesses involved accommodated to the regulatory setting. Some, like AT&T, continued to stress technological innovation as a crucial element of their long-term firm strategy, but others, like the American maritime companies, the airlines, and the truckers, gave greater emphasis to steady profits and security than they did either to technical innovation or to day-to-day efficiency of operations. Still, in the growth-oriented 1950s and 1960s, this sort of performance did not incur much criticism, in part because the entire business system was doing so well.

## THE CORPORATE COMMONWEALTH
## AT ITS PEAK

Complementing the regulatory agencies and oligopolistic markets was the new fiscal and monetary system for controlling the level of

*In steel and aluminum the standard form of billing eliminated transportation costs to the customer as a factor in sales.

economic activity. With strong business support, as we saw in the previous chapter, the federal government had begun in the postwar era to implement fiscal and monetary policies that stabilized aggregate demand. The policy mix was conservative throughout, emphasizing price stability and the balance of payments as much or more than unemployment. And behold: conservative Keynesianism and monetary controls worked! High cold war defense expenditures gave the government the fiscal leverage it needed on the economy, leverage that enabled the United States to avoid a major downturn and to weather its recessions without serious damage to domestic business firms. With the 1964 tax cut, the policy of business-oriented fiscal stabilization reached its highest stage of development. By that time America seemed to have discovered the proper way to harness corporate capitalism without seriously injuring the basic market-oriented process at its heart.

Business, for its part, had gradually adjusted to the emerging patterns of orderly expansion and profitable operations. For instance, most companies had gradually made important concessions to organized labor. With productivity increasing, corporations could better afford concessions to their employees than debilitating strikes. The managerial attitude that emerged was that of "satisficing." Instead of maximizing profits, as neoclassical economics suggested they should, the managers of the nation's leading firms sought to satisfy the several groups of clients with whom they had to deal. They paid higher wages and new fringe benefits to labor; some of the contracts involved built-in cost-of-living adjustments (COLAs) that tied future wages to the rate of inflation. They paid regular dividends to the stockholders while keeping the firm in a safe condition by using internally generated funds (that might, for instance, have been used to increase dividends) to finance growth. They gave their customers reliable products and services. If the products and services were somewhat less innovative than they might have been or slightly more expensive than they could have been, these were merely two more of the trade-offs that characterized this era of mass consumption. So long as American firms dominated the domestic market and held a strong position in foreign markets, those sorts of policies sufficed.

Who could seriously complain about the results achieved by U.S.

TABLE 7.1

Employment, Unemployment, and Women in the Work Force,
1945–1985

| | Total Nonfarm Employed (1,000) | Unemployed (1,000) | Unemployed as % of civilian workforce | % of Women in workforce |
|---|---|---|---|---|
| 1945 | 44,240 | 1,040 | 1.9 | 29.2 |
| 1946 | 46,930 | 2,270 | 3.9 | 27.8 |
| 1947 | 49,557 | 2,311 | 3.9 | 27.4 |
| 1948 | 50,713 | 2,276 | 3.8 | 28.0 |
| 1949 | 49,990 | 3,637 | 5.9 | 28.3 |
| 1950 | 51,760 | 3,288 | 5.3 | 28.8 |
| 1951 | 53,239 | 2,055 | 3.3 | 29.3 |
| 1952 | 53,753 | 1,883 | 3.0 | 29.4 |
| 1953 | 54,922 | 1,834 | 2.9 | 29.2 |
| 1954 | 53,903 | 3,532 | 5.5 | 29.4 |
| 1955 | 55,724 | 2,852 | 4.4 | 30.2 |
| 1956 | 57,517 | 2,750 | 4.1 | 31.0 |
| 1957 | 58,123 | 2,859 | 4.3 | 31.2 |
| 1958 | 57,450 | 4,602 | 6.8 | 31.5 |
| 1959 | 59,065 | 3,740 | 5.5 | 31.7 |
| 1960 | 60,318 | 3,852 | 5.5 | 32.3 |
| 1961 | 60,546 | 4,714 | 6.7 | 32.6 |
| 1962 | 61,759 | 3,911 | 5.5 | 32.7 |
| 1963 | 63,076 | 4,070 | 5.7 | 33.2 |
| 1964 | 64,782 | 3,786 | 5.2 | 33.6 |
| 1965 | 66,726 | 3,366 | 4.5 | 34.0 |
| 1966 | 68,915 | 2,875 | 3.8 | 34.6 |
| 1967 | 70,527 | 2,975 | 3.8 | 35.1 |
| 1968 | 72,103 | 2,817 | 3.6 | 35.5 |
| 1969 | 74,296 | 2,832 | 3.5 | 36.3 |
| 1970 | 75,165 | 4,088 | 4.9 | 36.7 |
| 1971 | 75,732 | 4,994 | 5.9 | 38.2 |
| 1972 | 78,230 | 4,840 | 5.6 | 38.5 |
| 1973 | 80,957 | 4,304 | 4.9 | 38.9 |
| 1974 | 82,443 | 5,076 | 5.6 | 39.4 |
| 1975 | 81,403 | 7,830 | 8.5 | 39.9 |
| 1976 | 84,188 | 7,288 | 7.7 | 40.5 |
| 1977 | 87,302 | 6,855 | 7.0 | 41.0 |
| 1978 | 91,031 | 6,047 | 6.0 | 41.7 |
| 1979 | 93,648 | 5,963 | 5.8 | 42.2 |
| 1980* | 95,938 | 7,637 | 7.1 | 42.4 |
| 1981 | 97,030 | 8,273 | 7.6 | 42.8 |
| 1982 | 96,125 | 10,678 | 9.7 | 43.5 |

TABLE 7.1 *(Continued)*

| | Total Nonfarm Employed (1,000) | Unemployed (1,000) | Unemployed as % of civilian workforce | % of Women in workforce |
|------|------|------|------|------|
| 1983 | 97,450 | 10,717 | 9.6 | 43.7 |
| 1984 | 101,685 | 8,539 | 7.5 | 43.7 |
| 1985 | 103,971 | 8,312 | 7.2 | 44.1 |

*All figures from 1980 on include the resident armed forces.

businesses between 1945 and the late 1960s? The national economy was growing (see table 7.1). Total employment had increased dramatically, and new groups—especially blacks and women—were finding more and better jobs. Women in particular were entering the work force in record numbers for peacetime in the 1960s (see figure 7.3). While experiencing these changes, U.S. firms had nevertheless increased their efficiency and maintained a satisfactory level of innovation. Internal structural changes had enabled the corporation to handle effectively a greater diversity of products and services and more widespread operations than ever before. Modern science and technology had, it seemed, been blended into the business system to good effect. The decentralized modern firm was triumphant in the U.S. market and a formidable competitor abroad. Multinationals had greatly extended the reach of the U.S. business system, which by the mid-sixties was as global as American diplomacy.

So successful were the largest U.S. firms that foreign governments feared their further expansion and foreign businesses began to pay them the ultimate compliment of emulation. As business began to recover from the war, firms in nation after nation began to adopt the new decentralized, vertically-integrated structure common to U.S. corporations. They began as well to invest in R&D and to explore new areas of high-tech operations. To a considerable extent, innovations abroad took place with the active support of the American government, which sought thereby to bolster the noncommunist economies against internal and external threats to their stability. This policy helped, and the indigenous efforts in Europe and Asia

FIGURE 7.3

Total Employment and Employment of Women, 1945–1985

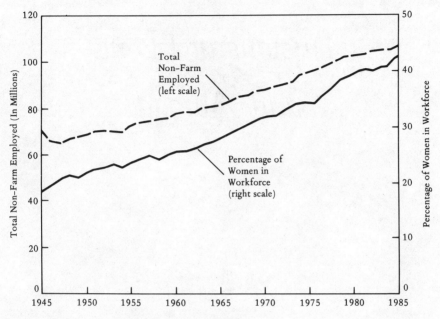

All figures from 1980 on include the resident armed forces.

paid off in a business recovery that would soon become so successful that U.S. companies would be challenged to improve their performance even more. Bear in mind, however, that from the perspective of the mid-1960s, the private and public institutions of the
American corporate commonwealth had compiled an amazing record of accomplishment in the postwar era. U.S. business stood
triumphant at home and abroad.

CHAPTER 8

# Tensions at Home
# and Abroad

EVEN DURING the period of its
greatest success, the new American commonwealth began to experience problems that foretold a second crisis. As the fundamental
conditions underlying the American Era started to shift, tensions
grew both at home and overseas. These strains were temporarily
masked by prosperity and business expansion, but by the late 1960s
some of them could no longer be easily ignored. The future was
most evident in the international realm, where aggressive new competitors to U.S. corporations had begun to emerge in Europe and
Japan and where the governments of nations producing raw materials had begun to assert their national interests. Within the United
States, there was evidence of managerial ossification as some established concerns began to lose touch with their changing technical
environments and markets. In part, America and its corporations
were victims of their own success. Two decades of good profits fed
an impulse to continue along familiar paths despite growing evidence of the need for change. Problems began to develop in rela-

184

tions with the government as well. Regulatory agencies that had long fostered orderly growth proved to be inflexible when the economic setting began to change. In the late sixties, mounting inflationary pressures in the United States began to strain a business system that was on the verge of a crisis. Lacking, however, was a sense of impending danger that might have fostered a consensus on the need for change.

## ECONOMIC RECOVERY IN EUROPE AND JAPAN

In the international economy, a unique set of circumstances in the years from 1945 to 1960 fostered U.S. dominance of world trade. The prolonged era of expansion, which Americans came to take for granted, rested squarely on the easy access of U.S.-based corporations to foreign raw materials and the leadership of those businesses in world markets. American enterprise had reached out aggressively into the international economy, thereby becoming a major part in an evolving, interdependent world system.

The initial advantage U.S. business had in that system was largely a consequence of the impact of the Second World War on the world's productive capacity. The United States emerged from the war with its industrial plant in excellent shape. Business-government cooperation during the war had produced a generation of new manufacturing plants that generally could be adapted to peacetime production. An extreme example was the petroleum and natural gas industries, where the war effort spawned heavy investment in modern facilities, including the first cross-country pipelines connecting the major sources of domestic oil and gas in the Southwest to markets in the Northeast. Related investments produced a robust new synthetic rubber industry, which hastened the expansion of petrochemical production. Much the same pattern held true in other vital sectors of the economy. In contrast, the war had devastated productive capacities in Europe and Asia. Pending the reconstruction of those economies and of a viable world trading order, U.S. dominance of international trade was assured.

The tensions created by the cold war reinforced the profit motive, encouraging U.S. corporations to move aggressively into the void in international trade. Here the needs of private enterprise and the goals of U.S. foreign policy came together, for U.S. multinationals were seen as representatives of "free world" values and agents of economic development. Coca-Cola and Fords were not just products; they were symbols of the promise of capitalism. The American way as embodied in its business system and products would help block the spread of communism.

U.S. concerns with the cold war overrode any efforts to define a coherent, long-range economic policy. From the perspective of American leaders, Europe and Japan needed strong economies to bolster them against the threat of communism; the long-term implications their development would have for the U.S. position in the international economy seemed largely beside the point. Thus while other nations sought to define national policies to help them expand their presence in world markets, the United States focused on containment of communism. This difference proved critical. The Marshall Plan and foreign aid encouraged capitalist development; the United States also encouraged the creation of a European common market. Massive U.S. expenditures on defense served to protect our allies, freeing our potential business competitors from the burden of large investments in national defense. These policies were successful. The United States had sufficient resources to assist in the recreation of a new world order, one that would eventually include numerous strong competitors.

While the Americans fashioned grand strategies to defend the free world, the Europeans of necessity focused on plans for economic recovery. The French, for example, created new types of planning institutions capable of guiding the growth process through the cooperative efforts of government, business, and labor. Not surprisingly, a crucial problem for the French planners and for those of other nations was to protect their businesses from the American economic challenge, rather than from communism. As the French and others got under way, they invested in state-of-the-art technologies to build up their industries. While the United States became the world leader in the production of military hardware, including nuclear weapons and delivery systems, its European allies concentrated on improving their basic manufacturing industries.

The evolution of Volkswagen illustrates what happened as European business returned to health. The "people's car" went back into production after the war. A car well suited to customers who demanded economy and durability, it found a steadily growing market as Europe recovered. When Volkswagen had built a strong base in Europe, the American market beckoned. After the mid-1950s, to the surprise of U.S. automakers and their workers, Volkswagen found a niche in the giant U.S. market. Efficient manufacturing and good quality, a modern distribution network, and creative advertising enabled Volkswagen to challenge American dominance in the industry that was the leading symbol of American corporate prowess. As yet, the big U.S. producers could take solace in the fact that Volkswagen was competing for a relatively small segment of the market. But the shape of things to come was suggested by the fact that the self-consciously "unAmerican" Bug, proudly promoted in ads asserting that "ugly is only skin deep," was able to build a base of loyal customers in this country.

Japan's recovery from the Second World War was more gradual than that of the European nations, but ultimately even more spectacular. As a defeated and occupied nation, Japan faced an uncertain future in the late 1940s. As was the case in Europe, however, the national security needs of the United States dictated economic assistance. U.S. foreign policy–makers viewed Japan as the primary bulwark against the spread of communism in Asia. The health of its economy was therefore a central concern and called for economic assistance and military protection. Of course Japan's steady expansion was facilitated, not created, by U.S. assistance. The nations hardest hit by the war looked inward to their traditional strengths and institutions for recovery. In the case of Japan, the government's Ministry of International Trade and Industry (MITI) had had several decades of experience in economic management (including wartime mobilization), and it emerged as the focal point of recovery. MITI drew on the national tradition of business-government cooperation and also used its substantial leverage over credit to help enforce the policies it devised. In sharp contrast to the American system, Japanese business thus had an integrative institution capable of defining and implementing a broad developmental strategy. MITI could, for example, target Japan's automobile manufactures for expansion as part of a national program aimed at increasing exports.

In both Japan and Europe, political leaders built on established traditions of strong central government in developing workable policies for their postwar business systems. Largely unhampered by the massive expenditures for defense that absorbed so much of the U.S. government's resources, they focused on ways to improve the performance and the competitive positions of their enterprises. In so doing, they developed a keener awareness of national economic strategy than did the United States during its heady era of economic dominance. As their strategies gradually succeeded, competition between the products of their companies and those of American corporations became more intense.

## OIL AND THE CORPORATE COMMONWEALTH

A different tension developed between the United States and the raw-material-producing nations throughout the world. The cold war gave America strong incentives to foster the economic development of these nations along noncommunist lines, particularly through foreign aid and the influence of U.S. multinationals. At the same time, American businesses needed the raw materials they had long obtained on favorable terms. Conflict broke out as these governments became increasingly adept at pursuing their national interests, changing the terms on which U.S.-based multinationals could acquire important materials.

Nowhere were these tensions more evident or more important than in the major oil-producing nations. The postwar prosperity of the United States and the reconstruction of Europe and Japan were fueled by oil and natural gas, which rapidly displaced coal in many energy markets. During the years 1945–1973, the international oil companies, their home governments, and the governments of the most important oil-producing nations worked out new understandings to keep these vital fuel supplies flowing. In earlier years, the oil companies had enjoyed considerable freedom in dictating the prices paid for raw materials and the terms of access. In the postwar era, however, first Venezuela and then the Middle Eastern producers began to bargain more aggressively. Confronted by a burgeoning nationalism, the threat of communism, and their growing dependence on these oil supplies, the companies and their home governments came up with a combination of oil tax revenues, foreign aid, military assistance, and loans from international development banks. For most of the era, the host governments were content to seek higher revenues, without trying to control the price of oil or the level of production. Although it produced considerable tension, this basic accommodation lasted for almost a quarter of a century, a remarkable accomplishment considering the value of oil, the volatility of the Middle East, and the passions of the cold war.

Gradually, however, this understanding was eroded away. There were not only numerous efforts by individual producing nations to assert greater control over their oil but the beginnings of a collective effort to do so through the Organization of Petroleum Exporting Countries (OPEC). Even before the war, the Mexican expropriation of U.S. and British oil properties in 1938 had sounded an alarm through the industry: access to foreign oil was by no means assured. Iran's attempt to nationalize the holdings of British Petroleum (BP) in the early 1950s reinforced this message. Although direct military intervention was frequently discussed as a possible response to nationalization, it was no longer a viable option in a world of nuclear weapons and cold war propaganda. Short of force, what could be done to assure access to oil? The U.S. government and the major multinational oil companies worked out a variety of answers to this question.

Taken as a whole, these responses were a long step toward a more equitable distribution of the benefits from oil production. Foremost, the oil-producing nations received more revenue. Oil taxes moved gradually upward after 1945, with Venezuela's 1948 decision to share profits equally with the oil companies setting a significant benchmark for the new era. Other producers quickly followed, and the U.S. Treasury paved the way with a ruling that these new levies could be treated as income taxes, not royalties, thus allowing U.S. firms to use them to offset domestic taxes on a dollar-for-dollar basis. In the Middle East this development allowed America to support friendly Arab oil producers through American oil companies (even though official U.S. policy strongly supported Israel). For their part, oil companies such as ARAMCO—a consortium of four U.S. corporations—were able to maintain relatively friendly relations with their host governments, without surrendering control over prices and production levels.

Another important element in the new package was improved treatment of the work force. The international oil companies learned to reduce tensions in their foreign operations with a combination of higher wages and better working conditions. They developed programs to assure the gradual movement of native workers into skilled jobs and ultimately into management. To preserve stable and profitable operations, the major oil companies began in effect to prepare the host nations to manage their own industries. There was no altruism involved here. The oil companies and their governments recognized the growing power of the producer nations to bargain forcefully, and they made significant concessions in order to protect their access to these critical oil supplies.

The great historical strength of the companies had been their capital, their technical knowledge, their access to world markets, and their ability to coordinate worldwide systems of production, transportation, refining, and marketing. Between 1945 and 1973, the producing nations steadily learned the business, from accounting systems to refinery operations. The educational process took place at American and European universities (including the Harvard Business School and the University of Texas), on the job, and through trade journals. The information was not secret. The producers had an overwhelming incentive to learn. Gradually they acquired the expertise they needed.

Such knowledge was of limited usefulness, however, as long as the companies could retain control by playing the producers off against one another. Venezuela, which had declining reserves and a poor competitive position relative to the Middle East, was the first to recognize this problem and to try to solve it through collective action. In response to price cuts in 1960, Venezuela's oil minister called together the initial meeting of the Organization of Petroleum Exporting Countries. OPEC's early focus was on the discussion of the producer nations' common problems. In the 1960s OPEC was more a forum than a fulcrum of power, but it nonetheless symbolized the growing maturity of the major exporters and the tensions between their aspirations and the existing international order in oil. By the end of the 1960s, America's oil business and the postwar accommodation with the producer nations were at risk.

In general the nations producing raw materials were becoming more assertive, and their new policies foretold the end of America's uniquely favored position in the world economy. The "American Century," so loudly proclaimed after the war, lasted for only about twenty-five years. It came to an end not so much because of any intrinsic flaws but because other nations became more successful in pursuing their self-interests. In achieving containment of Russian power, America actually hastened this process. By the late 1960s, the signs of impending change were visible: the United States and its corporations would soon be forced to adjust their policies to the new realities of the international economy. For Americans this transition would be particularly difficult because of their self-image as leaders of the noncommunist world and because U.S. businesses had grown comfortable in their dominant positions.

## INTERNAL PROBLEMS IN U.S. BUSINESS

By the late 1960s, problems were also developing at home, as the domestic economy began to sputter. During several decades of sustained expansion, corporate managers in many industries had honed their inherited management tools. All too often they had forgotten the basic impulses that had generated those tools—that is, the drives to achieve greater efficiency and to produce innovations. Management-by-the-numbers seemed to work in many industries in the years of American dominance abroad and of limited competition at home. The lure of short-term profitability appears to have dulled the incentive to think creatively about markets and technology. While there was ample evidence of business dynamism in such emerging industries as computers, examples of similar creativity in the established basic industries were more difficult to find.

The performance of the leading automobile companies is especially interesting in this regard. By any quantitative measure, the Big Three of American automobiles were extraordinarily successful after the Second World War. In the mid-1950s their preeminence in the world automobile industry made them a fitting symbol of the productiveness of the national economy (see figure 8.1). Their management was held up as a model for those in other industries and for other nations that wanted their businesses to adopt state-of-the-art management techniques. The managers of American automobile companies were clearly systematic, self-assured, and successful on their own terms.

In retrospect, however, they might also be described as short-sighted, conservative about innovations, and overly concerned with stability. Too often they delivered the form, but not the substance, of their predecessors in the industry. In part, this failing reflected the growing maturity of a business in which the fundamental breakthroughs had been made some decades ago. But this life-cycle explanation leaves much unexplained. These managers had opportunities to innovate. They chose instead to follow well-trod paths to stability and short-term profitability. In the process, they put off adjustments that would eventually have to be made in the midst of a crisis.

The disciples of Alfred Sloan embraced marketing as a substitute for a broader understanding of their customers. The Sloan revolution (see chapter 4, "Business Consolidates Its Control") had proceeded under the banner of "a car for every purpose and every pocketbook." By the 1950s, however, Sloan's concept of diverse offerings to fit diverse and changing markets had evolved into a philosophy of "bigger is better," as automobile makers tried to move the consumer up the ladder to bigger, more profitable models. The bottom of the line once symbolized by the inexpensive Model T had disappeared. The cars that passed for basic transportation increasingly became larger and loaded with "extras." To critics who decried the excesses of auto design in this era, managers smugly replied, "That's what American consumers demand." Had Henry Ford adopted the same philosophy, he would have made luxury cars such as the Pierce Arrow instead of opening up the mass market for automobiles.

FIGURE 8.1
World Motor Vehicle Production

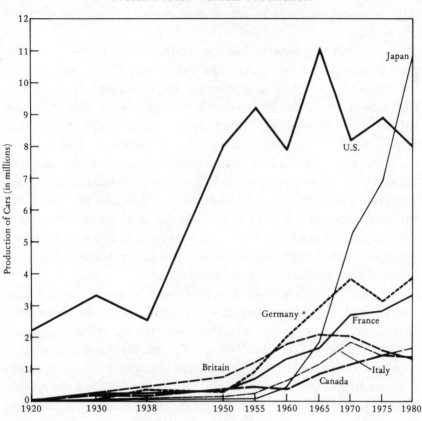

*Figures from 1950 on are for West Germany only.

SOURCE: John B. Rae, *The American Automobile Industry* (Boston: Twayne Publishers, 1984), 174.

Detroit's business leaders now seemed determined to prove that the American consumer would always want to buy longer, heavier, and less efficient cars—and to buy them more frequently. Their marketing strategy stressed "planned obsolescence." While spending millions of dollars to advertise, they appear to have given little creative thought to the basic markets for transportation in this country and throughout the world. The short-range perspective was dominant, as it was in many other U.S. businesses. Short-term profitability through the sale of bigger cars proved too seductive. The result was a lack of vision that Volkswagen exposed by demonstrating that there was in fact a market for a small, inexpensive, durable car.

Meanwhile, the basic technology of the internal combustion engine remained relatively static. The Big Three U.S. automobile makers refined the existing technology and emphasized developments that would contribute to driver comfort. While the auto industries in other countries were developing disc brakes, radial tires, diesel power, independent suspensions, fuel injection, and other basic innovations, U.S. technicians were spending their energies on power brakes, power steering, power windows, more powerful engines, air conditioners—features that improved the look and the feel of the product. One consequence was a decline in the average gasoline mileage of cars produced in America. So long as gasoline was inexpensive, of course, this was not a very pressing concern either to the automobile companies or to consumers.

Nor did the leaders of the business worry much about air pollution control. By the late 1940s, the growing use of the automobile in cities such as Los Angeles had aroused concern about the sources of air pollution and its possible impact on health. As various institutions and concerned individuals sought to understand the problem, representatives of the automobile industry faced some very interesting choices. They could conduct business as usual, disclaiming responsibility, at least until others could present irrefutable evidence that the automobile was a primary source of air pollution. They could rely on public relations and symbolic commitments to research in an attempt to maintain control of the issue both technically and politically by setting the terms of debate. Or they could study the impact of their chosen technology on the society as a whole and lead an effort to understand and control air pollution.

John D. Rockefeller had long ago proved the folly of the first alternative in an open society with numerous sources of information and an aggressive press. The third option would have required the Big Three to respond innovatively on a scale equivalent to Henry Ford's adoption of the $5 work day in an earlier era. It would have involved "entrepreneurship" on social issues, and admittedly, a collective effort might have run afoul of the antitrust laws. Yet the economic conditions of this era favored this choice. The Big Three companies were dominant and profitable; facing little foreign competition, they could have afforded larger expenditures on research aimed at controlling auto emissions. Such investments would have been in the long-term interests of the society—and of the companies.

Missing, however, was the recognition that the industry ultimately would be held accountable for the social impact of its technology. Missing too was the strategic insight that failure to provide leadership on new problems would assure that others ultimately would take the helm. In opting for a public relations approach, the companies stressed the lack of proof that vapors from automobiles were a significant source of pollution. They argued that automobiles were as clean as modern technology could make them. They pointed with pride to their meager expenditures on pollution research as evidence that they had the problem—if, indeed, there was a problem—under control. Such claims rang hollow in an era when annual model changes were absorbing billions of dollars of investment capital.

After the mid-1950s, industry spokespersons gradually gave ground as university and government researchers produced new evidence of the problems from auto emissions. Under pressure, the corporations finally embarked on a cooperative research program, but tensions over this issue mounted throughout the 1960s as the number of automobiles increased and the air quality worsened. After squandering a twenty-year head start, industry leaders had effectively forfeited their claim to leadership on this volatile issue.

Executives in the automotive industry and in most other industries also stored up problems for the future by locking their companies into expensive labor settlements. Business had no choice but to forge a workable accommodation with the new industrial unions that by the end of the Second World War had gained a solid foothold in the American political economy. The response of corporate CEOs was simple: they purchased stability and a relatively predictable labor force with a variety of expensive benefits. Walter Reuther and the United Auto Workers, in the vanguard of the American labor movement, demanded and received higher wages, cost-of-living adjustments, extended unemployment pay, excellent health and dental plans, and a variety of other benefits. Remembering the bitter disruptions immediately before and after the Second World War and aware of the strong threat of prolonged strikes in the postwar era, managers of the Big Three gradually conceded much of what Reuther and other union leaders demanded.

Good labor relations with long-term contracts removed one of the most threatening sources of potential uncertainty facing managers; improved public relations was an additional bonus. But managers paid dearly for stability. They locked themselves into expensive contracts and into the traditional format of adversarial labor relations. Instead of trying new approaches that might have brought their workers into a more creative role in the production process, (see Chapter 10, "Reconstruction Begins" on innovations such as the quality circle) managers paid them off—all too well—and looked to automation for increases in efficiency. Until the international context began to change, of course, the traditional approach to labor-management relations sufficed to achieve the companies' short-term objectives.

Along with concern for short-term profitability went a new emphasis on financial controls. Robert McNamara and his team of so-called "Whiz Kids" at Ford became early symbols of the role such controls were to play in the management of large-scale corporations. The proliferation of business schools, the development of increasingly sophisticated tools of financial analysis, and the age of computers all reinforced the tendency toward tighter controls. Inevitably, short-term profitability, which could be readily measured and analyzed, was the focal point of these evolving systems. Long-term corporate planning for technological and organizational innovation was harder to manage than bottom-line calculations, and planning depended to a significant degree on managerial vision, a soft factor that was difficult to specify and impossible to measure.

The growing sophistication of financial controls also helped ease business into the conglomerate merger craze of the 1960s. Using these tools, a relatively small central staff could coordinate the allocation of resources among numerous unrelated subsidiaries. In some instances, conglomeration proved spectacularly successful in producing profits. To firms in markets that were leveling off, conglomeration promised an escape from the lower profit margins associated with the last phase of the product cycle. To companies with specific growth targets in mind, this style of merger was particularly attractive. Perpetual expansion seemed possible, and firms like Xerox and the International Telephone and Telegraph Company compiled spectacular growth rates in this manner.

But in the longer term, conglomeration would create various problems for American business. Managers often had difficulties sustaining the much-touted "synergies" in companies with little in common except financial reporting systems. Corporations held together only by sophisticated financial controls accepted the *form* of traditional American management—that is, highly developed measures of costs and profits—without the *content*, the traditional integrative approach that includes not only the effort to discover areas in which to cut costs and increase efficiency but the development of new and improved products and new markets. The conglomerates could hardly develop the kind of unifying corporate culture that sustained businesses such as AT&T and IBM. Nor could their top managers generally offer expertise in technology or markets. Financial expertise alone did not necessarily encourage innovative performance. Conglomeration left many American firms poorly equipped to develop and sustain the sort of concentrated focus and expertise needed to produce quality products capable of competing in international markets.

## *GOVERNMENT POLICY TOWARD BUSINESS*

The shifting international economy also threatened many U.S. policies toward business that in the postwar era had on balance worked rather well. Most of these public programs—single-industry regulation of energy industries and financial institutions, for example, and cross-industry programs like antitrust—had initially been designed and implemented with a self-contained, domestic business system in mind. That was also true to a considerable extent of the fiscal and monetary policies that had functioned so successfully through the mid-sixties. As U.S. corporations began to lose their edge in the international economy, however, many of these policies became less of a boon and more of a burden to the corporate commonwealth.

It began to be apparent that in the regulated industries, some of the agencies had ignored—as did U.S. political leaders—the long-term health of the systems that delivered these vital goods and services to the economy as a whole. It was largely analysts outside of the government who first began to point out the economic costs and inflexibilities imposed by aging and increasingly outmoded regulations. By the mid-1960s, they had begun to stir up some political and economic tensions over issues that single-industry regulatory agencies had thus far been able to keep under control. Natural gas shortages, the high price of airline service, and long regulatory delays in the introduction of new technologies in cross-country freight shipment became subjects of concern. All pointed to a single conclusion: the existing accommodation between the businesses and the regulators in these vital industries was outmoded and threatening to break down.

The problems in the regulated industries emerged piecemeal for two reasons. All the difficulties at first seemed to be industry-specific. Natural-gas shortages focused attention on the FPC, not on regulation as such or even on the general energy problem. Moreover, the structure of American government had an effect on how issues such as this were addressed. As the administrative state grew larger and more complex in the postwar years, the functional agencies and bureaus acquired greater power. Integrative institutions like the political parties became weaker. Agencies and legislative committees established strong ties, further fragmenting and decentralizing authority in the new American state. The U.S. presidents found it increasingly difficult to direct the executive branch they headed. There were few government institutions with a mandate to analyze the economy as a whole or even to study problems such as those arising in the several regulated industries. The piecemeal expansion of government powers over separate segments of the economy had not added up to the power to observe general trends and integrate policy initiatives in different areas. Indeed, the institutions developed for partial planning in a specific sector of economic life often presented effective barriers to integration on larger issues. As long as the business system was prosperous and growing, this did not present a major problem. But in an increasingly interdependent domestic and world economy, the uncoordinated policies of a diverse collection of agencies proved a poor substitute for either market forces or a government agency with a general perspective on the entire business system.

The U.S. government came closest to achieving such an overview in its efforts at macroeconomic planning. Success in fostering a stable economic environment with conservative Keynesian fiscal policies had been an important ingredient in the overall success of the American business system after the Second World War. But effective macroeconomic planning proved difficult to sustain. In the late 1960s, amid intense political pressures for greater government spending (especially on defense and social welfare), inflation began to mount to uncomfortable levels. The beginning of the Great Inflation raised serious questions about the long-term outlook for the business climate in the United States.

President Lyndon Johnson (1963–1969) was caught in the middle of these pressures. Most of Johnson's political career had been spent in the Senate, helping to fashion the postwar corporate commonwealth. Not surprisingly, he refused to acknowledge the end of this era. The American system was, he insisted, capable of delivering guns for the war in Vietnam without straining its resources excessively; the industrial might of the United States could without question meet whatever challenges it faced. Communism could be stopped and poverty ended, without sacrificing prosperity at home. Yet Johnson learned all too quickly what the society as a whole was gradually coming to fear: there were limits to both American power and American prosperity.

The problems of the late 1960s involved the two most significant components of government spending, defense and social welfare. How much defense spending could the nation afford, and what were the implications of large military expenditures for the health of the business system over the long term? A quarter of a century of massive defense spending had already absorbed a significant part of the society's total resources and the trained personnel needed for advanced research and development. As defense spending for the war in Southeast Asia increased, and along with it the rate of inflation, these problems began to come into focus.

The debates on welfare spending were equally painful. Could the United States afford to finance a formidable social welfare system while the nation was accumulating substantial budget deficits and suffering from higher inflation rates? A series of urban riots turning on issues of social justice and human rights pointed to the need for measures that would deal with the problems of a no-longer-docile poverty class. But the price of giving these citizens a bigger stake in the system seemed to be an unbearable strain that might weaken the entire economy.

Several decades of heady prosperity and dominance on the world economic stage buoyed America's confidence that all these problems could be solved. There was reason to believe that U.S. corporations and the American government could cope with these challenges as effectively as they had the problems of postwar recovery and cold war containment. Even in the late 1960s when the country's economic problems were beginning to become obvious, international competition had not yet become so intense as to endanger the future of America's leading businesses. It was worrisome that small enterprises were having trouble raising venture capital and that some regulated businesses were in deep trouble. Growing tensions were evident at home and abroad. But not until the 1970s would the foundations of the corporate commonwealth visibly begin to crack.

# Part Four

## THE SECOND CRISIS OF THE

## CORPORATE COMMONWEALTH,

## 1970

## TO THE PRESENT

THE AMERICAN ERA was certain to end. As the world economy gradually recovered from the dislocations of the Second World War, renewed competition in international markets would inevitably reduce U.S. dominance. As raw-material-producing nations gained leverage over the pricing of their commodities, they were bound to assert greater control over the development of their resources. In retrospect, these changes seem natural and predictable, but by no means did they seem so as they began to occur. During the crucial transitional decade between 1965 and 1975, there were other more obvious problems—the war in Vietnam, the New Left and Black Power movements, the Watergate crisis—that occupied the public mind and preoccupied many of the nation's leaders. Moreover, a nation grown accustomed to a leading position in the international economy did not easily acknowledge that its economic power was on the decline. A business system that had been dramatically successful for a quarter of a century did not rush to make far-reaching adjustments.

Instead, the corporate commonwealth began to change slowly on several levels during the 1970s. Perhaps the hardest adjustments were psychological. From the president of the large corporation to the union worker to the consumer, many Americans had become very comfortable, even complacent. Just as the Vietnam War forced the nation to reassess its military and political power in international affairs, however, so the energy and environmental crises forced difficult reassessments in the nation's business system. Hard on the heels of these problems came the growing realization that U.S. business was vulnerable to effective competition from abroad. These challenges—any one of which would have required fundamental changes—together resulted in a mounting sense of panic. Shaken business and political leaders were frequently too quick to dismiss the historic strengths of America's business system and too eager to embrace new ideas borrowed with little discrimination from other nations. Suggestions that the United States could or should adopt radically different approaches to management or to business-government relations slighted the inherent strengths of the corporate commonwealth and ignored the barriers to rapid, basic change. The fascination with the "Japanese" or "West German" models of political economy seems at times to have deflected attention from the incremental adjustments which realistically and profitably could have been made in existing institutions.

Business organizations that had enjoyed several decades of sustained success frequently found these adjustments difficult to confront. Understandably, many company managers dug in their heels and resisted change, clinging to proven procedures and strategies long after the onset of difficult times. But the problems did not go away; the pressure for change mounted steadily. Regulated businesses like those in transportation that had molded political constraints on entry and innovation would have to learn how to compete; companies in mature industries such as automobiles and steel would be forced to give up attitudes and institutions they had developed during the flush decades after the Second World War. In the 1970s and 1980s, many American managers would have to relearn how to make their firms efficient and how to respond innovatively to new markets and intense competition from abroad.

The government as well as the corporation would have no choice but to change. Single-industry regulatory agencies would face strident demands that they alter their rules to allow more competition. In essence, these agencies were told to unlearn the lessons they had mastered during the Great Depression. At the same time, a number of new government agencies created to impose cross-industry regulations on business practices involving safety, health, employment opportunities, and the environment would force Americans to confront the choice between these laudable goals and the manifest needs of the business system. Finally, government-directed activities such as macroeconomic planning would also come under increasingly intense scrutiny. The government responded to these challenges by addressing whichever crisis seemed immediately most pressing—now environmental quality, now energy, now international competition. But as had been the case throughout the twentieth century, there was still little effort to use the considerable powers of government to understand and guide the general transition underway in the American system.

There was growing interest, however, in a more coordinated national approach to these problems, an approach that would involve new policies but also make use of the traditional strengths of the American commonwealth. The U.S. government and America's interest groups tended to lean in the opposite direction, away from a coordinated program. Yet even as the debates over the need for broader governmental powers continued, the United States had begun to define new accommodations among business, government, and the broader society. The outlines of this emerging order can now be seen both in business and in government.

# CHAPTER 9

# *New Directions and Misdirections in the Public Sector*

Aᴏᴏᴏᴏᴏᴏ BUSINESS conditions
turned sour in the 1970s, the tensions that had mounted during the
sustained prosperity of the postwar era could no longer be ignored.
Double digit inflation, an energy crisis, and international competition all put intense pressure on America's political leaders to develop solutions to the nation's economic problems. But the government's response was at first halting and feeble. Decision-makers
proved hesitant to reexamine the policies that had succeeded in the
previous decades. The fragmentation and lack of general direction
built into the public sector produced a debilitating confusion of
purpose among powerful but uncoordinated government institutions.

Beginning in the late 1960s, the federal government began to
grapple with some of the nation's difficult problems, but with
limited success. While macroeconomic management received a
great deal of attention, the results—including inflation, unprece-

dented deficits, and high levels of unemployment—were disappointing. Strong new initiatives in environmental policy met with a measure of success, but the price of these programs threatened to be more than the country's hardpressed firms could afford. Efforts in the energy field were contradictory and largely ineffective in addressing the underlying causes of the crisis. Moreover, these public policy initiatives introduced new uncertainties for business managers already struggling to cope with a complex, confusing situation. Gradually the postwar accommodation between business and government was undermined. In the 1970s, the traditional assumptions about business-government relations were severely challenged, but nothing approaching a consensus emerged regarding the proper role of government in the new order.

## MACROECONOMIC POLICY

Nowhere were the limits of the inherited government policies more evident or more troublesome than in macroeconomic planning. Of all the new functions of government that had emerged after the 1930s, management of the aggregate performance of the economy was probably the most important. In sharp contrast to the years immediately after the Second World War, the 1970s produced a disheartening record as the Great Inflation got underway. Unemployment was high by historical standards (see figure 9.1). Budget deficits were so large that they posed a threat to the business system for generations to come (see figure 9.2a). By the end of the seventies, the cumulative impact of government mismanagement of economic policy had generated severe problems for U.S. corporations operating in the domestic economy and in international trade.

The difficulties began in the 1960s, when the Vietnam War sharply increased defense spending at a time when a variety of new social programs were adding to the growing federal budget. The

### FIGURE 9.1
## Unemployment, 1945–1985

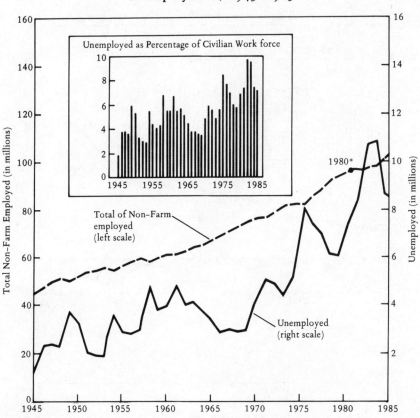

*All figures from 1980 on include the resident armed forces.

nation bought more guns and more butter, but at the cost of strong inflationary pressures. Presidents Kennedy and Johnson tried to control inflation by "jawboning"—urging corporate leaders to hold the line on prices—but even the most persuasive presidential arguments for voluntary constraints could not long hold the line on inflation (see figure 9.2b).*

When Richard Nixon assumed the presidency in 1969, he faced

*While "jawboning" primarily involved an effort to achieve government-business cooperation, there was perforce an implied threat that CEOs who did not help the White House deal with inflation could at the very least expect presidential criticism and at the most encounter some form of government retaliation against the company involved.

FIGURE 9.2

## Federal Budget Deficits and Inflation, 1960–1980

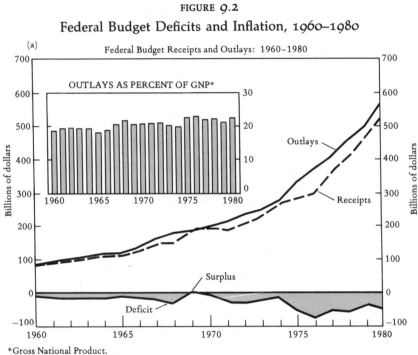

(a) Federal Budget Receipts and Outlays: 1960–1980

*Gross National Product.
Source: U.S. Bureau of the Census.

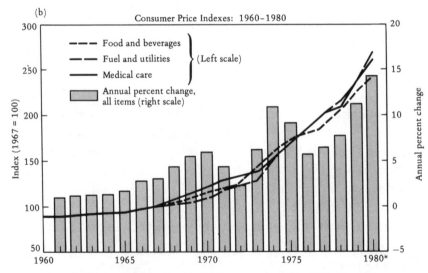

(b) Consumer Price Indexes: 1960–1980

*Annual rate for five months ending May. For 1980, percent change May 1979–May 1980.
Source: U.S. Bureau of the Census.

some difficult choices in macroeconomic policy. He neatly, if temporarily, sidestepped them and later used the traditional Keynesian prescription of budget deficits to stimulate a faltering economy before the presidential election of 1972. To reduce inflation, he chose wage and price controls. From the summer of 1971 through the spring of 1974, these controls held the line on prices and wages, but as always the rigid controls merely delayed the market adjustments that had to be made. They were, moreover, a departure in government powers unprecedented in peacetime, and few regretted the end of wage-price constraints in 1974. Almost no one judged them successful enough to recommend that they become a permanent federal policy.

The next six years witnessed numerous stops and starts, with each succeeding administration striking out in directions that generally contradicted those taken by its immediate predecessor. During the 1970s, presidents Nixon (1969–1974), Ford (1974–1977), and Carter (1977–1981) each implemented a different brand of macroeconomic policy. Each failed. To combat a persistent and debilitating "stagflation"—that is, a combination of high inflation, high unemployment, and a low growth rate—the government needed to develop new policies and apply them consistently over an extended period of time. Instead, the American government delivered a bewildering succession of policies that failed to confront the underlying causes of America's economic problems.

There were several attempts to correct this situation. Congress tried to foster more consistency and to enhance its own input into the budgetary process by creating the Congressional Budget Office (CBO) in 1974. The Office of Management and Budget (OMB) in the executive branch also took an increasingly active role in attempting to sort out the various spending and taxing proposals that poured forth from Capitol Hill and the White House. But still, most of the critical work of defining national economic priorities came in election campaigns, where political symbolism usually overwhelmed fiscal realism. Insulated somewhat from short-term political pressures by the fourteen-year terms of its members, the Board of Governors of the Federal Reserve had greater success in defining coherent monetary policies. But the Fed's tools, though powerful, were not capable of shaping the overall evolution of the economy unless they were used in conjunction with the fiscal program.*

During the Carter administration, Congress made one additional attempt to fashion a planning tool that could coordinate the government's policies. For several years, debate on jobs bills focused on the possibility of strengthening the Employment Act of 1946. But by the time Congress passed the Full Employment and Balanced Growth Act of 1978, the measure was even more ambiguous than the 1946 law. Instead of establishing specific public responsibility to manage the economy, the 1978 act used the vaguest of phrases, exhorting the government to

> promote full employment and production, increased real income, balanced growth, a balanced Federal budget, adequate productivity growth, proper attention to national priorities, achievement of an improved trade balance through increased exports and improved international competitiveness of agriculture, business, and industry, and reasonable price stability.

Business executives pondering this extensive list of goals could be pleased that they had only to develop for their firms a strategy that would balance the three major objectives of efficiency, innovation, and control. Compounding the problems for public-sector planners was the fact that Congress could pass the act only after agreeing *not* to define such words as "full," "increased," "balanced," and "reasonable." Government, the law proclaimed, should achieve these stated goals by relying "principally" on the private sector and by adopting fiscal policies that maintained federal expenditures at the lowest level "consistent with national needs and priorities." Boiled down to its essentials, this much-discussed act required an annual Economic Report of the President, which would enumerate statistical goals for the economy while explaining why previous goals had not been met. Explicit economic planning, as such, had yet to gather much support in Washington, D.C. All that the various interest groups and Congressional factions would approve was a measure that urged the government to adopt policies that would satisfy every important group of citizens in the country.

---

*Many reputable analysts would disagree strongly with this statement. The monetarist school has gained adherents in recent years, and the performance of the Fed in the 1980s has generated new evidence supporting that line of analysis.

By the late 1970s, however, the statistics on the performance of the economy were clearly signaling a red alert for the government's macroeconomic policies (see figures 9.1 and 9.2). As rising energy prices drove an already weak domestic economy further away from the levels of unemployment and inflation that had prevailed during the 1950s, economists and average citizens alike began to wonder aloud about the continued applicability of Keynesian solutions to the nation's economic problems. Something was wrong, but the experts could agree on neither the diagnosis nor the cure.

## GOVERNMENT SPENDING FOR DEFENSE AND WELFARE

In the absence of reasonable controls on government expenditures, the effective management of specific programs became all the more essential. But in the two largest areas of government expenditures, defense and social welfare, there was good cause to question the quality of the public management that Americans were receiving. In the 1960s and 1970s both of these "big ticket" items in the federal budget grew, almost as if increases were automatic and beyond control. Both had well-organized political constituencies with strong interests in increased spending. Both obviously had widespread appeal among voters; this was particularly true for defense spending in states that benefitted from defense contracts.

Defense spending surged forward in a spiral of new weapons systems and heavy expenditures overseas. Before the Second World War, the United States had spent a very small percentage of its peacetime resources on defense, but at the height of the Cold War, defense regularly absorbed about 10 percent of the nation's GNP and 50 percent of the federal government's budget. Largely as a reaction to the disastrous Vietnam War experience, these percentages declined somewhat in the late 1970s, but defense spending continued to grow in absolute dollars. Even when the United States finally gave up the war in Southeast Asia and withdrew, defense spending remained high. Preparedness seemed to be an infinitely expandable goal. Periodically politicians addressed the sensitive issue of the high cost of defense by calling for more efficient administration in security affairs. But these attacks of political indigestion usually passed rather quickly, leaving behind a large, expansive segment of American business—the "national defense industry"—which continued to function under rules and assumptions separate from those employed in the remainder of the business system. The hundreds of billions of dollars spent on defense in post–Second World War America were not available for other potential investments; nor was the technical personnel devoted to defense-related projects available for R&D in other parts of the business system. The price of national defense began to seem particularly high when businesses of the allies we were protecting began to push American corporations out of markets at home and overseas.

Defense spending competed for funds with the private sector and also with social welfare programs. The expanding Social Security system relied heavily for funding on direct contributions by individual workers and employers. In the 1970s the addition of new benefits and expansion of those eligible for payments, a trend encouraged by Social Security Administration officers, finally forced the system into a series of financial crises. Congress responded in predictable ways: task forces, tax increases, and a search for ways to improve the delivery system. A considerable amount of political rhetoric was directed at "cheats" who abused the welfare system. Meanwhile, the system continued to grow—in the late 1970s total welfare expenditures finally surpassed spending on national security—and the financial situation of Social Security became ever more threatening.

All these problems in government directed activities—social welfare, defense, and fiscal control of the economy—would not have been so serious had not the international setting changed so drastically. By the 1970s America's foreign competitors were thriving. American corporations were being squeezed out of markets abroad and in the United States. In effect, the corporate commonwealth lost most of its margin for error. It could no longer afford poor performance in either the public or the private sector. Government mismanagement posed serious threats to the overall health of the business system while absorbing a growing percentage of the nation's resources. "Politics-as-usual" in the budgeting process for welfare and defense assured considerable inflexibility in adjusting to changing conditions. Congress was practiced at adding benefits for defense contractors as well as recipients of social programs; it consistently refused to reexamine, much less to reduce or eliminate, these benefits. Meanwhile, growing deficits were fueling inflation and pushing up interest rates to uncomfortable levels. Business borrowing was adversely affected, as were the markets for venture capital for new enterprises. Instead of promoting national economic progress, government-directed activities in this new setting were becoming a millstone around the necks of American corporations.

## NEW AREAS OF GOVERNMENT REGULATION

The problems of business were compounded by the efforts of Congress, beginning in the 1960s, to use new laws to deal with a number of difficult situations that business and government had largely ignored in previous decades. As we saw in the previous chapter, business itself was in part at fault for not anticipating some of these problems and thus controlling the political responses. Government officials who had tolerated business's foot-dragging for several decades responded to mounting public pressures by demanding immediate solutions to a series of difficult problems. Policy-makers drove through a wave of new regulations in four major areas: employment practices, health and safety on the job, consumer protection, and environmental protection. Here the federal government made new rules that applied broadly across the economy. These regulations reached deeply into the decision-making process of most businesses, adding a layer of government supervision in areas where managers had traditionally enjoyed great autonomy. To enforce these regulations Congress had called forth a new generation of regulatory agencies, notably the Environmental Protection Agency (EPA), the Equal Employment Opportunity Commission (EEOC), the Consumer Products Safety Commission (CPSC), and the Office of Safety and Health Administration (OSHA). Each of these organizations needed specialized information from business in order to fulfill its mandate. The cumulative result was a considerable increase in reporting requirements for individual companies.

In the long-neglected area of employment opportunity, the government tried to reshape a century-long pattern of inequality for blacks, women, and other minorities. The Civil Rights Act of 1964 had created the EEOC with a mandate "to prohibit employment discrimination based on race, color, religion, sex or national origin." The agency was committed to reversing the impact of generations of job discrimination, inferior education, and a culture of poverty in the black population. Other groups grossly underrepresented in the skilled workforce—notably women—were granted new legal protection. Given the magnitude of this problem, it was hardly surprising that an agency intent on achieving quick results focused on the largest employers in the economy.

The EEOC wielded a heavy club in its drive for results, particularly after executive orders mandated affirmative action in government hiring and in hiring by concerns doing business with the government. While previous policies merely outlawed discrimination, affirmative action required employers to take positive steps to compensate for past discrimination against minorities (by giving blacks or women preference in hiring or promotion, for example). Because government purchases, especially those for defense, now reached so deeply into American business, affirmative action was quickly adopted by many large corporations. Historically, employers in the segregated South had acquiesced in the existing discriminatory social system, but they were now forced by law to institute hiring quotas and to implement new programs for training and promoting minorities. Such programs generated tensions, and these strains along with opposition to any new government regulations gave rise to the business rhetoric of resistance. Actually, as the policy was implemented, this far-reaching transition in hiring practices proved to be neither particularly painful nor expensive. By more aggressively recruiting and training women and minorities, major companies generally stayed at least a step ahead of the regulators. A good-faith effort usually satisfied the EEOC, which had far more work than resources. The resulting changes in hiring practices did not solve the broad societal problems of discrimination, nor did all businesses embrace the spirit as well as the letter of the law. But the improved access to new jobs was a significant step forward for the minority groups. At the cost of temporary disruptions in traditional policies, businesses were able to tap new reservoirs of talent and to contribute to the nation's progress in altering its historical patterns of job discrimination.

A somewhat different record was compiled in the area of pollution control laws. Until the 1960s the American public had largely given business the benefit of the doubt on air and water emissions. Efforts to force manufacturers to pay more attention to the environmental impact of their production processes had yielded few effective regulations. Growth, not clean air and water, was the nation's religion. The combination of individual self-regulation and weak pollution control laws had satisfied most Americans.

In the 1960s, however, business-dominated responses to environmental concerns gave way to a wave of strict governmental controls. Self-regulation and weak controls had not kept air and water contamination at levels acceptable to the society as a whole. Urbanization and the mounting level of pollution helped account for the shift in policy, as did improved scientific knowledge that made it possible to measure pollution more accurately and to analyze with greater precision its long-term effects. Increasing wealth in an era of prosperity provided the resources needed to address these problems as well as an enlarged middle class determined to solve them. In the aftermath of the Vietnam War a growing skepticism about large institutions also undermined the pleas of corporate leaders and their supporters in Congress for caution in passing new laws that would have profound influences on the business system.

The movement for stronger environmental protection peaked in the years 1969 and 1970. Dramatic television reports on substantial oil spills from tanker accidents and from off-shore drilling operations in California's Santa Barbara Channel fed the growing sentiment that something had to be done. Well-organized environmentalist groups capitalized on this support to organize effective, broad-based lobbying campaigns. These public-interest groups were successful in challenging business lobbyists on a broad range of environmental issues. Their success in setting the agenda of political debate and in using new legal and procedural safeguards to place business on the defensive altered—at least temporarily—the political balance of power on these issues. Business lobbyists long accustomed to sympathetic audiences in Washington and the state capitals suddenly faced an uphill battle in defending their traditional positions.

Elected officials ranging from liberal Democrats to conservative President Richard Nixon embraced reform of pollution control laws as an issue whose time had at last come. Those who opposed new laws or even argued for moderation found little support in Washington. Business lobbyists were powerless to stem the rush toward much stronger regulations. The environmental legislation in the years from 1969 to 1972 had an impact on business decision makers that rivaled that of any set of regulations in American history. The strict new laws forced managers to include in their calculations so-called "externalities"—costs (or benefits) that result from the activities of a business but are not accounted for completely by the business or by market transactions. The laws proved expensive and disruptive of traditional management procedures. Improvements in technology had long been the major means of improving efficiency, one of the primary business functions. Corporate R&D had been focused primarily on new products and new techniques of production, but now improved techniques of pollution control became a high priority as companies strove against short deadlines to meet strengthened standards on emissions.

The laws establishing new standards of air and water quality and timetables for achieving these standards in a sense embodied a form of affirmative action: they demanded that polluters not only move quickly to clean up their current operations but address the cumulative results of decades of neglect. These laws also created a planning mechanism—the environmental impact statement (EIS)—for anticipating the future impact of major construction projects. All federal agencies had to file such statements before approving any "major action significantly affecting the quality of the human environment." This requirement, a form of advance environmental planning, extended to all private projects applying for government permits. The law thus effectively encompassed all major construction projects in the nation.

The Environmental Protection Agency (EPA)—one of the most powerful regulatory agencies in the nation's history—was established to enforce this new array of laws. No mistake, these were "command and control" laws designed to force business to improve its performance in areas now deemed vital by the public and its elected representatives. The new standards were not created to persuade industry to cooperate; they were written to force the rapid adoption of technological innovations to improve environmental quality. Market-like regulations such as effluent fee systems under which polluters would pay taxes based on their levels of emissions received little support in the tense political atmosphere of the late 1960s.

In the rush to solve environmental problems, neither Congress nor the EPA gave much consideration to the long-term costs and benefits of specific policy choices. The overriding political question was "How can we clean up pollution most quickly, regardless of cost?" This approach reflected the optimism of the American Era and the "can do" psychology of a nation that had put men on the moon. Surely the corporate commonwealth was productive and innovative enough to solve these problems without any significant impact on the nation's productive capacities. On this point, the public was probably naive; it was certainly wrong—especially in the altered economic setting of the 1970s.

Consider, for example, the intense controversy over the use of catalytic converters to limit emissions from automobiles. After decades of allowing the automobile industry to proceed slowly on this issue, Congress suddenly cracked the whip. Automobiles were singled out because they were a major source of air pollution that could be sharply reduced through coercive regulations directed at a small number of manufacturers. After emotionally charged debates in which industry advocates found themselves with little effective voice, Congress passed the Clean Air Amendments of 1970. These stringent new standards mandated an approximately 90 percent reduction in the most dangerous pollutants from automobiles by 1975. The intent was laudable—to protect the nation's health and get results as soon as possible—but the means used reflected little thought about the cost or the effectiveness of the existing technology to control emissions. The standards were the same for all cars, and they were backed by the threat of fines of up to $10,000 per car manufactured or sold in violation of the law.

The race to compliance began amid much tension between government regulators and the automobile makers. About all that they could agree on was the catalytic converter, which most parties considered the best available means to make dramatic progress in meeting the new standards. This device could be added to existing internal combustion engines without fundamentally altering their design. The use of the converter did, however, require the phasing out of leaded gasoline. The road to compliance was quite rocky, and Chrysler, the smallest of the "Big Three," had particular difficulties in paying for the changes needed to meet these standards. After considerable confrontation and expenditure, the government's standards were finally met, with some modifications and several delays, in the late 1970s. The air was cleaner for it. But the automobile manufacturers complained with justice that the conversion costs—an estimated $500–700 per car—had weakened their positions at the very time that they were facing their most intense competition from lower-cost producers in the Far East. As charges and countercharges flew back and forth, the only thing beyond question was the fact that neither side could present a convincing social statement of the full costs and benefits of this policy innovation.

The building of the Alaska pipeline provides a similar example of how the new laws shaped business decision-making. The discovery of vast deposits of oil on the North Slope of Alaska in 1968 presented oil companies with both an opportunity and a challenge. To get this oil to market would require the construction of an 800-mile pipeline over terrain and under frigid conditions unlike anything in the history of the business. This was a formidable task, and the companies' specialists quickly forged ahead with plans for conquering the frozen reaches, imposing mountain ranges, and unpredictable rivers of northern Alaska. The Trans-Alaska Pipeline (TAP) was the most ambitious construction project yet undertaken by private companies, and it presented a range of technical problems—including those involving the environment—seldom before encountered in a single undertaking.

As history would have it, the TAP planners completed their preliminary designs just as Congress passed the National Environmental Policy Act of 1969, which required environmental impact statements. Suddenly the rules governing construction permits changed. Alyeska, the consortium organized to construct the pipeline, had to clear a new set of hurdles before it could begin construction. The impact statements provided opportunities for representatives of environmental organizations to challenge Alyeska's information and interpretation of the facts. Work on the project was put on hold as work on the impact statement began. A series of court challenges further delayed the acceptance of Alyeska's planning document, as did an unrelated court case involving preexisting claims on public lands by Alaskan natives. The resolution of both these disputes pushed the timetable back five years and dramatically altered the construction plans for the project. New safeguards for the fragile and largely undeveloped Alaskan environment were built into the pipeline's design. Even then, construction was begun only after the energy crisis of 1973–74 persuaded Congress to pass enabling legislation. The pipeline with supporting facilities was finally completed in 1977 at a cost of approximately $15 billion, a figure dramatically higher than the initial projections of approximately $2 billion.

The high cost of environmental protection was further illustrated by the unfortunate history of the Storm King power plant. Engineers at Consolidated Edison of New York conceived the idea for this plant in the early 1960s as the ideal engineering solution to the problem of supplying economical power to New York City during times of peak demand. Storm King would provide peak load power in a way that eliminated the need to construct numerous conventional plants. The idea was simple. A giant reservoir would be built approximately forty miles up the Hudson River from New York City, near Storm King Mountain. At night, water would be pumped through an aqueduct from the Hudson to this reservoir, using the idle capacity of a new generation of nuclear power plants. Then, during peak demand periods, water from the reservoir would be used to generate power for the city.

In the 1950s such a project would have gone from drawing board to completion in three to four years. In the 1960s and 1970s, it stayed on the drawing board for almost two decades. In a series of court cases stretching from the mid-1960s into the early 1980s, Con Edison never quite succeeded in gaining final permission to build the Storm King plant. Using the environmental impact statement and the courts, a variety of critics raised issues ranging from the destruction of the scenic beauty of the area, to the impact on fish life, to the potential harm to New York City's fresh-water aqueduct. As the dispute continued, Con Edison altered the plant's design to try to meet many of the objections. But compromise was blocked as much by the opposing world views of the opponents as by the specific issues involved. The firm's concept of progress through innovative engineering conflicted with the opposing concept of environmental quality as the overriding social good. By the late 1970s, the cases involving the Storm King permit had merged into a broader set of legal issues involving the overall impact of power plants on the Hudson River. In 1980, after eighteen years of futile effort, Con Edison's management finally decided to give up the Storm King proposal. Environmentalists had sued the project to death. Con Edison's managers had lost a traditional prerogative of utility managers, the right to choose technological innovations with little consideration of noneconomic factors.

As these examples indicate, the new regulations were achieving their objectives—environmental quality was improved to the benefit of all Americans—but the price was high. This new setting for business activity made innovation slower, more difficult, and more costly. At times, as in the case of Storm King, it made innovation impossible. The changes in public policy took place, moreover, just as the competitive pressures on American corporations at home and overseas were becoming intense. Before 1965 the American system could clearly have afforded these policies; after that date it was unclear whether or not it could. In the long term business would have to meet society's demands for clean air, soil, and water. It would have no choice in the matter, because the public seemed unlikely to change its mind about this issue. But at the end of the seventies it was not obvious that it could do so as quickly as government regulations required and at the same time achieve the efficiency and level of innovation it would need to compete in the new world economy.

### THE ENERGY CRISIS

International factors had an even more decisive impact on the country's energy policies. From 1973 through the 1980s, a series of sharp and unpredicted fluctuations in both the price and the supply of oil and natural gas jolted the United States. Coming on the heels of the environmental movement, the energy crisis severely tested the capacity of the political economy to cope with a complex problem that threatened both the nation's business system and its national security.

As the producer nations gradually asserted control over their supplies of crude oil, they built a new institutional framework around OPEC to facilitate international cooperation and cartelization. A succession of Arab-Israel conflicts hastened this process by creating unity among the Arab nations, a process of conciliation that then spread throughout all the member nations of OPEC. In October 1973, the outbreak of yet another war between Israel and the Arab nations encouraged the major Arab producers to initiate an embargo on oil shipments to the United States and other suppliers of military aid to Israel. With world oil supplies already tight, the embargo demonstrated the vulnerability of the major consuming nations to the cutoff of imported oil. When the embargo was lifted, OPEC quickly closed ranks and demanded much higher oil prices. After nearly quadrupling in 1973–74, oil prices remained relatively stable until 1979–80. Then the Iranian revolution removed large volumes of petroleum from world markets, pushing prices up to more than $30 a barrel in the early 1980s. In the short span of a single decade the price of the world's most important source of energy had increased tenfold. Fundamental changes took place in the flow of trade and of dollars in the world economy. In response, the U.S. government and the governments of other major consuming nations searched for policies that would cushion the shock of higher oil prices and reduce their vulnerability to OPEC.

Facing block-long gasoline lines in the winter of 1973–74, American consumers demanded quick action. The first response was to look for conspiracies and to blame "big oil" for the problem. President Nixon took to the airwaves to make hollow threats against the Arab nations before boldly proclaiming that the United States would embark on a crash program—Project Independence—that would eliminate oil imports by 1980. Having staked out the high ground, Nixon returned to the more pressing task of defending his administration against charges of misconduct stemming from the Watergate break-in.

Congress helped to make a shambles of national energy policy. The volatile debates on this issue splintered Congress by region, by party, by interest group, and by economic philosophy. At a time when unity of purpose and a long-term perspective were badly needed to address a real peril to the nation's business system and a potential threat to U.S. national security, the legislature failed to deal effectively with this fundamental transition in energy from surplus to shortage. Congress passed several major pieces of legislation: at different times it imposed price controls on domestic crude oil, created the Strategic Petroleum Reserve, searched for alternatives to oil, and fostered conservation. What was lacking was the consistent development of a policy attuned to market forces in the world economy.

During the eight years following the 1973 embargo, the government regulated domestic oil prices. The original justification for controls was the need to ease the runaway inflation likely to ensue from the quadrupling of OPEC prices. The controls no doubt helped to dampen the intense inflationary pressures from 1973 to 1981. But they had perverse effects. By limiting the revenues available for exploration, they stifled the expansion of oil production. More significantly, by holding down the price of domestic oil, they encouraged consumption at a time when other government policies were attempting to foster conservation. Moreover, the price controls were difficult to enforce. They fostered an adversarial relationship between the oil companies and the government at a time when national cooperation was needed.

The United States had little choice but to seek ways to reduce its dependence on OPEC oil, both in the long term and in the short term. The government was relatively successful in developing the Strategic Petroleum Reserve to deal with the latter problem. Vast amounts of crude oil were stored in salt domes along the Gulf coast, providing a form of insurance against actions of the producer nations. Although initially plagued by nightmarish technological and administrative problems, the Reserve reached more than 500 million barrels by the mid 1980s and promised to limit the short-term impact of a future oil embargo.

Considerably less successful were the long-term measures. There was much discussion of coal, of nuclear power, of solar energy, and of synthetic fuels, and the government subsidized experiments with each of these alternatives to imported oil. But the trials were sporadic and the government easily discouraged. Systematic, long-term commitments were not forthcoming.

The saga of synfuels tells much about the incoherence of the energy policies of this decade. As early as the 1950s, the U.S. Bureau of Mines had developed a program to produce fuel oil from coal and shale, but the plan had been abandoned at the urging of the oil industry. In the 1970s the program was revived, this time supported by private as well as public funds. Private concerns, notably the major oil companies, moved into this promising area of research. Finally, President Carter launched a massive synfuels program with the goal of producing 2,500,000 barrels of fuel per day by 1990. That objective was never achieved. When the OPEC cartel began to lose its grip on production in the early 1980s, oil prices dropped sharply, and the program was abruptly terminated despite indications that oil shortages were a predictable part of America's future. A good case could be made for investment in synthetic fuels produced from domestic sources. This policy would make the United States less vulnerable on the energy front. But almost fifteen years after the oil embargo of 1973 there was no evidence that such a program would go forward until the country had experienced another energy crisis.

Somewhat more successful were the government's efforts to encourage conservation of energy. Using a variety of programs ranging from tax incentives, to the speed limit of fifty-five miles per hour, to the publication of information, to laws aimed at making cars more fuel efficient,* the federal government tried to persuade Americans to change their long-established patterns of energy use. The most visible such program involved the automobile fuel standards. In the early 1970s, automobiles consumed approximately forty percent of all the oil used in the United States and almost one out of every nine barrels of oil consumed in the world. In 1974 the average gasoline mileage of American-made cars had declined slightly, to less than thirteen miles per gallon (MPG). One estimate

---

*In this particular case, government programs were working at cross-purposes. The anti-pollution regulations were increasing fuel consumption.

of the impact of doubling the gas mileage of U.S. automobiles projected a potential savings in twenty-five years of twenty billion
barrels of oil—double the estimated recoverable reserves of Alaska's
North Slope.

Congress moved on this front in 1975 by creating mandatory fuel
standards for American cars. The goal was to raise fuel efficiency
dramatically, from 18 MPG in 1978 to 27.5 by 1985.* The penalty
for noncompliance was $5 a car for each .1 MPG. This sliding scale
was meant to provide a strong economic incentive to come as close
to the standards as possible. A high tax on gasoline at the pump
would have had much the same effect, as European nations had
learned well before the 1970s, but Congress chose a less direct,
politically safer approach by placing the burden on the automobile
manufacturers, not on gasoline purchasers. In general the program
worked, reinforcing the drop in consumption brought by higher
prices. Fuel efficiency was improved, as mandated, at least until the
final increase was due, when the government gave the automobile
companies a temporary reprieve.

As part of a coherent program, this policy would probably have
been worth the additional costs it imposed upon the automobile
companies. But of course there was no coherent, consistent energy
program. Instead, the government tugged now one way (toward
conservation) now another (toward price controls) and then another
(toward greater domestic output). The internal contradictions were
reflected in and intensified by the varied institutions used to implement the federal programs. Before 1970 the primary agencies involved in energy included the Atomic Energy Commission (nuclear
power), the Department of Interior (oil and coal), and the Federal
Power Commission (natural gas). Government programs generally
were fuel-specific. In 1974 growing concern over the safety of nuclear power led to the creation of the Nuclear Regulatory Commission, and an impulse to foster research and development on various
energy sources prompted the formation of the Energy Research and
Development Agency (ERDA). Just three years later, in 1977, Congress collected many of the energy programs in one organization,
the Department of Energy (DOE). Still, the automobile fuel stan-

---

*This standard applied to the fleet average of each manufacturer. It provided a "back door"
to compliance, for a manufacturer could raise the fleet average, if necessary, by cutting back
on the production of the least efficient models.

dards remained with the Department of Transportation. The leasing of public lands for oil and gas exploration stayed in the Department of the Interior. The regulation of natural gas prices was lodged in the Federal Energy Regulatory Commission. As this hodge-podge indicated, neither Congress nor the presidents were as yet willing to make the hard decisions called for to implement a successful, internally consistent government energy program.

Left unresolved were the fundamental differences between the agencies involved in energy and those concerned with environmental quality. The decisions of the DOE and the EPA were often at odds. In several instances, notably that of the Alaska pipeline, Congress resolved the conflict by dictating a solution. In most cases, however, the need for trade-offs was simply ignored, and contradictory energy and environmental policies were supported. In an extreme instance, utilities forbidden from burning coal by environmental agencies could be mandated to burn coal by energy authorities.

This kind of confusion had always characterized American government, but in the late 1970s the costs associated with poor coordination of policy and weak leadership were higher than they had ever been. The public sector was now very large, and the direct and indirect effects of federal policies were greater than ever in our nation's history. The margin for error was also thinner than it had ever been. International competition made it essential that the United States develop a more effective energy policy, but with the failure of the Department of Energy to become a truly integrative institution, this burden fell back on Congress. Not surprisingly, the legislature continued to do what it always had done: it based policy on short-term considerations, moving only after issues had been forced to its attention by political necessity. In energy this meant a return to industry-specific legislation and a disregard for questions of long-term energy supply and demand. Congress demonstrated for all to see why independent regulatory commissions have been so popular in the past century. Faced with short-term political pressures, Congress was simply incapable of long-term systematic management of the complex technical issues that arose in energy policy.

By the end of the 1970s, it was obvious to most Americans that the country's economic policies had to undergo basic changes if the country's businesses were to compete effectively. It was not that all the programs had failed. Some of the energy and environmental policies had been successful. Job opportunities had been opened for women and minorities. Even the much-debated government bailouts of the nearly bankrupt Lockheed and Chrysler companies had met with success.* But the country's combination of welfare and defense spending with inadequate fiscal and monetary policies had fostered dangerously high levels of inflation and unemployment; the growth rate of the national economy was down, savings had been dissipated, venture capital was in short supply. Efficiency increases had dropped off sharply, as had expenditures for research and development. Neither single-industry regulations nor cross-industry policies were producing the results Americans wanted from their business system and their government. These public policies had been framed primarily in terms of domestic considerations; all seemed in need of refurbishing in light of the competition the United States and its corporations were facing in Europe and Asia. "Business as usual" was no longer possible. Disjointed, contradictory, and ineffective public policies had exacted a price from U.S. corporations, a price that many of them now had great difficulty paying. Significant changes were needed if reconstruction was to begin.

*The Chrysler policy is discussed in some detail in chapter 11.

# CHAPTER 10

# Reconstruction Begins

$B$Y THE LATE 1970s the American system was under tremendous pressure. Competition from overseas was undercutting many of the country's largest, most important businesses. Increases in efficiency, long the major source of growth in the corporate commonwealth, had declined precipitously; in 1979 and 1980, pivotal years, they evaporated entirely. If American firms were improving their efficiency, the results did not appear in the aggregate figures for the economy as a whole (see tables 10.1 and 10.2). R&D expenditures were low and continuing to decline. Inflation and high interest rates were weakening the position of established businesses and new ventures alike (see figure 9.2b). Spurred on by a dramatic increase in oil prices following the Iranian revolution, inflation surged ahead, accompanied by a disturbing deterioration in the nation's trade balance. Business in America was sick, and the nation's leaders—in business, labor, and government— were badly divided as to what should be done to cure the patient.

The next few years, however, saw the beginning of a process of reconstruction that demonstrated convincingly the single most important strength of the U.S. corporate commonwealth: its respon-

TABLE 10.1

Measures of the Problems and Progress of U.S. Business,
1970–1985

|  | % Growth Rate of GNP | Trade Balance* (billions) | % Growth Rate† of Productivity |
|---|---|---|---|
| 1970 | −.3 | 2.7 | .2 |
| 1971 | 2.8 | −2.0 | 2.9 |
| 1972 | 5.0 | −6.4 | .1 |
| 1973 | 5.2 | 1.3 | 1.7 |
| 1974 | −.5 | −4.5 | −3.1 |
| 1975 | −1.3 | 9.1 | 1.9 |
| 1976 | 4.9 | −8.3 | 3.5 |
| 1977 | 4.7 | −29.2 | 1.6 |
| 1978 | 5.3 | −31.1 | .5 |
| 1979 | 2.5 | −27.6 | −1.5 |
| 1980 | −.2 | −24.2 | −.7 |
| 1981 | 1.9 | −27.3 | 1.0 |
| 1982 | −2.5 | −31.8 | −.6 |
| 1983 | 3.6 | −57.5 | 3.3 |
| 1984 | 6.4 | −107.9 | 1.8 |
| 1985 | 2.7 | −132.1 | .5 |

*This is the merchandise balance.
†Output per hour in the private, nonfarm sector; per paid hour after 1971.

TABLE 10.2

Manufacturing Productivity Growth Rate of the United
States and Other Industrialized Countries

|  | Average annual percentage changes | | |
|---|---|---|---|
|  | 1960–1981 | 1960–1973 | 1973–1981 |
| United States | 2.7 | 3.0 | 1.7 |
| Canada | 3.6 | 4.5 | 1.4 |
| Japan | 9.2 | 10.7 | 6.8 |
| France | 5.5 | 6.0 | 4.6 |
| West Germany | 5.2 | 5.5 | 4.5 |
| United Kingdom | 3.6 | 4.3 | 2.2 |
| Italy | 5.8 | 6.9 | 3.7 |
| Sweden | 5.0 | 6.7 | 2.2 |
| Netherlands | 7.1 | 7.6 | 5.1 |

SOURCE: Sar A. Levitan and Diane Werneke, *Productivity: Problems, Prospects, and Policies* (Baltimore: Johns Hopkins University Press, 1984), 10.

siveness over the long term to the forces of change. The country's basic business institutions had, after all, been transformed twice in the modern era: once when the centralized combine replaced the entrepreneurial firm and again when the decentralized corporation became the normal form of organization among the nation's largest firms. Changes of similar magnitude had taken place in all three major areas of government involvement in the nation's business life: single-industry regulation, cross-industry policies, and government-directed activities. In both the public and private realms of the corporate commonwealth, change and not continuity had been an underlying theme of the nation's twentieth-century experience.

If the corporate order had major flaws, rigidity was not one of them, although there was some evidence of inflexibility both in the business system and in public life. The most obvious shortcoming was the lack of effective integrative institutions that would enable the United States to recognize the interrelated nature of its problems and to implement intelligent, system-wide solutions. In both the polity and the economy, there were abundant experiments with new organizations, new policies, and new objectives. But there were few means of generalizing those experiences, of translating micro-improvements into macro-advantages. In previous eras such institutions had not been needed. Piecemeal change had sufficed, and market forces had provided an adequate impetus to innovation. But now the playing field was political as well as economic, and countries with effective means of centrally guiding their business systems were providing much of the competition that was undercutting U.S. firms, even in their home markets. As yet unclear is the extent to which America will be able to develop institutions that are both suited to its traditional political forms and capable of making full use of the innovations that will make U.S. business healthy and competitive in the years to come.

## DE-CONGLOMERATION AND SCALING DOWN

In the private sector, several significant patterns were being traced by corporations bracing to cope with the new era of international competition. One such pattern involved a retreat back into traditional, core lines of production. De-conglomeration began to take place as companies spun off some of the diverse divisions and departments acquired in previous decades. The conglomerate style of organization had promised to protect firms against the product cycle in one industry, enable the corporation to sustain a high rate of growth, and keep the total package of corporate assets earning the highest possible return on investment over the long term. But along with this type of company came a new attitude toward managing. Instead of being product- or service-centered, as the best managers had been when companies were in a single line of business or serving just a few closely related markets, the top executives of highly diversified conglomerates approached their jobs as portfolio asset managers. They had neither the time nor the incentive to develop an intimate knowledge of a single product, service, or market. They tended to be dedicated to short-term earnings and insensitive to long-term growth patterns and the positioning of their organizations to achieve market and technological advantages. Conglomeration shifted the culture of management in ways that made it difficult for many U.S. businesses to compete effectively with foreign producers.

De-conglomeration offered one means of getting back to the idea that an automobile company should excel at making cars and a steel firm at producing metal. ITT, one of the most diversified of America's leading corporations, embarked on a major effort to spin off unrelated divisions and restore the company's central, unifying focus on certain classes of high-technology products and services for sale in world markets. Gulf and Western, which as a conglomerate had compiled one of the most dramatic growth records in U.S. business history, threatened to set equally dramatic records for spin-offs of diverse subsidiaries. Exxon, confronted by growing evidence of the poor financial performance of its conglomerate subsidiaries, sought to refocus its efforts on its traditional markets. The giant oil firm's experience with diversification into unfamiliar industries had been costly, and by the mid-1980s it had convinced management to move the corporation back toward its area of historical strength, the technology and markets of oil. On a smaller scale, Firestone, Rohm and Haas, and other producers narrowed their focus and attempted to improve their efficiency and innovativeness in the markets they still served.

The books are far from closed on these developments. Some longtime conglomerates such as Tenneco have apparently built balanced, diversified holdings that continue to be profitable. Other highly successful firms are still buying into unrelated industries, as was the case with Du Pont's purchase of Conoco. Then too some of the struggling giants of American business have found at least temporary solace in the purchase and operation of subsidiaries in divergent fields; this seems to be the case with the acquisition by U.S. Steel (now USX) of Marathon Oil. Despite these counterexamples, however, it is safe to conclude that the conglomerate fever that gripped U.S. business in the 1970s has broken. The main trend is now in the opposite direction.

In addition to concentrating on a smaller range of functions, many American firms are looking for ways to scale down their operations to make them more efficient and innovative. In an earlier day, as we saw in chapter 7, this was one of the rationales for decentralization. Autonomous divisions and central offices specializing in long-range planning were introduced to improve a corporation's entrepreneurial capabilities. By the late seventies, however, this type of structural change was being pushed to much greater extremes. Companies were breaking down authority according to their several lines of business or market segments. Discretionary power and responsibility were being pushed to lower levels of the firm. Many firms were being fragmented in the belief that "small is beautiful" and that only small units could be innovative enough to meet the challenges currently facing business.

Two successful companies that provided models for scaling down were Johnson & Johnson, a producer of pharmaceuticals and home health products (best known to the public for Tylenol and Band-aids), and Minnesota Mining and Manufacturing (3M), a manufacturer of various adhesives (Scotch Tape, for example) and technologically similar materials. At Johnson & Johnson, the process of subdivision into separate companies has accelerated in recent years. By 1980 there were in J & J 150 companies, each of which did its own research and marketing as well as production, and each of which enjoyed a high degree of autonomy. At 3M new-venture teams consisting of only four to ten persons worked as entre-preneurial task forces in developing an almost unbelievable range of new products. The innovative styles of these two companies were popularized by Thomas J. Peters and Robert H. Waterman, Jr., whose *In Search of Excellence: Lessons from America's Best-Run Companies* became a best-seller in the early 1980s. Their study was one of the most successful of a flood of books and articles explaining where U.S. companies had gone wrong and what they should do to recover their preeminence.

Although scaling down was one popular solution, managers in some businesses discovered that there were economies of scale, of scope, and of system that could not be ignored in the rush to become more innovative. Alcoa learned this lesson. In its basic processes of smelting and refining, the aluminum producer had more to lose than to gain by way of decentralization. The managers of post-divesti-ture AT&T appear to have reached a similar conclusion about its long-distance business. In the steel business, too, the international leaders were neither small nor decentralized; they were giant, inte-grated producers who in traditional ways achieved low unit prices by maintaining very high levels of output. In these and other cases, big was still beautiful, and so it would remain for the foreseeable future.

Even in these firms, however, big no longer applied to the com-pany's staff. De-staffing—in some cases cutting out entire levels of managers, especially those in planning and related functions—became a popular means of reducing costs and improving the firm's ability to innovate in a timely fashion. In the flush years following the Second World War, it had been common for busi-nesses to build very large staffs at several levels of the multidivi-sional firm. These staffs generated substantial studies of every as-pect of the firm's behavior, promising thereby to reduce some of the risks of decision-making. In the 1970s and 1980s, however, as competition became more intense, many companies found that they had to be more nimble in taking advantage of market op-portunities and new technologies. They could no longer wait to staff out the problem. Moreover, good decisions seemed most often to be the product of experienced, talented decision-makers, not cumbersome staffs. This aspect of bureaucracy in the private as well as the public sector had become the enemy of efficiency and innovation. De-staffing cut overhead costs and made for faster decision-making. The fact that Johnson & Johnson's central office included no staff planners was not lost on managers in other large corporations. At ITT, the chairman of the board, Rand Araskog, sliced his headquarters staff by more than half in the 1980s.

The new model is a lean organization. In the oil business, a wave of consolidations in the 1980s has been accompanied by widespread job reduction through decreased hiring, early retirement, and permanent layoffs (sweetened at times with severance pay and retraining). Even when jobs are not completely eliminated, managers have instituted "off-staffing" programs that use temporary workers or specially trained employees of independent contractors. The consulting business is also growing as more and more corporations cut back sharply on the number of regular employees they use. At the obvious cost of alienating the unions, such programs have lowered labor costs while giving management greater flexibility in deploying the work force. They have also provided new opportunities for entrepreneurial firms in the fast-growing service sector; relatively small operations providing consultants or temporaries have thrived by taking advantage of the efforts of giant firms to improve their productivity.

Reconstruction along these lines seems to have succeeded in making U.S. companies more efficient and innovative without increases in R&D expenditures. Funds budgeted for R&D (non-defense-related) have not turned back up after they dipped in the years following 1965. Nor is there any strong evidence that American business executives have become much more adept at the tricky business of managing research and development. Certainly some major firms have logged good track records in this regard, but many others have not. RCA, once an industry leader, bounced from one major disaster (computers) to another (the videodisc), leaving the company so weakened that it was obliged to accept a buy-out offer from General Electric. ITT had a similar (but as yet not so devastating) experience with a digital switching system designed for the U.S. market; in 1986 ITT wrote off over $100 million in losses on this single product. Managing R&D is an area of business performance where precious little of a formal nature is known; what we do know suggests that there are no major structural developments taking place comparable to the creation of the early industrial labs at the turn of the century.

Public policy, in particular tax policy, has certainly encouraged U.S. businesses to introduce new technologies. There have been some indications in the last few years that these programs are having their desired effect, especially when measured by aggregate figures on increases in efficiency (see the figures on productivity in table 10.1). The declines in the rate of increase in productivity that characterized the late 1970s have been arrested; the figures began to rise as the nation rebounded from the long recession of 1980–82. Robotics have become a watchword of the big three automobile manufacturers. New continuous casters are making their way into American steel mills. In large computers and telecommunications switches, the leading U.S. corporations—IBM, Northern Telecom, and AT&T—seem to have maintained their overall lead in the worldwide competition. Even in those businesses the margin has narrowed, especially in particular niches of the market. But progress on this front is clearly being made in the 1980s, as U.S. corporations gear up for what promises to be a long and difficult phase of intense international competition.

While some of these trends are largely positive, the rate of change—especially in innovative technologies and in increased efficiency—is still disappointing when one surveys the entire business system. The American response to the competition of the new era is still in its early stages, more a promise than a formidable movement. Some leading firms have made considerable progress in improving their efficiency and flexibility. Some have positioned themselves on the leading edge of the new technologies. But the majority of U.S. businesses are still struggling to adapt to the new environment, to find a workable balance between efficiency, innovation, and control. The current obsession with "self-help" books to improve management performance suggests the extent to which executives are looking for appropriate models to use in striking this balance. What many of these firms have discovered is that their major changes must involve not hardware but new forms of management and of labor relations.

## NEW CONCEPTS OF LABOR RELATIONS

The impulse toward improved efficiency has inevitably brought managers face to face with one of the most significant barriers to change in the American system: the traditional adversarial relationship between labor and management. From the nineteenth century to the present day, that has been the dominant type of labor relations in this country. It was confirmed in the New Deal settlement, the new institutional setting created under the aegis of the National Labor Relations Board after 1935. Labor unions acquired a stronger position in the marketplace and in politics. Management was encouraged to continue treating the work force as a factor of production to be managed, not as a source of ideas about the effective organization of the workplace. During the flush years of the American Era, many firms avoided conflict by buying off workers with high wages and benefits, and these patterns have proved difficult to alter in the 1970s and 1980s. No greater challenge faces the American system today than that of defining an equitable new accommodation between big business and big labor. Yet in no area does the historian's search for useful precedents in our past produce less evidence for optimism.

Bear in mind that our adversarial system does not embrace violence, any more than our adversarial legal system does. But what it does presume is a lack of cooperation between workers and managers as they each struggle—according to the rules, we hope—to achieve their own best interests. It is normally assumed that this is a zero-sum game: what the employers lose, the workers gain, and vice versa. As we have seen in the previous chapters, this adversarial approach is the hallowed, traditional style, as much a part of the American way as competition. From the early-nineteenth-century factories, from the immigrant work forces of the early twentieth century, from scientific management, from the welfare capitalism of the 1920s, from the government-sanctioned independent unions of the 1930s and the postwar era, we have inherited a system in which workers are seldom consulted about or held responsible for the efficient organization of their work. To tap this previously neglected source of ideas and to enlist workers in the search for greater productivity will require fundamental adjustments in our institutions and attitudes.

There are at hand two models of how this end can be achieved. One is provided by the U.S. factories of Japanese automakers such as Honda. This company's managers have tried to adapt Japanese-style labor relations to a predominantly American work force. Thus far, Honda has stalled the entry of the United Auto Workers union into its plants by granting workers wages and benefits only slightly lower than the union scale. Meanwhile the firm has encouraged the workers to be active participants in the company-wide quest for higher productivity and product quality. If such companies succeed in the long term, they will provide a tempting model for American managers seeking to escape the rigidities of traditional work rules and disruptive disputes with their unionized workers. A slightly different model was provided by A&P's successful efforts to refurbish its image (becoming "Super Fresh") and improve its position in the highly competitive retail food market. The company implemented a new plan for labor, sharing with the employees the savings stemming from increases in efficiency. While less all-embracing than the Honda plan, the Super Fresh model appears to be working, enabling the firm to cut its labor costs drastically and improve its performance.

Many other American firms are launching similar experiments, frequently looking outside of the United States for useful models. Firms in a variety of industries have begun to explore the so-called quality circle technique, in which workers have regular meetings to discuss what they might do to improve productivity and product quality. Many American service companies have traditionally utilized similar approaches in managing the white-collar work force, but few industrial concerns had even explored such programs until faced with the rising tide of international competition in the recent past. In the automobile industry, all three of America's leading producers have now experimented with cooperative arrangements to enlist the support of the men and women on the shop floor in improving performance. GM set up its first such program in the early seventies and quickly discovered how difficult it would be to reverse the flow of the industry's deepset adversarial traditions.

Labor was skeptical; managers lacked the skills and attitudes they needed to innovate in labor relations. GM created pockets of excellence but not a new system—at least not at first. The company persisted, working now with its new Japanese partners in production and attempting in some of its new plants to bypass the UAW entirely. The results to date appear impressive in terms of higher quality products, lower rates of absenteeism, and shop-floor innovations. Whether labor will ultimately be satisfied with these gains and the jobs they protect remains to be seen. Steel firms driven to the wall by foreign competition have also begun to try this new approach to increasing efficiency. In this industry the tradition of hierarchical authority and adversarial relations has been deeply planted and nurtured by decades of harsh labor strife. The accommodation that followed the New Deal and the Second World War was at best tense. Even today the businesses that have sought to use Japanese techniques of labor relations have experienced significant tension between this imported method and U.S. traditions and values.

The institutions most commited to assumptions and procedures inherited from the American Era have been the country's labor unions. Having fought for half a century to achieve a secure place in the economy, they had at best two decades to enjoy the full benefits of strong unions. By the mid-1950s the combined American Federation of Labor and Congress of Industrial Organizations had reached their peak membership of approximately 16 million. In the prosperity of the American Era, the unions and management seemed assured of a growing economic pie to divide. Understandably, the unions concentrated on getting a larger slice for their members. Productivity was a problem for management, not for the workers or their unions. But since the 1960s these conditions have changed drastically, and the prospects for organized labor are poor. The unions have been losing members, in relative and real terms, a trend that has accelerated sharply in the 1980s (see figure 10.1). Most new jobs in the recent past have been created in the service industries where the unions have frequently found it difficult to organize workers. Both there and in the smokestack industries where their strength has been centered, the basic problem for labor

FIGURE 10.1

Union Membership
in the United States,
1897–1985

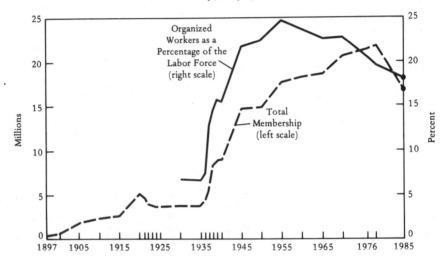

All figures are for employed wage and salary workers and union members.

organizations has been to find a strategy that will enable them to preserve their own position in labor markets while allowing U.S. business to respond creatively to foreign competition. At present this quest has been largely unsuccessful from the perspective of the unions. When companies are able to develop intra-firm circles and other innovations to introduce flexible, cooperative methods of improving efficiency, loyalty to the union has inevitably been eroded. The firm, not the union, has become the central focus of the worker's group loyalty. But where unions have fought the new techniques, they have faced an even worse fate: companies have either closed or moved offshore—that is, to other countries—where they can obtain cheaper, more pliable work forces.

The impact of these developments can be seen most clearly in the major manufacturing businesses. The extreme example of a union undermined by technological and economic changes is the Oil, Chemical and Atomic Workers (OCAW), whose strongholds were in the capital-intensive businesses of petroleum refining and petrochemical production. In the era from the 1930s to the 1950s, the OCAW established itself firmly in the industry's large manufacturing plants. The union's demonstrated ability to shut down a company's manufacturing operations with effective strikes was the foundation of its power. By the 1970s, however, automation made it possible for supervisory personnel to operate these plants at near-full capacity during strikes, removing the union's primary bargaining weapon. As the number of workers required to run a refinery declined and as more and more of the world's refining capacity moved outside the United States, the power of the union waned. A similar process undermined industrial unions in other, less capital-intensive manufacturing industries.

The move outside U.S. labor markets has reached formidable proporations in the past decade. AT&T recently responded to its new situation as a competitive firm in intensely competitive markets by shifting its production of telephone sets to Asia. The union—in this case the Communications Workers of America—had been unwilling to make concessions that would enable AT&T to price its products competitively with those of other major producers. AT&T responded by transferring its Shreveport telephone production to a new facility in Singapore. This scenario has become a common one in the past decade. The United States now has an older population accustomed to high wages and a relatively high degree of job security, whereas Asian, Latin, and African nations have younger populations accustomed to low wages and arduous working conditions. This situation hangs over the heads of American workers, forcing them to choose between making concessions on wages and working conditions or losing their jobs entirely. Even in some service industries—in the handling of bills and accounts, for example—recent advances in telecommunications and computing technology have made offshore operations feasible. Insofar as these businesses tend to be labor-intensive, more and more are likely to move outside U.S. borders.

In the short term, offshore operations provide American companies with an attractive means of lowering labor costs and improving quality control. But in the long term, this strategy might well backfire. The American market is attractive to domestic and foreign firms alike because of the buying power of American white-collar and blue-collar workers. When their jobs go to Taiwan, however, unemployed workers will not be able to buy new cars, wherever they are produced. This suggests that the only good long-range solution to the problem is for American companies and their workers to push down the trail blazed by GM, Super Fresh, Honda, Chrysler, Corning Glass, Honeywell, and many other innovative firms in recent years. If adversarial labor relations can be replaced by greater cooperation in the workplace—using, for example, the quality circle and production team approach, with or without unions—the American worker and indeed the entire nation will benefit. If in the course of this transition U.S. corporations are able to provide their employees with some of the guarantees of security that their unions used to give them, this new accommodation might well become more productive and perhaps even more stable than the New Deal synthesis was.

Public policy will, of necessity, play a major role in easing labor and management through this transition, just as the NLRB successfully mediated a new accommodation in the tense days of the New Deal. Without the active involvement of a revitalized NLRB—or another agency with an even broader mandate to oversee industrial revitalization—labor and the unions will probably find it very difficult to accept the trade-offs essential in the present day competitive setting. Management too should find it easier to negotiate a new settlement with active federal government participation. Otherwise the pressure to take short-term gains—lower wages, longer hours, fewer work rules, lower fringe benefits—will probably override the more difficult long-term task of engineering a new style of labor participation in the firm.

In the mid-1980s, all the major parties—labor, business, and the federal government—seem to be drifting toward accepting the need for significant change. Business has little choice. It will be forced to adapt to the new conditions in the world market for labor, if not through negotiated arrangements then through continued automation and offshore operations. Even devoted union employees will probably recognize, if they have not already done so, the futility of trying to freeze in place a New Deal policy that will cause a steady loss of jobs at home. The government has a large stake in devising a policy that will protect American jobs while encouraging U.S.

firms to become more competitive. The government can of course offer certain tangible trade-offs, including temporary tariff or quota protection for businesses in the transition period. Job-training programs are another possibility, as is a new policy that would provide workers making sacrifices with a government-backed measure of security. Using the Super Fresh model, employers might well be required to share with their workforce the gains achieved through greater productivity.

The NLRB experience provides a useful model in the 1980s. The Board established in the thirties a new forum for mediation and new, legally sanctioned rules for bargaining. The NLRB worked. The agency helped both the unions and corporations to shift gears and learn how to function in a new setting. Now that the environment for U.S. business has again changed decisively, another federal effort is probably needed if the corporate commonwealth is to strike a new bargain between labor and management. If anything, the task this time is even more difficult than it was in the thirties. But those who would focus on the difficulties of designing such a forum should consider the even higher price to be paid by all Americans if the business system cannot overcome the fundamental barriers to reconstruction thrown up by the adversarial tradition.

## DEREGULATION

In the public as well as the private sector, significant adjustments have already been made to the new era of international competition. One of the most startling changes has taken place in single-industry regulation. Since the mid-1970s, a strong surge toward deregulation has shaped the evolution of most of the industries subject to single-industry controls. As a result, many large companies active in transportation, communications, finance, and energy are now experiencing increased competitive pressures and much less direct government involvement in their operations. Although the long-term impact is as yet far from clear, deregulation of public industries long subjected to control of rates and entry is now an established fact. Deregulation is one significant aspect of the reconstruction of the American system that has moved beyond debate and into practice.

The first movement in this direction came in the airline industry in the middle 1970s. Since the 1930s the CAB had managed the airline industry as a cartel, with impressive results. Close control over rates and routes assured the profitability of existing airlines and the expansion of air service after the Second World War. But the lack of competition also produced some unfortunate results, which became the focus of much public concern by the 1970s. Much of the criticism focused on ticket prices. Consumers took notice that nonregulated intrastate airlines were charging much lower fares for flights between cities within a state than those charged by regulated carriers for flights of roughly the same distance between cities in different states. Passengers who flew frequently between the heavily populated cities on the East and West Coasts could not help but question why they should pay high fares to subsidize more costly service between less well-populated areas. With consumer complaints mounting, politicians began to take an interest in the issue.

An unlikely coalition drove this issue ahead. It included consumer advocates seeking lower costs and better service, conservatives concerned with reducing the size and power of government, and economists turned regulators who sought greater efficiency. Variants on this combination of advocates began to exert pressure for deregulation in other industries. Their crusade gathered support as the business system faltered in the 1970s. They were helped as well by the post-Watergate skepticism about government and the related desire to minimize its powers. Regulatory analysts reinforced the attack by describing how the "dead hand of regulation" had undermined the incentive to manage creatively, reducing innovation by the airlines and other companies. Secure rates of return and business as usual in a government-sanctioned cartel, the critics said, had stifled the desire to innovate and to achieve efficient operations.

The interest-group struggles over deregulation were intense, but the movement, with support from liberals as well as conservatives, proved impossible to stop. Not surprisingly, some well-established airlines (but not all of them) strongly opposed deregulation on the grounds that the industry was still healthy and in little need of change. Small carriers with ambitions to grow beyond their traditional boundaries disagreed. Spokespersons for cities and regions that had reaped the benefits of cross-subsidization favored the status quo, while those from the big cities that stood to gain dramatically from lower fares supported the movement. The political sentiment for change was potent. It culminated in the passage of the Airline Deregulation Act of 1978, a measure that destroyed the cartel and put the CAB completely out of business by 1985.

The immediate results in this industry and in interstate trucking (where the ICC had begun to eliminate regulation in the late 1970s and Congress had confirmed this action in the Motor Carrier Act of 1980) were encouraging if somewhat unsettling. As barriers to entry began to fall, new competitors rushed into both businesses. Prices readjusted to fit competitive conditions. An intense wave of competition eliminated some carriers and forced others to consolidate. Large businesses and large population centers benefitted. Small businesses and more isolated parts of the country lost their subsidies. Managers long accustomed to stable markets were hardpressed to improve the efficiency of their operations as margins narrowed. Labor costs were slashed, and longstanding union agreements crumbled as the cartels gave way.

In telecommunications, somewhat similar results emerged from an entirely different political process. In this case the Federal Communications Commission and the courts had gradually and hesitantly opened particular markets (equipment, then private-line service, and finally long-distance service) to competition. The hesitancy stemmed largely from the fact that the American Telephone & Telegraph Company, which had a near monopoly in all these markets, had long provided Americans with the best telephone service in the world. The Bell System was technologically progressive and was clearly the world leader in most types of telecommunications equipment. But AT&T was also the largest corporation in the world, and its size and reputed power—as well as its dominance of a vital, expanding industry—encouraged regulators and the courts to chip away at the Bell System's control of telecommunications. The Department of Justice also decided that AT&T had taken advantage of its powerful position in actions against its competitors and in 1974 brought an antitrust suit against the firm. When the suit was finally settled out of court in 1982, AT&T gave up its Bell Operating Companies (the horizontal component of the combine) in order to preserve its long-distance business and basic vertical integration (it kept Bell Labs and Western Electric, its research and manufacturing subsidiaries).

The immediate consequences of these decisive changes were in part similar but in part very unlike what had happened in the airline and trucking businesses. In this case the elimination of cross-subsidies pushed up the prices for local telephone service while cutting sharply the prices for long-distance calls. Equipment markets became intensely competitive, and for the first time foreign firms became major players in the U.S. industry. New firms rushed into long-distance service, protected by the fact that AT&T's prices were still regulated. The FCC, instead of going out of business as the CAB had, found itself fully occupied with the problems of trying to control a business that was partially regulated (local service and AT&T's long-distance service) and partially competitive. Looking over its shoulder and making significant decisions about these issues was the federal court, which still had charge of the antitrust settlement. Deregulation, in brief, was far from complete, and telecommunications was far less competitive than either the trucking or the airline business.

Deregulation in financial institutions also took place in a unique way. The process, which was gradual, stemmed in large part from the chorus of complaints by commercial banks and by savings and loan organizations that they were forced to compete on an "unlevel playing field." Security-oriented controls had fostered the growth of stable financial institutions that had proved quite profitable and reliable during the American Era. But new opportunities for profits created by the use of computers in filing and analyzing financial information gradually eroded the market positions of commercial banks, long the backbone of the financial system. Interest-free checking accounts had given these banks a substantial margin to finance their operations. But during the 1960s, first large depositors and then others began to find more profitable uses for their funds. In the following decade these banks and the savings and loan institutions looked to deregulation to provide them with the opportunity to recoup their position.

The impulse toward deregulation climaxed in the passage of two major laws, the Depository Institutions Deregulation and Monetary Control Act of 1980 and the Garn-St. Germain Depository Institutions Act of 1982. These laws and other regulatory changes encouraged three major trends: greater quality competition, as boundaries between once-distinct services were broken down; greater price competition, as interest ceilings were removed; and a trend away from geographical limits to bank expansion, as various types of banking across state lines were permitted. Consumers—in particular large corporate customers—benefitted from lower interest charges on loans and from higher payments for the use of their funds (either in checking or in savings accounts). A wider array of services was offered in more convenient locations. Bank customers had greater flexibility in the deployment of their financial resources. The entry of new competition in markets heretofore controlled stimulated banks of all sorts to adopt new procedures that appealed to their customers. A stodgy, complacent business clearly became more innovative.

## THE REAGAN PROGRAM

While deregulation fostered competition in some of America's crucial businesses, the administration of President Ronald Reagan, who took office in 1981, attempted with partial success to clamp the lid on social welfare spending and on the kinds of cross-industry regulations that businesses had protested about in recent years. Social Security had for decades been a politician's dream—benefits could be broadened and deepened at little obvious cost to any individual—but in the 1970s it had finally become an accountant's nightmare. The number of persons paying into the system had long been exceeded by the number drawing benefits. Social Security has *not* operated as a national collection of individual retirement funds. Instead, it has functioned as an administrative system for accumulating revenues targeted specifically for social welfare expenditures—retirement, unemployment, Medicare and Medicaid payments—and for transferring these funds to beneficiaries. Using this approach and combining an aging population with a lower birth rate turned out to be a prescription for fiscal disaster. The United States approached this state in the 1970s. Finally, in 1983, the administration and Congress, Republicans and Democrats, joined forces to reduce future benefits, increase social security taxes, and stabilize the System's finances for the near term. A long-term solution awaits some future administration.

The Reagan team found it painfully difficult to trim transfer payments, initially one of its major goals, and to relieve business of the burdens imposed by cross-industry regulations. In both cases, deeply entrenched interests fought successfully to preserve the programs they supported. Allied with the government agencies that implemented the programs and with Congressional representatives dedicated to their preservation, they were forced to retreat slowly but they held the line on most of the major policies. Pollution control provides an interesting example of how this process worked. Many businesses were opposed to the controls on the grounds that they were too costly in an era when U.S. firms were under fierce competitive pressure from abroad. Basically the administration agreed with these protests, and where the White House could control policy (in delaying the implementation of certain standards, for instance), it came down on the side of the regulatees, not the environmentalists. But while most Americans liked the president, they also favored the pollution controls. Widespread support and highly effective lobbying by environmental groups brought the Reagan campaign to a standstill. Some environmental programs lost funds; some were administered less vigorously than before 1981. But on balance the environmental controls that most Americans wanted—for obvious reasons—remained intact.

Even the calls to replace command and control regulation with an entirely different style of program failed. Professional economists led the way in arguing that market-like regulations would be more efficient than existing standards: they would minimize the social costs of protecting the environment. Proposals for regulatory reform centered around the idea of effluent fees. A tax system would be created under which a fee would be paid for the right to discharge wastes, with fees set high enough to produce either an economic incentive to save money by eliminating pollution or a source of government funds earmarked for cleaning up the resulting pollution. This approach had theoretical advantages over the command and control system, and briefly it appeared to be gaining political support. But the friends of the existing regulations beat back the advocates of this new approach. The nation had paid a high cost for the introduction of command and control regulations in the 1970s; as long as the existing controls seemed to be functioning satisfactorily, neither business managers nor environmentalists were eager to pay for the transition to a new fee-based system. Here, as elsewhere, the Reagan administration played to a tie, and the United States kept the existing set of cross-industry pollution controls.

Considerably greater success was achieved in bringing inflation under control (see figure 9.2b). Just as oil price shocks in the 1970s had fed high inflation rates, the precipitous drop in world oil prices in the eighties helped reduce inflation to more acceptable levels. International competition also helped. The Federal Reserve Board, working with the administration's support, used monetary policy effectively to reinforce the downward trend of prices. By restricting the growth of credit and the money supply, by tolerating a long recession with high rates of unemployment in the early 1980s, and by refusing to implement programs that would have accelerated growth at that time, the Fed and the Reagan administration squeezed the inflationary pressures out of the economy. Interest rates eventually came down, making it easier for businesses to borrow to modernize their plants and for consumers to buy such big-ticket, durable items as automobiles and houses.

All too often the automobiles were imported, but the administration moved—very cautiously—to bring the imports under control. In general the Reagan administration resisted the pressures coming from some businesses and unions—particularly those in manufacturing industries long shielded from competitive pressures—to protect their traditional market positions against foreign competitors. Nevertheless, several industries secured temporary protection. So-called "trigger pricing" was used with partial success to limit the dumping of foreign steel in U.S. markets at prices below the cost of production. The Japanese (after intense negotiations) imposed voluntary quotas on the number of their automobiles exported to the U.S.

These measures were designed to give U.S. companies a breathing space in which to adapt to increased international competition by improving their manufacturing facilities and operations. In automobiles, at least, the Big Three firms initially responded with strong promises to meet the foreign challenge on all levels of the market. They have since backed off from this strategy and are beginning instead to explore ways of striking alliances with their foreign competitors. GM, for example, is cooperating at least temporarily with Toyota in building small cars in Fremont, California. In the meantime all the domestic firms have upgraded the efficiency of their plants and the quality of their products. Nevertheless, in automobiles and steel the future of American companies is by no means clear. In the short term, public policy in the form of direct or indirect import restrictions will certainly play an important role in shielding U.S. corporations from the full impact of foreign competition. In the long term, the efficiency and innovativeness of the companies will be the deciding factor in determining the outcome for these industries. Today there is strong support for the policy of long-term protection. It may be necessary, its advocates contend, to match the subsidies and trade advantages many foreign governments provide to their businesses. Before dismissing such protectionist measures out of hand, Americans should reflect on the fact that one of the few trumps in the modern, high-stakes game of international trade is the U.S. government's power to set the rules for entry into the most attractive market in the world for many products—the United States.

## PROBLEMS IN THE PUBLIC SECTOR

Not all the recent developments in the public sector have contributed positively to the task of reconstructing the corporate commonwealth. The Reagan administration—like the administrations of the 1970s—has wanted to buy more than it could afford and has generated a continuing budget deficit that is unusually, even dangerously, large by U.S. peacetime standards. At the end of the

American Era in the 1970s, the growing problems of business were accompanied by a rising sentiment that new styles of macroeconomic management would be required in the "post-Keynes" age. The first major prescription for change came from Ronald Reagan, who put forward the idea that massive tax cuts would reinvigorate the American economy. A burgeoning business recovery would generate higher government revenues, which would be used to balance the budget. No one could argue with the inherent political appeal of this "supply side" approach to planning. But the miracle cure failed. In practice, supply side economics produced unprecedented budget deficits that posed a threat to the normal workings of capital markets while shifting a substantial bill for current expenditures onto future generations of taxpayers. The results were not all negative; the deficit fueled and helped sustain the economic recovery after the deep 1981–82 recession.* With considerable help from overseas, the United States was able to pay all its bills. But the long-term price for these short-term benefits—especially in the loss of flexibility in macro-planning—was and will be very steep.

Our recent attempts at controlling government spending have failed. The quest for better management of funds produced such experiments as zero-based budgeting, which was aimed at forcing government departments and agencies to justify every increase in spending; they did so. Agencies adopted temporary hiring and wage freezes until public managers learned how to hide new employees and disguise pay raises. Then, frustrated by the growing deficit, many of our political leaders turned to more radical solutions. For some it was a balanced budget amendment, which would in theory force Congress to do what it had the opportunity and the obligation to do already. Next in line was the Gramm-Rudman Act, which mandated across-the-board constraints on increased spending but which failed its first court test. To date, what Gramm-Rudman has inspired is innovation in government accounting techniques instead of good sense in the legislature. What such measures could not resolve was the basic split between a president who wanted to increase defense spending sharply while cutting non-defense ex-

---

*Although the Reagan administration explicitly rejected Keynesian prescriptions, the policies of sustained government expenditures and reduced taxes produced a deficit à la Keynes, and this deficit helped drive the economy ahead. The deficit (in current billions of dollars) was: 1980, 73.8; 1981, 78.9; 1982, 127.9; 1983, 207.8; 1984, 185.3; 1985, 212.3; and 1986, 220.7.

penditures and a Congress willing to go along with the first request but not the second. That stalemate, plus a significant tax cut, left the country with the largest peacetime deficits in the nation's history.

A second area of public policy that has had unfortunate effects on the reconstruction effort is antitrust policy. Under the Reagan administration, the traditional antitrust restraint on mergers of large firms has given way to a new sense of laissez-faire in the merger market. At no other time in the twentieth century, for example, would prevailing interpretations of the antitrust laws have allowed the acquisition of Gulf Corporation by Standard of California, a major competitor in an already concentrated industry. This new permissiveness has been justified by the need for consolidation in industries undergoing rapid changes. Market forces—as represented by the decisions of business executives and the availability of credit to finance acquisitions—have largely replaced government regulations in determining which mergers should go forward.

This shift in federal policy seems likely to have some favorable results. Institutionalized antitrust policy was framed almost exclusively in terms of a domestic economy; in the new era of international competition even the most powerful monopoly at home is not likely to go unchallenged by efficient foreign competitors. Moreover, in many industries only firms with very large-scale operations, able to afford high-technology innovations, and well suited to mass production and mass distribution are likely to survive in the years ahead. Insofar as the Department of Justice no longer attacks such firms because of the size and structure they now need to be successful, the business system will be well served, as will the public, by the new permissiveness. If this policy survives, the breakup of AT&T may well mark the end of that aspect—the structural aspect—of the American antitrust movement.

Unfortunately this shift in policy has also sparked a wave of hostile takeovers that have on balance weakened rather than strengthened the American business system for its long-term struggle in the international economy.* Boone Pickens and other leading

*The availability of large amounts of credit to finance acquisitions and the willing market for the low-grade ("junk") bonds frequently used to finance them have contributed to this development. But public policies at the state and federal levels have clearly been the major factor prompting the recent merger/takeover mania.

financiers of takeovers have defended their policies on the grounds either that the corporations they acquired have sluggish managers who have not made maximum use of the company's resources or that the takeover targets have been grossly undervalued. The market, they contend, should rule in the interest of stockholders, not professional managers. But the results have thus far not sustained this line of reasoning unequivocally. Companies fighting takeovers have overloaded themselves with debt (the "poison pill") or have bought off the takeover artists ("greenmail") to the detriment of their company's long-range financial security. Equally damaging is the manner in which the takeovers have driven managers to sacrifice everything to immediate considerations of return on investment and the enhancement of stock values. This has happened at a time when American companies need above all to develop effective business strategies for long-term positioning in domestic and foreign markets and for technological innovation. Although necessary retrenchment and reorganization have accompanied the takeover process in many companies, the price of such change—in uncertainty and wasted managerial energies, as well as in dollars—seems unnecessarily high.

Nevertheless, there is a strong possibility that the American business system will move in the direction of an even stronger emphasis on short-term planning and profits. Immediate market considerations will then dominate the system. Fluidity will be achieved by breaking up all those giant corporations whose parts can be sold for more than the takeover price. In this scenario the trends charted in our previous chapters will be sharply reversed. The types of corporations we have described have been successful by developing long-term business strategies that achieved a balance between innovation, efficiency, and control. These companies have accumulated and coordinated vast resources and have built up enduring corporate cultures that sustained their successful operations. If the vulture capitalism of the takeover movement is indeed the wave of the future, few of these firms will exist, an outcome that seems not to have been anticipated by America's current political leaders.

Even the deregulation movement has had some results that were unanticipated and that run counter to the budding reconstruction effort. Among financial institutions, for instance, the new competition has produced a rash of bank failures unmatched in number and size since the 1930s. The failures have severely taxed the resources of the Federal Deposit Insurance Corporation and raised serious questions about whether local and regional economies can remain prosperous when credit institutions fundamental to their businesses are unstable. In this setting, the near failure in 1984 of Continental Illinois Bank and Trust Co. of Chicago, which was then the nation's sixth largest commercial bank, splashed cold water on the urge for further deregulation. Continental Illinois had been a fast-growing, highly visible bank in the 1970s and early 1980s. It had used the new freedom allowed by deregulation to increase its lending in expansive industries such as oil. Signs of weakness in the early 1980s, including devastating losses on energy loans, precipitated an international run on the bank's deposits. At this point, the FDIC orchestrated a $4.5 billion bailout of Continental Illinois. After the regulators dictated changes in management, funding, and lending procedures, a considerably smaller Continental Illinois survived under the temporary direction of the government.

This episode helped persuade numerous experts to reconsider the movement toward deregulation of financial institutions. The suspicion grew that the pendulum might have been allowed to swing too far toward unrestrained competition. Instability in the nation's banking business—a business vital to the country's economic health—threatened to undermine the flow of credit and funds that fed the expansion of every other type of economic activity. America's brief experience with banking deregulation suggests that future generations of Americans may have to decide again how much risk society is willing to allow its vital banking system to incur.

Similar questions were raised about other industries. In air transport, Americans seemed to have traded competition and lower prices for less reliable service, frequent layoffs, and new concerns about air safety. A rash of bankruptcies and takeovers appeared to be working against the goal of creating efficient and innovative companies in this important industry. In telecommunications as well, fears began to arise that the United States may have given away its technological edge by breaking up the Bell System. What all these experiences suggest is that the new era of competition still calls for large-scale corporations that over the long term are innovative, efficient, and capable of achieving a stable accommodation with their changing economic and political environments. Insofar as deregulation drove some of the nation's leading firms away from an excessive emphasis on stability and control of risk, it served the nation well. Insofar as it has prevented those businesses from achieving the optimal long-range balance between the three objectives of innovation, efficiency, and control, some efforts at partial re-regulation or at government tolerance of private efforts to achieve the same end will probably gather support.

The various political impulses favoring deregulation played themselves out in an uncoordinated series of changes, pushed through here by a judge, there by a determined head of a regulatory agency or a congressional committee. There was little concern for the broad, long-term implications of deregulation of specific industries for the business system as a whole. Too little thought was given to managing the transition from regulation to competition. Missing was any sense of orderly, directed change. Some sort of oversight—either by Congress or by an agency designed specifically to monitor business conditions—might have reduced the transition costs of deregulation. A more gradual, managed process would perhaps have prevented some of the disruptions that accompanied the abrupt introduction of competition.

## CAN RECONSTRUCTION BE SPEEDED UP?

There are several ways that government might be able to accelerate reconstruction. The process is well under way in the private sector (although there, too, much remains to be done), but significant changes in the public sector will also be needed. Some are obvious. A healthy business system can probably not be achieved today unless the federal government can improve its recent performance in managing those activities over which it exercises direct control. One of the top priorities in future years will probably be a reduced federal deficit, which will again enable the government to use fiscal policy as a countercyclical tool of macroeconomic planning. To achieve that goal, government leaders will have to rethink the assumptions of our national security policies, which are still grounded in the conditions that existed when the United States was the world's dominant business and military power. America has lost its economic dominance; why should the nation continue to channel disproportionate amounts of its resources and technological expertise into the defense of allies who, less burdened by military expenditures, are trouncing U.S. firms in international markets? America's allies should be forced to share those defense expenses more equitably. This approach to U.S. foreign relations would reduce the power of U.S. leaders to shape world affairs, forcing them to consult and cooperate more actively with the country's allies. It also would significantly reduce defense spending and—if non-defense expenditures were only held steady—cut deeply into the deficit.

Consistent with that new concept of America's global role and capabilities would be a judicious use of protectionist measures in two ways. In most cases, protection, either through tariffs or quotas, would be employed (as it is today) selectively and temporarily to help ease U.S. businesses through reconstruction. Congress can probably achieve that goal effectively only by giving discretionary power, within specific limits, either to the president or to an independent agency. In a smaller number of cases, protection may be needed over the long term, because even the most efficient U.S. firms will not be able to match the low labor costs of some third-world countries. U.S. labor costs are being cut and productivity is being improved. But as we have noted before, Americans should remember that one reason their market is so attractive to Asian and European firms is that high wages here have long sustained U.S. buying power. The possibility of receiving protection—whether long- or short-term—could be used to persuade American business and labor to make needed adjustments in the adversarial system. It might also be employed to serve notice on foreign governments that the United States demands equality of access to international markets.

In addition to protection, direct aid to strategic firms can fit comfortably in U.S. traditions. Some large enterprises in important industries that need to be resurrected may need financial assistance such as the U.S. government gave to Chrysler in 1980 and earlier to Lockheed. Both the Chrysler and Lockheed bailouts worked. But every large enterprise that can present a similar reconstruction proposal cannot go directly to Congress for assistance. The country probably needs a narrowly focused independent agency, organized like the Fed or the SEC, to serve as a combined mediator and investment banker during this difficult business transition. The new agency could help a selected number of vital corporations reorient their managerial and labor policies and reequip their plants for new era competition. Like the RFC in the Great Depression, an agency for economic revitalization could focus on temporarily troubled companies that are deemed salvageable and important to the nation's economy. Such temporary aid would come with strings attached, as it did in the Lockheed and Chrysler bailouts. In effect, the agency would coax private interests to make the adjustments needed to stay viable over the long run in competitive markets.

It has also been proposed that the United States follow the lead of other countries and implement an even more ambitious program of government assistance and direction. This policy would provide the United States with the equivalent of Japan's MITI, a true central planning agency. Opponents of this concept suggest, however, that the U.S. economy is too large and complex, and that our traditions are too oriented to competition, individualism, and political independence, to enable us to use effectively a MITI-like institution. The objections notwithstanding, these and other proposals will be debated again and again, because the conditions of intense international competition that now exist seem unlikely to give way to another American Era. Whatever the outcome of those debates is, U.S. businesses will have to strike their new balance between efficiency, innovation, and control in the marketplace and the polity under intense competitive pressure. They will be able to return neither to J. P. Morgan's world nor to the American Era. All that we can be certain of today is that the processes of reconstructing the corporate economy and the American commonwealth are well underway in a nation with all the resources it needs to complete those tasks. The history of the corporate commonwealth strongly suggests that those resources will be used effectively and reconstruction will succeed, as it already has in some of America's leading enterprises.

# CHAPTER 11

# The World
# According to Iacocca

HE WALKS toward you, explaining his product and the company that makes it. Square-faced, serious. He is an intense and vigorous salesman. The CEO and spokesman for one of the country's leading industrial firms, he is also a fitting symbol for the reconstruction of the corporate commonwealth. If you have not seen one of the commercials Lee Iacocca has made for Chrysler automobiles, you have probably not been watching network television in the 1980s. If you have, you know quite well the image this chief executive officer conveys: honesty, dynamism, the common touch, an earnest desire to communicate directly with you, the American consumer. "If you can find a better car," he says, "buy it."

The same man smiles at you from the shelf of your corner bookstore. *Iacocca—An Autobiography* was a wildly successful best-seller, already translated into several foreign languages. On the book jacket, the shirt-sleeved author smiles as he leans back in his chair with his hands behind his head. He looks successful and satisfied with himself. He is pictured on the back of the jacket taking his mother back to Ellis Island, where she had disembarked when she immigrated from Italy sixty-three years ago. You can understand why Iacocca put so much energy into the campaign to refurbish the Statue of Liberty in time for its centennial celebration. Making it in America has long been the immigrant dream, and Iacocca has made it to the top of the American business system.

In his own way he has been as successful as J.P. Morgan was in 1900, and in certain regards the two men are similar. Intense men, they dedicated most of their lives to their business. While they accepted substantial civic responsibilities, they above all focused their immense energies upon their careers in America's emerging corporate system and pursued singular visions of how that system should function. Both men were unusually successful in picking the associates to whom they assigned crucial tasks in their business activities. While Iacocca makes less of a fuss about "character" than Morgan did, he has been no less assertive about the role that his carefully selected colleagues played in his successful effort to rebuild the Chrysler Corporation. This ability to make good choices about other men and women and to mold an effective corporate team eludes precise definition and probably cannot be taught. But in the careers of these two outstanding men, it has clearly been a major reason for their success.

In some regards, too, both men viewed the proper role of government in the United States as that of a junior partner to business. The future, in this construct, is primarily dependent upon what happens in the private sector. Without the profits of corporate enterprise, without efficient business systems, without innovative firms, the United States cannot be successful in the twentieth century. Government can help—and about the precise nature of that help they would strongly disagree—but ultimately only good business performance can provide the country with the jobs and the goods and services it needs in order to have a secure future. In that sense both men exemplify the sort of ideology which has been one of the foundation stones of the American system.

So much for similarities. The differences between Morgan and Iacocca are far more prominent, and they capture to a considerable degree the changes that have taken place in the corporate commonwealth in the decades since 1900. The society, the economy, and the polity have all been transformed. By 1980 the social distance between a top business leader and the workers in the factories was no longer so great as it had been in 1900. While Iacocca can use a company airplane for his business trips, so can the union leaders with whom he has to deal. Iacocca's economic system is also incredibly complex by Morgan's standards. Instead of the simple concentric circles of the Morgan-centered universe, the Iacocca economy would have to be compared to a great galaxy of organizations, including numerous, largely autonomous solar systems. At the center of the American system is the government, not the investment banks. In Iacocca's world the modern administrative state is fully articulated, a participant in almost all the major business decisions a corporate leader has to make. Outside the American system is an international economy that is beyond the control—although not the influence—of even the most powerful of America's political or business leaders.

Morgan's environment was different, as was his career. As an investment banker, he was in a strategic, central role in the entire U.S. economy—especially in the vital sectors of his time, transportation and manufacturing. By contrast, Iacocca built his career in a single industry, automobiles. He spent most of his career earning a salary, moving up through the executive ranks at the Ford Motor Company. Marketing was his forte. Despite his engineering background he was above all a salesman, although by his own account he was not a natural. He learned his art from a number of talented mentors.

Iacocca's career at Ford stretched from 1946 to 1978, following the great parabola the U.S. industry made from postwar expansion through ascendancy in world markets to the beginnings of decline. These were the years at Ford when Henry Ford II and the so-called Whiz Kids were introducing modern techniques of management, the Sloan-GM system of decentralization and control (see chapter 7). As Ford became a modern corporation, one of the largest in the world, Iacocca climbed the corporate ladder from salesman to zone manager, to district manager, and by 1956 to divisional head of car and truck sales. His goal? "At that time . . . it wasn't prestige or power I wanted. It was money."

Money he made. By the age of thirty-six, this son of Italian immigrants was running the Ford Division, with 11,000 employees. He had become an expert on managerial talent and motivation and had built effective teams that developed and produced the Mustang, a car that required an initial investment of seventy-five million dollars and made net profits of $1.1 billion for the firm. In 1970 accomplishments such as these persuaded the Board of Directors and Henry Ford II to appoint Iacocca president of Ford. He was earning about a million dollars a year by mid-decade and could proudly point to the fact that under his leadership the company had compiled the best earnings record it had ever enjoyed. He had cut costs, encouraged his managers to be more decisive, and spun off the losers (largely in the appliance and electronics operations) in this diversified corporation. Despite the oil crisis in 1973 and the invasion of U.S. markets by the mini-cars, both Ford and its president made a great deal of money in those years.

Pride came before a fall. Iacocca's performance and the company's earnings records could not protect him when Henry Ford II turned against him. In 1978 Iacocca suddenly found himself out of work, fired from the top position in the company. He was dismayed by a turn of the wheel that J.P. Morgan could not have contemplated, let alone experienced. Perhaps this helps explain the thin thread of insecurity that one senses in the man. After all, he is the self-made man who pushed himself up from an immigrant background to the top of one of the country's most formidable businesses. He is also the quintessential salesman and like most, he has a touch of Willy Loman in his personality.* Oriented toward the people (his customers), determined to be liked, and braced for the inevitable rejections, the salesman is perforce what sociologist David Riesman once called an "other-directed" person. Morgan was an "inner-directed" man, determined to shape the world according to that innate sense of order that he brought to all his activities. Morgan paid a price for that, his severe migraines, but he certainly did not worry about whether he was liked. Iacocca clearly does.

In 1978, he was certainly not liked by Henry Ford II, and Iacocca

*Willy Loman is the central character in Arthur Miller's magnificent drama *Death of a Salesman.*

had to decide what to do with the rest of his life. He was already wealthy. But he decided to stay in business and to stay in the automobile industry: "cars were in my blood." In that same year he took command of the ailing Chrysler Corporation, a large diversified manufacturing firm that was on the brink of bankruptcy.

Thus began one of American business's most intriguing tales of corporate revival. Chrysler's problems had been mounting for more than a decade. In the 1960s and 1970s the company's managers had focused on the production of large cars while providing a full line of models in the tradition of Alfred Sloan. In addition, they had overextended the company with a series of international investments. To the problems caused by this questionable strategy were added the obligations of meeting government-mandated standards for both emissions control and fuel efficiency during the 1970s. All this had to be done in a period of high inflation and amid growing pressures from Japanese imports. Iacocca arrived at Chrysler to find a company in total disarray from top to bottom. The secretaries were "goofing off" and the executives casually used the president's office as a shortcut to the coffee machine. "Dry rot." "Anarchy."

Iacocca set out to provide the company with a prescription that J. P. Morgan would have approved: "a dose of order and discipline—and quick." While Chrysler's new head had cut costs before, his career had been largely focused on sales, not questions of administrative order and efficiency. He scorned financial officers who were obsessed with these matters as "bean counters." They were by nature "defensive, conservative, and pessimistic." "Salesmen," he opined, were "aggressive, speculative, and optimistic"—that is, like Iacocca. But at Chrysler reorganization had to be the order of the day. New financial controls were introduced. Coordination was achieved between departments heretofore operated as separate feudal domains. Inventory was brought under tight control, as was quality in the production process. Purchasing was systematized and the firm's marketing refurbished. The company was top-heavy, and many staff positions simply had to be eliminated, along with the managers who held the jobs. Very quickly these measures began to show up in the ledger books as savings of about $600 million a year. In a period of four years, the corporation cut its break-even point from 2.3 million to 1.1 million cars and trucks.

Iacocca built up an entirely new managerial team. He drew many of his experienced executives from Ford and some from General Motors. Meanwhile, he fired thirty-three of the company's thirty-five vice presidents in an effort to clear out the "dry rot" and instill a new sense of mission, cooperation, and accomplishment. One can imagine the strain this created for a man who wanted to be liked as well as respected. This aspect of his personality showed in his favorite managerial technique, the quarterly review system. Every manager had to set personal goals for the next quarter and then review with his or her boss the extent to which these objectives had been accomplished. This plan kept a dialogue going between the executives. It gave each manager a precise set of personal targets and a sense of immediacy about his or her performance. It also neatly shifted the psychological burden of monitoring behavior down from the boss to the manager, just as surely as the scientific management of J. P. Morgan's era had transferred the burden of decision-making up from the foreman to the boss.

Despite these innovations and the success Chrysler enjoyed with its new line of K-cars, Iacocca found himself in a severe financial bind in 1979 and 1980. He had sold off the company's lucrative tank division and laid off 7,000 blue- and white-collar workers, but the recession and oil crisis had dampened the market for American automobiles. Faced with the possibility of bankruptcy, Iacocca took a step that Morgan would have found almost impossible to understand, let alone accept: he went to Washington to sell the federal government on the idea of a guaranteed loan that would carry Chrysler through its fiscal crisis.

The arguments against the bailout were powerful. How could a democratic government give credit to Chrysler while it allowed thousands of smaller enterprises to fail? Should not Chrysler's managers and stockholders pay the price for their errors? In the future how would the United States ever stop pouring public funds down the rathole of failing companies? As William Proxmire explained, "We live in a free enterprise economy, and free enterprise means the freedom to fail as well as the freedom to profit." Many prominent business leaders and academicians went public, using newspaper advertisements to urge Congress to let Chrysler survive or die without government assistance.

Iacocca and his supporters countered with a full-barreled lobbying and public relations campaign. The government, they said, should be willing to provide temporary assistance to a company driven to the wall *in part* by regulatory demands for cleaner emissions, higher fuel economy, and greater safety. They reminded Congress that government had been helping businesses, farms, and other Americans for many years. Chrysler deserved assistance now because it was in a central position in a vital industry under seige by aggressive foreign competitors. It was a major defense contractor. As a Department of Transportation study indicated, a Chrysler failure would cause the loss of about 300,000 jobs, a 1.5 percent decline in the GNP, a $1.5 billion increase in welfare benefits, and a $1.5 billion loss on the U.S. balance of payments. Unemployment in Detroit would jump from 9 percent to 15–16 percent. These harsh statistics were persuasive, as was Lee Iacocca. As he later explained, his Dale Carnegie training helped him frame the issues in terms acceptable to Congress. He left the nation's capitol with one and a half billion dollars in loan guarantees granted on the condition that Chrysler would raise a similar sum in private financial markets. He quickly converted these pledges into the cash the business needed to turn the corner to profitability.

Before that corner was passed, however, Iacocca had introduced another round of cost-cutting measures that he sold as "equality of sacrifice." He shrewdly started with his own salary and the salaries of his fellow executives. The union had to take sharp cutbacks as well; some plants had to be closed; and the banks that had lent money to Chrysler had to scale down their demands significantly. Other innovations followed. A representative of organized labor was added to the company's board of directors, and a stock ownership plan for workers—reminiscent of the 1920s—was introduced. Labor paid a big price for these changes. Well-established work rules were junked, and the wage/benefit concessions cost the average worker thousands of dollars of income during the first two years of the turnaround.

By 1983 these several measures were paying off in profitable operations. Iacocca had struck the right balance, making Chrysler a more efficient and innovative business without losing sight of the giant corporation's need to have a measure of stability in its domestic markets and political relationships. He focused his business on a narrower range of products, reversing a long tradition of competing with GM and Ford with cars of all sizes. Concentrating on a smaller number of cars seemed to help the firm become more innovative, and Chrysler led the world in the development of popular "mini-vans." As Iacocca explained, Chrysler now had the right "people, product, and profits." In a stunning grandstand move, Iacocca, the master of public relations, paid back the entire government-guaranteed loan seven years before it was due! The publicity associated with that unexpected maneuver, along with his effective TV ads and his activities on behalf of the restoration of the Statue of Liberty, prompted media discussion of Iacocca as a political candidate. As is usual in such cases, he was ticketed at once for the top job, the presidency. While Iacocca denied any ambitions for elective office, the speculation about his political future continued—as did his columns and speeches outlining proposals for reconstructing the U.S. economy.

Iacocca is, after all, a man with a political program, a platform announced in his best-selling autobiography. His proposals provide an interesting guide to many of the significant structural changes that have taken place in the American political economy between 1900 and the 1980s. Iacocca is a frank advocate of national planning, of his own form of industrial policy. All large organizations plan for a successful future, he says, and the United States government must do that as well. The Japanese challenge makes such planning inevitable. For a planning agency he looks to a Critical Industries Commission. In the New Deal's NRA style, the Commission would bring together labor, management, and government to develop plans for economic recovery in industries willing to adopt the Chrysler model of "equality of sacrifice among management, labor, suppliers, and financial backers." Protection would be provided for those industries and others; it is time, he says, to limit very carefully the foreign share of the U.S. market. Meanwhile, the government needs to ensure energy independence, limit federal entitlement programs,* promote technological advances, and restore our

---

*These are social programs—Social Security, for instance—under which beneficiaries are entitled to the specified benefits without the passage of an appropriations measure by Congress.

transportation infrastructure. Labeled "a Marshall Plan for America," Iacocca's program would embrace some of the policies being promoted in Washington today by the Reagan administration—policies discussed in the previous chapter. But Iacocca would combine them with a far more positive role in economic planning than the current administration has advocated.

Seen in the light of our review of the rise of the corporate commonwealth, Iacocca's program of direct assistance would be well within American traditions. Periodically, the United States has developed new institutions and refurbished old ones to cope with a changing economic setting. Business executives themselves have been some of the most creative institutional innovators. They have developed a new business organization—the centralized combine—and then replaced it with another type of private bureaucracy, the decentralized firm. These two forms of organization have been vital elements in U.S. business success during this century. Along the way, business managers balanced the goals of control, efficiency, and innovation in ways that promoted the growth of the American economy. They developed multinational operations that carried U.S. products and business techniques around the world. They internalized the R&D function and helped to improve the nation's productivity and products, keys to higher income in the past eight decades.

No less impressive have been the innovations in the country's political institutions. In the past century Americans have built and then rebuilt a new administrative state. The rise and fall of the independent regulatory commission played an important part in that history, as did the pioneering ventures in the promotion of science and engineering through government support. Through single-industry regulation, cross-industry policies, and direct government involvement, Americans have built a tradition of and acquired substantial experience in planning for their business system. Many of those policies have been successful over the long term. All have from time to time logged impressive accomplishments that, like the innovations in the private sector, have become constituent elements of the American commonwealth. It is that experience that Iacocca and others would exploit in pushing forward with economic reconstruction.

If that course is adopted—and it is only one of several possibilities, as we have seen—it will be essential for Iacocca and others to recognize two additional lessons that our history teaches us. One is that you cannot, à la Iacocca, revitalize the government side of our business-government relations merely by taking a new team of aggressive, experienced corporate executives to Washington and turning them loose. "With twenty-five of these guys," Iacocca tells us, "I could run the government of the United States." Alas, it has been tried—repeatedly. It always fails, for reasons that should be obvious to the readers of this history. The U.S. government balances goals, just as business leaders do, but in the case of government the constituencies are so varied and their objectives so complex that no team of Whiz Kids—even the Best and the Brightest—can possibly satisfy all their needs and quickly drive the government down a new path to more efficient operations. America's political institutions have been molded by these group needs, and while few citizens may be satisfied with all the results, that is the price of having representative government.

A second lesson involves the fundamental changes that are required in labor-management relations in this country. History teaches us that this transition will be painful and costly to complete. It is far from complete today. Iacocca himself illustrates why American managers will find it as difficult as organized labor will to make this change. Iacocca has promoted the quality circle plan and dealt effectively with organized labor—even placing a UAW representative on the board—during the recovery phase at Chrysler. But he is more critical of than sympathetic with labor's problems during the turmoil of reconstruction. His ideas are grounded in the traditional adversarial relations that American firms can no longer afford to sustain. One can understand, then, why Chrysler might slip back into the customary mode of labor-management relations once the immediate crisis had passed. But American business needs something more than a temporary fix; it needs a long-term transformation to a new mode of labor relations.

Still, the Iacocca saga illustrates just how far American corporations have come and how much the nation's political institutions have changed as reconstruction got underway. There is every reason to believe that the task can be finished. America's track record suggests that similar transitions have taken place before in the past century and that the previous institutional accommodations between business and government were relatively successful. By the end of the Progressive Era just such a new balance of forces and goals had been created. Again, in the 1930s and 1940s the American system changed dramatically and laid the foundation for the country's postwar economic success. By the 1970s that accommodation had been undercut by a shifting international environment, and today the United States has just begun another era of major institutional change. As history indicates, fundamental adjustments of this sort have been—and no doubt will continue to be—the essence of the American experience.

# Suggestions for Further Reading

The serious reader interested in probing more deeply into the two subjects surveyed in this book—business history and business-government relations—will not want for additional books and articles. So voluminous is the literature that a short guide to some of the most important and readily available publications is all that we can provide here. We have not tried to be complete, nor have we mentioned all the materials we drew upon in writing *The Rise of the Corporate Commonwealth*. Instead, we have tried to indicate materials that are likely to be accessible and interesting to our readers.

Those who are indeed seriously concerned with the history of American business should turn first to the single most important volume in the field, Alfred D. Chandler's magisterial *The Visible Hand: The Managerial Revolution in American Business* (Cambridge, Mass.: Belknap Press, 1977). Also useful is Alfred D. Chandler and Richard Tedlow, eds., *The Coming of Managerial Capitalism: A Casebook on the History of American Economic Institutions* (Homewood, Ill.: Richard D. Irwin, 1985). For a recent cogent overview of developments in the public sector, see Thomas K. McCraw, *Prophets of Regulation: Charles Francis Adams, Louis D. Brandeis, James M. Landis, Alfred E. Kahn* (Cambridge, Mass.: Belknap Press, 1984). There are also a number of up-to-date essays on public policy in Glenn Porter, ed., *Encyclopedia of American Economic History*, in three volumes (New York: Charles Scribner's Sons, 1980) and Jack P.

Greene, ed., *Encyclopedia of American Political History*, in three volumes (New York: Charles Scribner's Sons, 1984).

CHAPTER 1

On J. P. Morgan, all the previous studies have been superseded by Vincent P. Carosso, *The Morgans: Private International Bankers, 1854–1913* (Cambridge, Mass.: Harvard University Press, 1987). The reader who finds this long and detailed account daunting can turn to Frederick Lewis Allen's lively *The Great Pierpont Morgan* (New York: Harper, 1949) for a brief study. Robert Wiebe, *The Search for Order, 1877–1920* (New York: Hill and Wang, 1967) provides an excellent introduction to the reform movements at the turn of the century, and Glenn Porter, *The Rise of Big Business, 1860–1910* (New York: Thomas Y. Crowell, 1973) is also a fine survey of that important subject. The best source on Standard Oil is still Ralph and Muriel Hidy, *Pioneering in Big Business: History of Standard Oil Company (New Jersey)* (New York: Harper, 1955).

CHAPTER 2

While the history of the entrepreneurial firm has of late attracted less attention than that of large enterprise, all the following books include a treatment of relatively small nineteenth-century businesses: Thomas C. Cochran, *The Pabst Brewing Company: The History of an American Business* (New York: New York University Press, 1948), Ralph W. Hidy and Frank Ernest Hill, *Timber and Men: The Weyerhauser Story* (New York: Macmillan, 1963), David A. Hounshell, *From the American System to Mass Production: The Development of Manufacturing Technology in the United States* (Baltimore: Johns Hopkins University Press, 1984), Anthony F.C. Wallace, *Rockdale: The Growth of an American Village in the Early Industrial Revolution* (New York: Alfred A. Knopf, 1978), Philip Scranton, *Proprietary Capitalism: The Textile Manufacture at Philadelphia, 1800–1885* (New York: Cambridge University Press, 1983), and Glenn Porter and Harold C. Livesay, *Merchants and Manufacturers: Studies in the Changing Structure of Nineteenth-Century Marketing* (Baltimore: Johns Hopkins University Press, 1971). Also of interest is Harold C. Livesay, *Andrew Carnegie and the Rise of Big Business* (Boston: Little, Brown, 1975) and Maury Klein's well-crafted biography, *The Life and Legend of Jay Gould* (Baltimore: Johns Hopkins University Press, 1986). For a less favorable view of Gould, see Charles Francis and Henry Adams, *Chapters of Erie* (Ithaca: Cornell University Press, 1956). On labor, the following are informative: Alan Dawley, *Class and Community: The Industrial Revolution in Lynn* (Cambridge, Mass.: Harvard University Press, 1976), David Brody, *Steelworkers in America: The Non-Union Era* (Cambridge, Mass.: Harvard University Press, 1960), and Herbert G. Gutman, *Work, Culture, and Society in Industrializing America: Essays in American Working-Class and Social History* (New York: Vintage Books, 1977). Reese V. Jenkins, *Images and Enterprise: Technology and the American Photographic Industry, 1839–1925* (Baltimore: Johns Hopkins University Press, 1975) effectively blends the history of business and technology, as does Thomas P. Hughes, *Networks of Power: Electrification in Western Society, 1880–1930* (Baltimore: Johns Hopkins University Press, 1983). In addition to the books already cited by Chandler and Porter, see Naomi Lamoreaux, *The Great*

*Merger Movement in American Business, 1895–1904* (New York: Cambridge University Press, 1985), for a contrasting interpretation of the sources of combination.

## CHAPTER 3

On the early regulatory movement, Ari Hoogenboom, *A History of the ICC: From Panacea to Palliative* (New York: W.W. Norton, 1976) offers a brief overview, while Albro Martin, *Enterprise Denied: Origins of the Decline of the American Railroads, 1897–1917* (New York: Columbia University Press, 1971) is highly critical of the ICC. Robert E. Cushman, *The Independent Regulatory Commissions* (New York: Oxford University Press, 1941) elaborates on the legislative debates. In addition to these accounts, see Alan Stone, *Economic Regulation and the Public Interest: The Federal Trade Commission in Theory and Practice* (Ithaca: Cornell University Press, 1977), Eugene White, *The Regulation and Reform of the American Banking System, 1900–1920* (Princeton: Princeton University Press, 1983), and Peter Temin, *Taking Your Medicine: Drug Regulation in the United States* (Cambridge, Mass.: Harvard University Press, 1980). The early history of the antitrust movement is recounted in great depth in Hans Thorelli, *The Federal Antitrust Policy: Origination of an American Tradition* (Baltimore: Johns Hopkins University Press, 1955) and in more compact form in William Letwin, *Law and Economic Policy in America: The Evolution of the Sherman Antitrust Act* (New York: Random House, 1965). Of interest as well is John G. Clark's survey of *Energy and the Federal Government: Fossil Fuel Policies, 1900–1946* (Urbana: University of Illinois Press, 1987).

## CHAPTER 4

On the centralized combine, see Alfred D. Chandler, *Strategy and Structure: Chapters in the History of the Industrial Enterprise* (Cambridge, Mass.: MIT Press, 1962), Richard S. Tedlow and Richard R. John, Jr., eds., *Managing Big Business: Essays from the Business History Review* (Boston: Harvard Business School Press, 1986), Alfred P. Sloan, Jr., *My Years with General Motors* (New York: Doubleday, 1963), Robert Lacey, *Ford: The Men and the Machine* (Boston: Little, Brown, 1986), and George S. Gibb and Evelyn H. Knowlton, *The Resurgent Years: History of Standard Oil Company (New Jersey), 1911–1927* (New York: Harper, 1956). The early history of the Bell System is treated in Robert W. Garnet, *The Telephone Enterprise: The Evolution of the Bell System's Horizontal Structure, 1876–1909* (Baltimore: Johns Hopkins University Press, 1985) and George David Smith, *The Anatomy of a Business Strategy: Bell, Western Electric, and the Origins of the American Telephone Industry* (Baltimore: Johns Hopkins University Press, 1985).

Research and development in a corporate setting are well treated in Leonard Reich, *The Making of American Industrial Research: Science and Business at GE and Bell, 1876–1926* (New York: Cambridge University Press, 1985). Also see Neil H. Wasserman, *From Invention to Innovation: Long-Distance Telephone Transmission at the Turn of the Century* (Baltimore: Johns Hopkins University Press, 1985) and George Wise, *Willis R. Whitney, General Electric and the Origins of U.S. Industrial Research* (New York: Columbia University Press, 1985).

The changing patterns of labor relations are treated in Donald Nelson, *Managers and Workers: Origins of the New Factory System in the United States, 1880–1920* (Madison: University of Wisconsin Press, 1975) and in Sanford Jacoby, *Employing Bureaucracy:*

*Managers, Unions and the Transformation of Work in America* (New York: Columbia University Press, 1985). Richard C. Edwards provides a perceptive synthesis in *Contested Terrain: The Transformation of the Workplace in the Twentieth Century* (New York: Basic Books, 1979), and David Brody, *Workers in Industrial America: Essays on the Twentieth Century Struggle* (New York: Oxford University Press, 1980) gives a particularly deft treatment of the 1920s.

On smaller businesses and associations, the following are helpful: Thomas C. Cochran, *American Business in the Twentieth Century* (Cambridge, Mass.: Harvard University Press, 1972), Sheldon Hochheiser, *Rohm and Haas: History of a Chemical Company* (Philadelphia: University of Pennsylvania Press, 1986), August Giebelhaus, *Business and Government in the Oil Industry: A Case Study of Sun Oil, 1876–1945* (Greenwich, Conn.: JAI Press, 1981), Louis Galambos, *Competition and Cooperation: The Emergence of a National Trade Association* (Baltimore: Johns Hopkins University Press, 1966), and Ellis W. Hawley, *The Great War and the Search for a Modern Order* (New York: St. Martin's Press, 1979).

CHAPTER 5

An excellent introduction to the New Deal is William Leuchtenburg, *Franklin D. Roosevelt and the New Deal* (New York: Harper & Row, 1963). Ellis W. Hawley carefully dissects *The New Deal and the Problem of Monopoly* (Princeton: Princeton University Press, 1966). Particular policies are addressed in the following: Michael Parrish, *Securities Regulation and the New Deal* (New Haven: Yale University Press, 1970), Thomas McCraw, *TVA and the Power Fight, 1933–1939* (New York: Lippincott, 1971), William Childs, *Trucking and the Public Interest: The Emergence of Federal Regulation* (Knoxville: University of Tennessee Press, 1985), David Prindle, *Petroleum Products and the Texas Railroad Commission* (Austin: University of Texas Press, 1981), and Donald Ritchie, *James M. Landis: Dean of the Regulators* (Cambridge, Mass.: Harvard University Press, 1980).

The politics of high finance are examined in Joel Seligman, *The Transformation of Wall Street: A History of the Securities and Exchange Commission and Modern Corporate Finance* (Boston: Houghton Mifflin, 1982), Robert Sobel, *The Big Board: A History of the New York Stock Market* (New York: Free Press, 1965), and Walter L. Buenger and Joseph A. Pratt, *But Also Good Business: Texas Commerce Banks and the Financing of Houston and Texas, 1886–1986* (College Station: Texas A & M University Press, 1986). Still useful is Jesse Holman Jones, *Fifty Billion Dollars: My Thirteen Years with the RFC, 1932–1945* (New York: Macmillan, 1951).

In regard to labor policies, Christopher Tomlins, *The State and the Unions: Labor Relations, Law, and the Organized Labor Movement in America, 1880–1960* (New York: Cambridge University Press, 1985) revises the conventional story. David Montgomery, *Workers' Control in America: Studies in the History of Work, Technology, and Labor Struggles* (New York: Cambridge University Press, 1979) takes a somewhat similar tack. See also John Barnard, *Walter Reuther and the Rise of the Auto Workers* (Boston: Little, Brown, 1983), Melvin Dubofsky and Warren Van Tine, *John L. Lewis, A Biography* (New York: Quadrangle, 1979), and Irving Bernstein, *Turbulent Years: A History of the American Worker, 1933–1941* (Boston: Houghton Mifflin, 1970).

CHAPTER 6

For a good introduction to the public policies of this era see Murray Weiden-baum, *The Modern Public Sector* (New York: Basic Books, 1969). See also Otis Graham, *Toward a Planned Society: From Roosevelt to Nixon* (New York: Oxford University Press, 1976), James Clayton, ed., *The Economic Impact of the Cold War* (New York: Harcourt, Brace & World, 1970), and Louis Galambos, ed., *The New American State: Bureaucracies and Policies Since World War II* (Baltimore: Johns Hopkins University Press, 1987).

Marver Bernstein, *Regulating Business by Independent Commission* (Princeton: Princeton University Press, 1955) should be read along with James Q. Wilson, ed., *The Politics of Regulation* (New York: Basic Books, 1980). Particularly important is Richard Vietor, *Energy Policy in America Since 1945: A Study in Business-Government Relations* (New York: Cambridge University Press, 1984).

Herbert Stein, *The Fiscal Revolution in America* (Chicago: University of Chicago Press, 1969) should be paired with Robert Collins, *The Business Response to Keynes, 1929–1964* (New York: Columbia University Press, 1981). Aaron Wildavsky examines *The Politics of the Budgetary Process* (Boston: Little, Brown, 1984 edition), and Stephen Bailey describes the intricate legislative history of one important measure in *Congress Makes a Law: The Story Behind the Employment Act of 1946* (New York: Columbia University Press, 1950). Another helpful volume is Theodore Kovaleff, *Business and Government During the Eisenhower Administration: A Study of the Antitrust Policy of the Antitrust Division of the Justice Department* (Athens: Ohio University Press, 1980).

CHAPTER 7

For a sparkling overview, see John Kenneth Galbraith, *The New Industrial State* (Boston: Houghton Mifflin, 1967). Robert Averitt's *The Dual Economy: The Dynamics of American Industry Structure* (New York: W.W. Norton, 1968) covers some of the same ground. More detailed is Harold G. Vatter, *The United States Economy in the 1950's* (New York: W.W. Norton, 1963).

Diversification is discussed in Chandler's books and in Richard P. Rumelt, *Strategy, Structure and Economic Performance* (Boston: Division of Research, Harvard Graduate School of Business Administration, 1974). The conglomerate movement is treated in Milton Leontiades, *Managing the Unmanageable: Strategies for Success Within the Conglomerate* (Reading, Mass.: Addison-Wesley, 1986) and Jesse W. Markham, *Conglomerate Enterprise and Public Policy* (Boston: Division of Research, Graduate School of Business Administration, Harvard University, 1973). There are several excellent books on the multinationals: Raymond Vernon, *Sovereignty at Bay: The Multinational Spread of U.S. Enterprises* (New York: Basic Books, 1971), Mira Wilkins, *The Maturing of Multinational Enterprise: American Business Abroad from 1914 to 1970* (Cambridge: Harvard University Press, 1974), and Mira Wilkins and Frank Ernest Hill, *American Business Abroad: Ford on Six Continents* (Detroit: Wayne State University Press, 1964).

The automobile business is surveyed in John Rae, *The American Automobile Industry* (Boston: Twayne Publishers, 1984) and Lawrence White, *The Automobile Industry Since 1945* (Cambridge, Mass.: Harvard University Press, 1971). Ford is discussed in Allan Nevins and Frank Ernest Hill, *Ford: Decline and Rebirth, 1933–1962* (New York: Charles Scribner's Sons, 1962). Especially helpful in analyzing the businesses in this industry and others is Paul R. Lawrence and Davis Dyer, *Renewing American Industry: Organizing for Efficiency and Innovation* (New York: Free Press, 1983).

Other valuable volumes on postwar developments are Samuel Hollander, *The Sources of Increased Efficiency: A Study of DuPont Rayon Plants* (Cambridge, Mass.: MIT Press, 1965), Gerald Brock, *The United States Computer Industry* (Cambridge, Mass.: Ballinger, 1975), the same author's *The Telecommunications Industry: The Dynamics of Market Structure* (Cambridge, Mass.: Harvard University Press, 1981), Howell John Harris, *The Right to Manage: Industrial Relations Policies of American Business in the 1940s* (Madison: University of Wisconsin Press, 1982), and Henrietta M. Larsen et al., *New Horizons, 1927–1950: History of Standard Oil Company (New Jersey)* (New York: Harper & Row, 1971). On RCA see Margaret B.W. Graham's perceptive history, *RCA and the VideoDisc: The Business of Research* (New York: Cambridge University Press, 1986).

CHAPTER 8

On the pattern of emerging tensions during the American era, Anthony Sampson, *The Seven Sisters: The Great Oil Companies and the World They Shaped* (New York: Bantam Books, 1975) is a popular account. Peter Odell, *Oil and World Power* (New York: Penguin Books, 1983) deals with OPEC. Other volumes on this same industry are David Painter, *Oil and the American Century: The Political Economy of U.S. Foreign Oil Policy, 1941–1954* (Baltimore: Johns Hopkins University Press, 1986) and Irvine Anderson, *Aramco, the United States and Saudi Arabia: A Study of the Dynamics of Foreign Oil Policy, 1933–1950* (Princeton: Princeton University Press, 1981).

Other useful volumes include David Halberstam, *The Reckoning* (New York: Morrow, 1986), Chalmers Johnson, *MITI and the Japanese Miracle: The Growth of Industrial Policy, 1925–1975* (Stanford: Stanford University Press, 1982), and Robert B. Reich and Ira C. Magaziner, *Minding America's Business: The Decline and Rise of the American Economy* (New York: Harcourt Brace Jovanovich, 1982). See also James Krier and Edmund Ursin, *Pollution and Policy: A Case Essay on California and Federal Experience with Motor Vehicle Air Pollution, 1940–1975* (Berkeley: University of California Press, 1977) and Charles Schultze, *The Public Use of Private Interest* (Washington: Brookings Institution, 1971).

CHAPTER 9

On environmental problems there are a number of informative studies, including J. Clarence Davies and Barbara Davies, *The Politics of Pollution* (Indianapolis: Bobbs Merrill, 1975), John Quarles, *Cleaning Up America: An Insider's View of the Environmental Protection Agency* (Boston: Houghton Mifflin, 1976), and David Vogel, *National Styles of Regulation: Environmental Policy in Great Britain and the United States* (Ithaca: Cornell University Press, 1986). Two popular case studies are James Roscow, *800 Miles to Valdez: The Building of the Alaska Pipeline* (Englewood Cliffs: Prentice-Hall, 1977) and Allan Talbot, *Power Along the Hudson: The Storm King Case and the Birth of Environmentalism* (New York: E.P. Dutton, 1972).

On other areas of public policy see Robert Stobaugh and Daniel Yergin, *Energy*

*Future: Report of the Energy Project of the Harvard Business School* (New York: Random House, 1979), Joseph Kalt, *The Economics and Politics of Oil Price Regulation* (Cambridge, Mass.: MIT Press, 1981), M. Elizabeth Sanders, *The Regulation of Natural Gas: Policy and Politics, 1938–1978* (Philadelphia: Temple University Press, 1981), and Crauford Goodwin, ed., *Energy Policy in Perspective: Today's Problems, Yesterday's Solutions* (Washington: Brookings Institution, 1981). Three additional books that touch on recent problems are Douglas Ginsburg and William Abernathy, eds., *Government, Technology and the Future of the American Automobile* (New York: McGraw-Hill, 1980), Lawrence White, *Reforming Regulation: Processes and Problems* (Englewood Cliffs: Prentice-Hall, 1981), and Stephen Breyer's important volume on *Regulation and Its Reform* (Cambridge, Mass.: Harvard University Press, 1982).

## CHAPTER 10

Recent developments in the public and private sectors have received considerable attention in the press and in popular magazines. In addition to these accounts, see Thomas McCraw, ed., *America Versus Japan* (Boston: Harvard Business School Press, 1986), David Teece, ed., *The Competitive Challenge: Strategies for Industrial Innovation and Renewal* (Cambridge, Mass.: Ballinger, 1987), and Robert Reich and John D. Donahue, *New Deals, the Chrysler Revival and the American System* (New York: Times Books, 1985). One of the most popular of the recent books is Thomas J. Peters and Robert H. Waterman, Jr., *In Search of Excellence: Lessons from America's Best-Run Companies* (New York: Warner Books, 1982). For a different view see George C. Lodge, *The American Disease* (New York: Alfred A. Knopf, 1984).

From the extensive literature on deregulation, see in particular Martha Derthick and Paul Quirk, *The Politics of Deregulation* (Washington: Brookings Institution, 1985), Elizabeth Bailey, David Graham, and Daniel Kaplan, *Deregulating the Airlines* (Cambridge, Mass.: MIT Press, 1985), and S. Kerry Cooper and Donald Fraser, *Banking Deregulation and the New Competition in Financial Services* (Cambridge, Mass.: Ballinger, 1984).

## CHAPTER 11

On Lee Iacocca and Chrysler, the best source is Lee Iacocca, with William Novak, *Iacocca: An Autobiography* (New York: Bantam Books, 1984).

A final word: we drew heavily upon the works of our colleagues and students, most of whom we did not mention by name. Two exceptions are Kenneth Lipartito, whose dissertation, *The Telephone in the South: A Comparative Analysis, 1877–1920* (Johns Hopkins University, 1986), provided us with some important ideas, and Ann Boggs, whose research on Armco helped us understand that firm's interesting, early history.

# Index